Heavenly
POWERS

Heavenly
POWERS

UNRAVELING
THE SECRET HISTORY
OF THE KABBALAH

Neil Asher Silberman

Grosset/Putnam
A MEMBER OF
Penguin Putnam Inc.
NEW YORK

Grosset/Putnam
a member of
Penguin Putnam Inc.
375 Hudson Street
New York, NY 10014

Library of Congress Cataloging-in-Publication Data

Silberman, Neil Asher, date.
Heavenly powers : unraveling the secret history
of the Kabbalah / Neil Asher Silberman.
p.   cm.
Includes bibliographical references and index.
ISBN 0-399-14448-X
1. Cabala—History.   I. Title.
BM526.S59   1998   98-20347 CIP
296.1'6—dc21

Printed in the United States of America

1   3   5   7   9   10   8   6   4   2

This book is printed on acid-free paper. ∞

Book design by Judith Stagnitto Abbate
The Tree of Life Chart by Jeff Ward

For Trude and Moshe Dothan

CONTENTS

ACKNOWLEDGMENTS

I n this book, I have departed from earlier subjects of digs, diggers, and biblical discoveries to examine the characters and hidden history of a more recent cultural and spiritual phenomenon. It was Jane Isay, my longtime editor and friend, who first suggested that I write about the social history of the Kabbalah and explore some of my longstanding ideas about the intertwining of religion, politics, and economics in an entirely new context. From the beginning, we agreed that this was to be a different kind of book about the Kabbalah. I would not offer any novel meditative techniques or paths to spiritual self-awareness. My challenge would be to craft a narrative, placing the Kabbalah in a down-to-earth context, weaving in the events, the often exotic locales, and the vivid characters who contributed to the Jewish mystical tradition over the centuries.

This has obviously been a long process of research and reflection. I want to thank Professor Jacob Lassner of North-western University for allowing me—at the very beginning of the research—to participate in an international conference on "conflicts of culture and absorption" among Jews, Christians, and Muslims in the sixteenth century. It was there in Evanston in the spring of 1996 that I first had the chance to meet a number of important scholars in the fields of Kabbalah and early modern Jewish history. I benefited greatly from conversations with Professor Lassner and with Professors David Ruderman and Moshe Idel.

I want to extend my appreciation to the staffs of the Sterling Memorial Library and the Divinity School Library at Yale University for their invaluable assistance during my research for this book. My thanks also go to Rabbi Howard Sommer of Temple Beth Tikvah in Madison, Connecticut, who took time to read an early draft of this manuscript and who, as always, generously pointed out ways I could improve it. Many other congregation members of Temple Beth Tikvah helped me refine my ideas on the history of the Kabbalah in a series of lectures and discussion groups. I am especially grateful to Stan and Myra Josephson for their continual, enthusiastic support; and to Scott and Carly Casper and Ron and Bette Zollshan for their friendship and their lively discussion with me—over the last couple of years—of many of the themes in this book. Steve Horn, as usual, was a sage advisor and ready source of knowledge on the nuances of Jewish culture and history. And over the years, Professors Moshe and Trude Dothan of Jerusalem have profoundly influenced my historical and archaeological perspective. It is no exaggeration to say that as friends and mentors, they have shaped the course of my career.

In the world of publishing, I offer my continuing appreciation to my literary agent, Carol Mann, who has been instrumental in making this book—like the five others we have worked on together—a reality. At Putnam, David Groff skillfully shepherded the manuscript through the production process, even as my original text was being refined by the editorial oversight of Michael Lowenthal, and the perceptive copyediting of Timothy Meyer, to whom I owe—as in two previous books at Putnam—special thanks. Most of all I want to acknowledge support for this project by Riverhead Books President and Publisher Susan Petersen and the constant, helpful encouragement of Putnam's director of religious publishing, Joel Fotinos, whose sound judgment, patience, and encouragement always made me feel that the idea of writing a narrative of the Kabbalah's political and social history was a worthwhile thing to do.

My family hardly needs to hear again how much I love them and cherish their confidence in me. My parents, Barbara and Saul Silberman, and my sister, Ellen Silberman Lemoine, have always been a source of great encouragement and emotional support. My wife, Ellen, has once again gracefully adapted her life—and our family life—to the sometimes painful rhythms of a book-in-progress. Over many years and many books, she has helped me in ways too numerous to count. And to my daughter, Maya, whose Bat Mitzvah year has been filled to the brim with schoolwork, school sports, and the challenge of memorizing and chanting her portions of biblical Hebrew, I can only hope she will, someday, enjoy the story I've presented here.

—N.A.S.
June 13, 1998

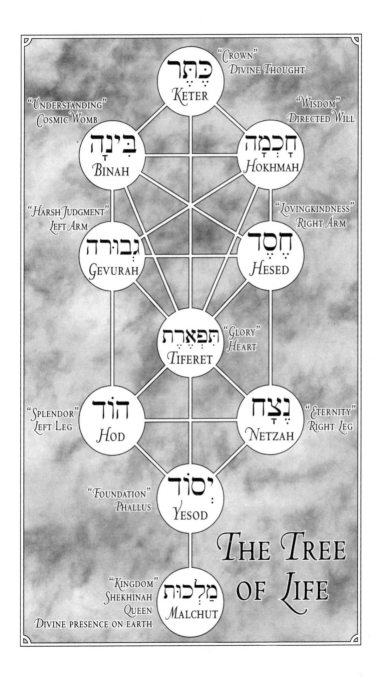

"CROWN"
DIVINE THOUGHT

כֶּתֶר
KETER

"UNDERSTANDING"
COSMIC WOMB

"WISDOM"
DIRECTED WILL

בִּינָה
BINAH

חָכְמָה
HOKHMAH

"HARSH JUDGMENT"
LEFT ARM

"LOVINGKINDNESS"
RIGHT ARM

גְּבוּרה
GEVURAH

חֶסֶד
HESED

תִּפְאֶרֶת
TIFERET

"GLORY"
HEART

"SPLENDOR"
LEFT LEG

הוֹד
HOD

נֶצַח
NETZAH

"ETERNITY"
RIGHT LEG

"FOUNDATION"
PHALLUS

יְסוֹד
YESOD

THE TREE
OF LIFE

"KINGDOM"
SHEKHINAH
QUEEN
DIVINE PRESENCE ON EARTH

מַלְכוּת
MALCHUT

SECRETS OF CREATION

The Kabbalah is a way of mystical knowledge dedicated to understanding and harnessing the awesome forces unleashed at the time of creation. Just as astrophysicists explore the mysteries of the Big Bang theory to explain the origins of the universe and everything in it, kabbalists are also committed to a theoretical quest. Over the centuries, Jewish mystics have reflected deeply on the initial verses of the Book of Genesis, probing the symbolism of each of God's actions in creating and maintaining the world. Their goal has always been to understand how the dazzling variety and changeability of creation—the spectrum of light and colors, the form of the human body, the structure of plants and snowflakes, the alphabet, the numbers, and even the course of human history—are all symbols as well as tangible manifestations of a single divine reality.

In the whirling, spiral patterns of fractal geometry, in the random flames of a roaring fire, and in the ups and downs of stocks and political parties, kabbalists believe that we can see the patterns of flowing energy that created the universe. Some have been content to use this insight for short-term gain and personal motives. Some have fashioned amulets and chanted prayer-spells to influence the heavenly powers. But the aim of this brand of mysticism is far more than casting spells for love, revenge, or profit. Its ultimate object is restoring a balance between light and darkness, good and evil. And the participation of the followers of the Kabbalah in that process of cosmic repair—so say the ancient sages—is the true destiny of the righteous throughout history and all over the world.

The main theme of this book is that the Kabbalah is and always has been a politically explosive underground tradition that speaks about power, oppression, resistance, and freedom. In each period of its development, economic and political changes have created great opportunities for prosperity and progress, but they have also often resulted in tyranny and inequality. The Kabbalah offers an alternative way of wisdom, looking to the heavens for visions of eternal truths and principles of cosmic balance that—if applied on earth—would utterly transform the world. The magic, the particular symbols, and techniques of meditation are all powerful ways to help us recognize that the structures of society all around us are not divinely created or inevitable but artificial patterns imposed by private interests that hunger for power in our day-to-day reality.

If we trace the evolution of kabbalistic concepts through time and across continents, we can begin to see how its sages and innovators skillfully responded to the changing fate of the Jews under specific regimes, international conflicts, and economic trends. For the Kabbalah is neither a modern fad nor an ancient superstition but a great and complex philosophy of down-to-earth struggle cloaked in the symbols of heaven. It is an epic of determined resistance to earthly power, in which the protagonists forged a breathtakingly coherent system of metaphors and understandings. Their goal in every age and in every stage of the struggle was to transform the world from its present chaos and violence to a state of harmoniousness. And it is only by tracing the long-overlooked details of the lives and times of the kabbalists themselves—who they were, how they lived, dreamed, and died—that we can perhaps gain a new understanding of the meaning of the ancient mystical tradition that remains very much alive today.

FROM BABYLON TO NEW YORK CITY

In the following chapters, as we trace the history of the Kabbalah over the centuries from ancient times to the present, we will see how specific events, personalities, and misfortunes changed lives and influenced the development of the Jewish mystical vision. As ideas—especially mystical ideas—that were given life and meaning in their own historical context, we will see how each of the Kabbalah's main stages of development was an unambiguous response to the social changes and political challenges of the Babylonians, the Roman Empire, medieval Christendom, Renaissance Humanism, the Reformation, and the rise of modern Industrial Society. Sometimes the followers of the Kabbalah retreated into closed, secretive circles. Sometimes they arose as the leaders of violent, messianic movements. And sometimes they emerged as respected community leaders to apply their insights in reconstructing their society and economy. Yet in all its historical and theological variations, the Kabbalah's most crucial insight has been the belief that the most powerful sources of energy possessed by every community and individual lie not in blind obedience to earthly ideologies of power but in transcendent patterns of cosmic harmony.

Over centuries of crisis and upheaval, the teachers and sages of this mystical school, whose name roughly means "received tradition" in Hebrew, have experienced intense bursts of mystical revelation and creative theological innovation. They have produced a rich literature of speculation, meditation, prayer, and practical techniques for harnessing the powers of heaven for community renewal and intensified personal spirituality. In their use of exacting techniques of inward meditation and hypnotic incantation, the greatest of the kabbalists have recounted their personal ascents through heavenly worlds to gaze upon fiery chariots and breathtaking palaces. In some extraordinary cases, they have recounted the details of angelic instruction about past lives and future events. Some have even claimed to have glimpsed the indescribable brilliance of the realm of the Divine Presence. Yet their goal has never been escape from the suffering and conflicts of earthly existence. In every era, the purpose of the kabbalists' otherworldly adventures has been to help restore a shattered balance of power in the heavenly worlds. For that imbalance in the relationships of metaphysical forces—tragically generated in the earliest stages of creation—is, they fervently believe, the root cause of all the bitter sufferings, violence, and injustices of human history.

Today, the Kabbalah is experiencing an unprecedented renaissance of interest. In self-help workshops, evening seminars, weekend retreats, and university courses across Europe and America, the Kabbalah is once again gaining enthusiastic adherents among Christians as well as Jews. Many eager students, with little religious education or experience, are finding it a source of spiritual nourishment otherwise unavailable in our increasingly secularized society. In an age of individual quests for self-fulfillment, the Kabbalah is now promoted in tracts, videocassettes, and slickly produced workbooks. No longer scorned as superstition, it is embraced by celebrities and harried urban professionals as a powerful New Age explanation of life, death, and destiny—and a metaphysical key with which a modern individual can open up his or her deepest personal potentialities.

Not unexpectedly, many bitter critics of this new mystical renaissance have arisen, branding this New Age kabbalistic interest as—at best—a fraudulent corruption of an ancient tradition and, at worst, the resurrection of medieval superstition in modern guise. Indeed, this new Kabbalah does not require that its study be grounded in a meticulous observance of Jewish ritual law, religious rites, or dietary restrictions. It utilizes metaphors from astrophysics, computer science, and fractal geometry as often as it refers to biblical or Talmudic passages. And the teachers of this neo-Kabbalah promise their eager students if not a straighter path to the heavens, then perhaps an effective escape from their personal hells. Traditional rabbinic authorities and kabbalistic scholars assert that this new mystical melange has nothing whatever to do with the Kabbalah's place in the history of Jewish thought. For them, the Kabbalah is *not* just a constellation of abstract spiritual principles, of relevance to anyone—of any background—who happens to find personal fulfillment in them.

Yet there may be another way to apprehend the kabbalistic vision, neither reducing it to a particular branch of traditional Judaism nor presenting it as an almost entirely non-denominational meditative technique. All forms of kabbalistic expression—those of the traditionalists and the New Age dabblers—can be seen as subtle expressions of social and cultural protest. The aim of this book is to examine the long history of the Kabbalah over the centuries and see how the various forms of kabbalistic rituals—at least in their initial stages—expressed symbolic yearnings for down-to-earth political ideals, formulated under particular historical conditions, with particular earthly injustices in mind.

Most modern works on the Kabbalah tend to homogenize its doctrines into a single, comprehensive system of theology. Yet as we will see, the Kabbalah is an ever-changing intellectual *process* and perspective rather than a dogmatic system of belief. Changing material concerns with down-to-earth problems of crops, trade, textiles, political power, and day labor are as relevant to understanding the development and significance of the Kabbalah as the influence of ancient philosophical schools and theological trends. In the layers of its literary production—and in the layers of human experience it represents over centuries of struggle for survival—the Kabbalah can, at its heart, be seen as a passionate expression of faith that a deeper and truer reality lies beneath the surface appearance of things. And as one of the world's most mysterious and powerful mystical traditions, the Kabbalah is also an explosive *political* doctrine, dedicated to challenging the rule of the earthly powers that be.

Chapter 1
VISIONS OF THE CHARIOT

In the beginning was Ezekiel's vision, a series of stunning, surrealistic images, miraculously appearing in the heavens above the ziggurats and hanging gardens of Babylon:

> In the thirtieth year, in the fourth month, on the fifth day of the month, as I was among the exiles by the river Chebar, the heavens were opened, and I saw visions of God . . .
>
> . . . As I looked, behold, a stormy wind came out of the north, and a great cloud, with brightness round about it, and fire flashing forth continually, and in the midst of the fire, as it were gleaming bronze. And from the midst of it came the likeness of four living creatures.
>
> And this was their appearance: they had the form of men, but each had four faces, and each of them had four wings. Their legs were straight, and the soles of their feet

were like the sole of a calf's foot; and they sparkled like burnished bronze. Under their wings on their four sides they had human hands . . .

. . . As for the likeness of their faces, each had the face of a man in front; the four had the face of a lion on the right side, the four had the face of an ox on the left side, and the four had the face of an eagle at the back . . . And their wings were spread out above; each creature had two wings, each of which touched the wing of another, while two covered their bodies. And each went straight forward; wherever the spirit would go, they went, without turning as they went . . .

. . . Now as I looked at the living creatures, I saw a wheel upon the earth beside the living creatures, one for each of the four of them. As for the appearance of the wheels and their construction: their appearance was like the gleaming of a chrysolite; and the four had the same likeness, their construction being as it were a wheel within a wheel. When they went, they went in any of the four directions without turning as they went. The four wheels had rims and they had spokes; and their rims were full of eyes round about . . .

. . . Over the heads of the living creatures there was the likeness of a firmament, shining like crystal, spread out above their heads . . . And when they went, I heard the sound of their wings like the sound of many waters, like the thunder of the Almighty, a sound of tumult like the sound of a host; when they stood still, they let down their wings. And there came a voice from above the firmament over their heads; when they stood still, they let down their wings.

And above the firmament over their heads was the likeness of a throne, in appearance like sapphire; and seated above the likeness of a throne was a likeness as it were of a human form. And upward from what had the appearance of his loins I saw as it were gleaming bronze, like the appearance of fire enclosed round about; and downward from what had the appearance of his loins I saw as it were the appearance of fire, and there was brightness round about him.

Like the appearance of the bow that is in the cloud on the day of rain, so was the appearance of the brightness round about. Such was the appearance of the likeness of the glory of the Lord. And when I saw it, I fell upon my face, and I heard the voice of one speaking. And he said to me, "Son of man, stand upon your feet, and I will speak with you."

(Ezekiel 1:1–28)

The thirty-year-old priest Ezekiel was an unlikely figure to receive such a disturbing vision. Born around 623 B.C.E. in the Holy City of Jerusalem, he was raised and educated in the most privileged stratum of Judean society. He grew to adulthood at a time of great national revival and prosperity: the city had reached the apex of its physical grandeur with its great broad walls, plazas, palaces, and Temple to the God of Israel — crowning the summit of its highest hill. A new confidence and pride blossomed in the court of King Josiah, a scion of the House of David and visionary political leader who had been brought to the throne by popular acclamation and became the patron of a great reform of the national cult away from idolatry. Remembered in the Book of Kings as one of Judah's most righteous rulers, his saintly reputation was not merely a matter of rituals observance or ethical piety. Josiah was a champion of Israel's independence from the era's great empires, and in the ancient world, religion, politics, and economics were all inseparably intertwined.

Since his boyhood, Ezekiel had been trained in the scribal schools and priestly academies of Jerusalem in the soaring poetry and somber epic of the great national story of liberation whose central focus was on Israel's liberation from a tyrannical Pharaoh and its solemn covenant with God in the wilderness. Yet in 609 B.C.E., the Pharaoh returned with a vengeance. King Josiah was killed by an invading Egyptian army at a fateful battle near the ancient city of Megiddo (Armageddon in the later woeful memories of the apocalyptic struggle), and within just a few years, the Kingdom of Judah would become a helpless possession of the rising Babylonian Empire. The aristocracy of Jerusalem would be humiliated, stripped of their possessions, killed, and scattered. Famine and plague would ravage the countryside, and the deserted public squares of Jerusalem would become the haunt of jackals. Weeping would echo throughout the land, and—as the Book of Lamentations would put it—holy stones would lie scattered at the head of every street. The Babylonians' usual practice in the case of rebellious provinces was to eliminate the rebellious aristocracy. And so it was done with Judah. A new ruler, Zedekiah, was placed on the throne with the Babylonians' blessings while King Jehoiachin and eight thousand Judean courtiers, priests, and craftsmen were placed under guard and transported hundreds of miles eastward to be resettled as refugees by the waters of Babylon.

The young priest Ezekiel, son of Buzi, was among the exiles, forced to live in a cluster of half-ruined villages along the Tigris River and its dense network of irrigation canals. He and the other displaced Judeans tried their best to piece their lives together, but God's verdict seemed to be clear: the People of Israel had not been resolute enough in their shunning of foreign powers and their gods of greed and oppression. Both before and after the noble Josiah, the leaders of the Kingdom of Judah had willingly consorted with tyrants, and they would have to taste the bitterness of exile until the sinfulness and arrogance of their ways was acknowledged and overturned. Now in Babylon, some bided their time and dreamed of a miraculous return to their homes and property as they dutifully collected rations from the government granaries. Others quietly plotted rebellion as letters and messengers arrived from Judah, telling of a secret alliance between King Zedekiah and the Egyptians that might destroy Babylon's imperial grip. Yet for Ezekiel the priest, Egypt was the land of Pharaoh, a pit of darkness and death into which Israel must not be allowed to fall. In its current power and grandeur, Babylon was merely acting as God's agent and would not be easily defeated. Something had to be done to stop the suicidal plans for rebellion. And wandering out to the banks of the Chebar Canal, Ezekiel gained an indelible glimpse of the terrible Majesty of God.

Ezekiel was hardly the first Israelite priest to gain a direct glimpse at the heavenly powers. As far back as the time of the Israelite king Ahab, nearly three hundred years before, Micaiah ben Imlah had been granted a vision of the heavenly court, with God seated, surrounded by an angelic council. And in the time of Hezekiah, just over a century before, the prophet Isaiah had described the appearance of winged cherubs in the Divine Presence, endlessly chanting hymns of praise. Ezekiel's vision, however, was not one of static majesty but rather of a mobile, world-conquering divinity, supported by the four bizarre figures propelled by fiery "wheels," and blazing above an icy ceiling into the limitless depths of the sky.

For centuries, Jewish sages and mystics have read and studied the enigmatic words of Ezekiel's description, convinced that here was an eyewitness account of a close encounter with God. Scholars have speculated on the meaning of the prophet's words and the accuracy of the description—and the uncanny resemblance of many of its features to the gods of the Mesopotamian pantheon. Yet the stance and hymns of the winged figures supporting the divine Chariot became models for a unique new mode of prayer and meditation. And, as we will see, those heavenly figures—called in Hebrew *seraphim, cherubim,* and *ofanim*— were ultimately regarded as metaphysical intercessors for the prayers and requests of humanity. Yet at the core of the vision was an astute political warning. As the exiles spoke of the coming triumphs of the Egyptians and the independent Judean people, Ezekiel knew that even greater disasters loomed before them. He had lived through the first Babylonian siege of the city and recognized that the Babylonians would surely return at the outbreak of a new rebellion and leave little but ruins and corpses in their wake. For the time being, the Temple still stood in Jerusalem, but its days were numbered if the new king and court in Jerusalem persisted with their plans. Instructed by the spirit of the fiery Chariot to warn the People of Israel of the impending disaster, Ezekiel acted like a madman enflamed by the spirit, lying in the dust and prophesying doom for the Holy City and its leaders. He raged and fulminated—and ate a bitter bread of coarse grain mixed with dung that the people of Judah would eat under the boot of Babylon.

Yet the People of Israel didn't listen to Ezekiel—even as they also refused to listen to the prophet Jeremiah, who was sending word at the same time from Jerusalem that the political adventurism of the "bad figs" left to rule Judah would soon bring the vengeance of the Lord. In the winter of 588 B.C.E., King Nebuchadnezzar of Babylon marched on Judah, intending to punish the perfidious client-king Zedekiah and reduce the rebellious province to rubble as quickly as he could. Step by step the Babylonian armies advanced through the country spreading terror and destruction. "Their horses are swifter than leopards," wrote the prophet Habakkuk, "more fierce than the evening wolves." Jerusalem was surrounded, besieged, destroyed, and thoroughly plundered. King Zedekiah was hunted down and blinded. The terrible cruelty of that Babylonian campaign, culminating in the destruction of Solomon's Temple, is commemorated by Jews all over the world in the solemn yearly fast of Tisha b'Av.

As news of the fall of Jerusalem reached the exiles in Babylon, Ezekiel received a vision of the future in which the earthly activities of the heavenly powers would play a prominent role. God promised Ezekiel that despite the catastrophe that had befallen the People of Israel, He would "let a few of them escape from the sword, from famine and pestilence, that they may confess all their abominations among the nations where they go, and may know that I am the Lord" (12:16). In time, Ezekiel was filled with new visions: of the transformation of the scattered survivors, each imbued with a new spirit of loyalty to God and abhorrence of earthly tyrants (36:24–32); of a valley filled with dry bones that suddenly rose to life with a clatter, as the spirit of God resurrected the righteous dead who had so long lain in their graves (37:1–14). And Ezekiel was also granted a vision of the intertwined scepters of Israel and Judah, symbolizing righteous rule over the People of Israel by a divinely anointed Davidic king (37:14–28).

Ezekiel's visions became the foundation of a new mystical understanding. In his detailed description of the New Temple (chapters 40–44) that would someday be built by the righteous survivors of Israel (with dimensions and architectural features reflecting a heavenly pattern), Ezekiel recognized that Israel had a crucial role to play in its own redemption. If the Israelites could separate themselves from the sources of evil and reproduce patterns of divine power, they could tap unimaginable energy for the improvement of the world. Ezekiel's closing image of rivers gushing from the entrances of the rebuilt Temple to give life to the world anticipates countless later kabbalistic images. "And on the banks, on both sides of the river," concludes Ezekiel 47:12, "there will grow all kinds of trees for food. Their leaves will not wither nor their fruit fall, but they will bear fresh fruit every month, because the water from them flows from the sanctuary. Their fruit will be for food and their leaves for healing." From Ezekiel's vision of the Chariot and its attendants would come incantations and magical rituals aimed at enabling individuals to pass through the heavens and, like Ezekiel, enter the presence of God. Ezekiel's Chariot vision was a first step toward understanding how heaven and earth were intimately connected. And in that sense, it marked the birth of the Kabbalah.

WARS OF THE SONS OF LIGHT

Babylon fell to the rising kings of Persia. And Persia eventually fell to the advancing Macedonian armies of Alexander the Great. Once established, the principle of worldwide empire proved to be one of history's permanent features. It seemed that the People of Israel could never regain the right to live in their land and worship their God without bowing low (and paying tribute) to earthly powers who presumed to rule over everyone and everything. Yet even as the "Great Kings" of the Persian Empire permitted some of the Judean exiles to return to Jerusalem to raise up the ruins of Solomon's Temple, the mystical science of the heavens went on. Generation after generation of mystics—convinced of the omnipotence of the God of Israel—expanded and elaborated Ezekiel's original vision of the heavenly powers and the larger plan God had for humanity.

Sometimes the visions contradicted each other in details. Though Ezekiel had identified the four-winged creatures in God's retinue as *hayyot*, "living beings," or cherubim, Isaiah 6:1–4 had described them as seraphim, each having *six* wings. But their function was similar in both of the prophetic descriptions: hovering around the Divine Throne, with their beating wings producing an energized vibration, perceived by human ears as either a roaring "like the sound of many waters" (Ezekiel 1:24), or continuing hymns of praise to God (Isaiah 6:3). And where Ezekiel had seen only one divine Chariot streaking across the heavens, the Book of Zechariah, apparently composed about fifty years later, at the end of the sixth century B.C.E., mentions several.

"And again I lifted my eyes and saw, and behold, four chariots came out from between two mountains; and the mountains were mountains of bronze. The first chariot had red horses, the second black horses, the third white horses, and the fourth chariot dappled gray horses. Then I said to the angel who talked with me, 'What are these, my lord?' And the angel answered me, 'These are going forth to the four winds of heaven, after presenting themselves before the Lord of all the earth'" (Zechariah 6:1–5). Yet slowly the conflicting details coalesced as the early descriptions of close encounters with the divine Chariot were superseded by texts containing far more complex narratives.

These later works provided striking new details about the relationship between the earthly and heavenly powers and differentiated between good and evil factions within the divine retinue. In the Book of Enoch, written during the Hellenistic era, we no longer hear of a static constellation of powers surrounding the Divine Throne, but a narrative of great conflict and drama that lies beneath the surface of human history. The text tells of a great rift among God's attending angels that began soon after the creation of the world. One group of two hundred rebellious angels descended to earth and mated with human women to create a race of giants "who consumed the produce of all the people until the people detested feeding them." These wicked fallen angels also introduced to the earth the arts of weapon-making, astrology, and sexual deviation — making them obvious spiritual patrons for the Hellenistic dynasts, priests, and commanders who were currently ruling much of the eastern Mediterranean world. But the Book of Enoch also offered a complex understanding of the cosmos that stood in sharp opposition to Greek science and philosophy.

Enoch was first mentioned in Genesis 5:24 as an extraordinary figure "who walked with God" and was taken by God into the heavens, and the book that bears his name describes much of what he was permitted to see. After passing through a white marble wall surrounded by flaming tongues of fire, he was led into a great house containing the Chariot throne guarded by the cherubim. From there he was taken to see the inner workings of creation: the river of fire that fills the world's oceans, the heavenly mountains that spawn the great storms of the winter, and the storeroom of all the winds. Guided by Uriel, one of God's most powerful and trusted attendants — known as an archangel of the Divine Presence — Enoch embarked on a flying tour of the heavens. He was introduced to other archangels, soared through the gates of heaven that bellow cold, hail, frost, and snow, and was finally shown the seven lofty mountains of the northwest that guarded the Tree of Life. All these were elements of a divine order that far transcended the earthly desires and violence of the fallen angels and their earthly kin. Yet Enoch was assured that a time was soon coming when wickedness would be defeated and when the barrier between heavenly and earthly spheres would be removed. God would eventually dispatch the archangel Michael and other heavenly forces to do battle with the fallen angels and their earthly hordes. "And the earth shall be cleansed from all pollution, and from all sin, and from all suffering" (Enoch 10:22). And following the great battle between the forces of light and darkness, God promised to "open the storerooms of blessing which are in the heavens, so that I shall send them down upon the earth, over the work and toil of the children of man. And peace and truth shall become partners together in all the days of the world, and in all the generations of the world" (Enoch 11:1–2).

In oracles contained in the Book of Daniel, written in Judea at the start of the Maccabean revolt against the rule of the Seleucid king Antiochus IV in 167 B.C.E., the actions of the various heavenly forces were arranged in a definite timetable, suggesting a divine chronological plan for the events of human history. Where before the divine Chariot soared through the heavens as a timeless manifestation of God's potential power, the prophet Daniel now suggested that the long succession of worldly empires of Assyrians, Babylonians, Medes, Persians, and Greeks was just a prelude to God's direct intervention on earth. After the world had suffered under the yoke of those evil empires, Daniel prophesied, the heavenly powers would finally swing into action. "As I looked, thrones were placed and one that was Ancient of Days took his seat; his raiment was white as snow, and the hair of his head like pure wool; his throne was fiery flames, its wheels were burning fire. A stream of fire issued and came forth before him; a thousand thousands served him and ten thousand times ten thousand stood before him" (Daniel 7:9–10). And at the appointed time, God's lieutenant, the archangel Michael, "the great prince who has charge over your people," would defeat the forces of darkness—both heavenly and earthly. "And many of those who sleep in the dust of the earth shall awake, some to everlasting life, and some to shame and everlasting contempt" (Daniel 12:2).

Under the banner of the God of Israel, the Maccabean militia routed the Seleucids and liberated Jerusalem—suggesting to even the most skeptical and hard-headed Judeans that reliance on the powerful heavenly beings described in the mystical visions was not such a bad strategy after all. And in the coming decades, the mystical dream of the Chariot—and increasingly specific images of heavenly savior figures who served as its agents and emissaries—endured.

By the late first century B.C.E., new threats endangered Israel's freedom. The Romans had conquered most of the Mediterranean and had proclaimed their emperor Augustus to be a living deity. The people of Judea seemed powerless to throw off the yoke of the Romans' onerous system of tribute and taxation. Little wonder, then, that precisely at this time, they experienced one of their most intense outbreaks of visionary prophecy.

The writings of the time are filled with continuing elaboration of the well-established pattern: myriads of avenging angels in the heavens, timetables for divine intervention, and a mysterious savior figure enshrouded in glory who would answer God's command to destroy the forces of evil from the world. If we look to the ideological foundations of the time—the righteous rage of John the Baptist, the apocalyptic fervor of the Dead Sea Scrolls and the Zealot movement, and even the Gospel accounts of Jesus' battle with demons and demonic powers—we can see the mystical worldview that all of them shared. By the time of the mad, sybaritic emperor Nero, the apocalyptic tension was building. And in the aftermath of an especially brutal act by the Roman governor of Judea in the spring of 66 C.E., the people of Judea and Galilee believed that the time was right for the forces of heaven to reveal their power. Guided by visions of heavenly armies marching across the heavens above the Holy City, they expelled the Roman garrison and declared their independence from the empire.

Such a violent act of national rebellion, entirely dependent on mystical revelations of an ancient tradition, was unique in the Roman period—and perhaps in the history of the world. For the Romans, it posed a dire political danger. For if successful, the Judeans' appeal to heavenly powers could become the model for seditious ideology by Rome's other subjects throughout the Mediterranean world. So with the arrival of legions with cavalry, siege machinery, and a determined scorched-earth policy, the

Romans attacked, systematically reducing the Galilee to a waste-land, battering down the walls of Jerusalem, and burning the Temple of the God of Israel to the ground.

In the wake of the terrible suffering and destruction, the People of Israel were forced to reevaluate their ideas of heavenly powers intervening on earth. Some came to believe that the sinfulness of the People of Israel had denied them redemption — with the Romans merely acting as God's punishing agents, as the Babylonians had once done. Others believed that the timetable had merely been misinterpreted and that the heavenly forces would indeed descend to earth to throw off the yoke of all worldly empires at a later date. A few came to believe that the obscure Galilean prophet named Jesus was the anointed or "messianic" figure mentioned in the prophecies, though the salvation he offered was more in the realm of spiritual rebirth than political liberty. And then there were those who remained faithful to the original vision as it had been expressed and gradually elaborated since the time of Ezekiel.

Even as the survivors of the First Great Revolt against Rome began to pick up the pieces and reformulate their traditions without the rituals of the Temple or the presence of a priesthood, visions from beyond the ken of human senses influenced early rabbinic Judaism. No less a figure than Johanan Ben Zakkai, the founder of the first rabbinic academy at Yavne, remained deeply involved in mystical speculation. And when his students gathered to expound on the Chariot, they sometimes felt explosive effects. "Although it was a summer day," the Talmud later remarked of one of their mystical meetings, "the earth shook, and a rainbow was seen in the cloud." The early rabbis were, for the most part, reluctant to expound on this subject in public under the watchful eyes of the Roman authorities and the informers in their midst. Speaking of *another* power far greater than the empire was regarded as a clear subversive act. Thus external suspicion and internal commitment combined to give the Jewish mystical tradition even more pronounced and unmistakable political aspects.

When, in 132 C.E., the Emperor Hadrian presumed to erect

a pagan shrine in the ruins of the Temple, Rabbi Akiva—a respected scholar and inveterate mystic—served as the spiritual leader of a new national rebellion. Its focus was on God's anointing of a new messianic figure named Simon Bar-Kosiba, better known as *Bar Kokhba*, "Son of the Star." And even though this revolt, too, was brutally crushed by the Roman forces, the determined followers of Rabbi Akiva—among them the legendary sage and resistance leader Simeon Bar-Yohai—would not be cowed into believing that the Roman emperor was anything but a brutal dictator. Their faith rested in their conviction that the true power in the universe lay in the heavenly realms.

The image of the Chariot and the angels still remained vivid for Bar-Yohai and his disciples, but the problem was now how best to maintain communication with those forces and draw down their energy. The Jews would never again plan an armed revolt against Roman power, but the intensity of their national quest to bring about the earthly redemption of Israel through the intervention of the heavenly powers would continue— through the development of radically new expressions and mystical techniques.

INTO THE
HEAVENLY MANSIONS

In the sullen silence and powerlessness of life under Roman occupation, a new expression of Jewish piety was born. It was a far cry from the messianic fervor of earlier generations, yet it kept the hope for divine intervention in the course of human history very much alive. In synagogue meetings across Palestine, throughout the cities and towns of the Mediterranean, and even among the large Jewish communities of Mesopotamia (living under the rule of the other great empire of the time—the Parthians), the mystical apprehension of the heavenly powers became an increasingly important part of synagogue ritual. More than just an element of the cycle of prayers that were being standardized by the rabbinical academies for uniform worship by

Jews all over the world, it was a far deeper, emotional response to the heartlessness of the strutting officials of the imperial system. Each week's reading of the Torah offered a different lesson in the possibilities of God-given liberty.

The celebration of the late springtime festival of Shavuot, the Feast of Weeks (known as Pentecost to the Christians), became particularly important. In their commemoration of God's giving of the Torah to Moses on Mount Sinai, assembled congregations listened to the portion of the Book of Exodus describing God's fiery appearance on the summit of the mountain, accompanied by thunder and lightning, mighty quaking, and a deafening trumpet blast. And it was hardly coincidental that this Shavuot passage had been supplemented from an early date with the public reading of the first chapter of Ezekiel—and his description of the brilliance of the Chariot. These formal public readings were far removed from the context of the original prophetic visions. Instead of bursting spontaneously from the mouths of spirit-filled seers, they were now intoned from set texts and explained in prepared sermons by the leaders of the congregations. But they nevertheless underlined the core concept that would continue to characterize Jewish mysticism long after the Roman Empire was gone. In the tradition of Israel, those scriptural passages—and other texts soon to be written— reassured the faithful of the tangible and perceptible existence of heavenly powers dedicated to principles of justice that were greater than those of any earthly king.

The vivid Exodus image of the cloud-enshrouded brilliance of Sinai offered a stark contrast to the bleakness of the earthly reality for the People of Israel in the second century C.E. Throughout the Middle East and the entire Mediterranean, the patronage system was expanding its grip on society, smothering and destroying all earlier or competing forms of social and economic relationships. The cult of the emperor, embodied in the familiar statues and marble monuments that became fixtures of the landscape of modern cities throughout the empire, created a vast, homogeneous cultural ocean in which it was nearly impossible for distinctive cultural or religious minorities not to drown.

In the Land of Israel—now renamed *Palaestina* to rub the noses of the defeated rebels in the latinized name of their ancient Philistine enemies—the Romans evinced particular interest in wiping out or at least domesticating all native and independent traditions. They used the sticks of arbitrary arrests, unfair taxation, and land expropriation to break up traditional communities and families. And they used the carrots of material prosperity and social status to lure ambitious merchants and craftspeople to put aside their people's traditions and join in the free-for-all of an expanding consumer culture.

We have no idea of the number of Jews who succumbed to the lure of the dominant Roman order, yet it must certainly have been substantial—further depleting a Jewish population that had already suffered catastrophic casualties in the course of the two revolts. Under the rule of the Antonine emperors (138–192 C.E.), in the midst of a great building boom in the vast cities of Gerasa, Caesarea, and Scythopolis, the Jews of the Land of Israel were reduced from a majority of the population to a pitiful minority. The impact of official discrimination and the consequent economic hardships brought about a steady, mass emigration. The sages who did not agree to reconcile their ancestral laws to the pervasive Roman culture were branded as religious fundamentalists and the leaders of terrorist rings. At a time when they were being hunted, martyred, or compelled to live a fugitive existence, popular leaders like Rabbi Akiva, Rabbi Simeon Bar-Yohai, Rabbi Nehuniah ben ha-Kanah, and Rabbi Ishmael became subjects of heroic legends that were preserved in rabbinic texts. And it was during this period of intensified repression that biblical visions of the heavens were transformed from a passive appreciation of God's power to an active quest to appeal for His help.

The geography of the heavens grew ever more elaborate, as individual mystical trances grew more common. In fact, the circle of the Zodiac—representing the movement of the stars and the passage of the seasons—became an extraordinarily popular motif for the mosaic floors of synagogue sanctuaries throughout the Land of Israel in the later Roman and Byzantine periods. Scholars have long debated the significance of this decorative innovation, noting the biblical prohibition of the use of images. But images they are: Gemini, Cancer, Leo, Virgo, Libra, Scorpio, and all the others—labeled in Hebrew and executed in various degrees of artistic sophistication. And often placed at the center of these zodiac circles is an image of a heavenly Chariot blazing through the skies. To the Jews' pagan neighbors, this figure would almost certainly have appeared to be the Greek sun god Helios or the Roman god Sol Invictus, the unconquerable sun, ruling over all the heavenly bodies, days, and seasons. But to those who participated in the yearly synagogue recitation of the first chapter of the Book of Ezekiel, there could be no mistaking the identity of this Chariot or its role in the universe. It was the throne of God's blazing glory, propelled across the heavens by the seraphim and ofanim. The words of Ezekiel, the visions of the mystics, and the vivid, visual decoration of the synagogue thus all combined to express faith in the reality of the heavenly powers and their influence on earth.

We have numerous texts from this period that offer extraordinary detail on heavenly journeys. The prophetic tradition of more ancient times was now expressed in the visions of a special class of scholars who developed intense meditative techniques centered on Ezekiel's description of the Chariot. In time, the Chariot became the innermost image in a complex labyrinth of celestial chambers, guardian angels, and dangerous passages through which the mystic journeyed in an attempt to reach the presence of God. Such experiences were recorded in a vibrant body of literature called the texts of the *Hekhalot,* or "Heavenly Palaces," though the relatively few surviving examples are undoubtedly just a tiny selection of countless experiences whose descriptions are now lost—or were never written down. Yet they all conform to a certain basic pattern, an uncanny response of the politically powerless to their own refusal or inability to navigate the hierarchically arranged halls of Roman power from the local *praetorium*, to the provincial governor's palace, to the seat of the imperial government in Rome.

In one particularly vivid text called *Re'iyyut Yehezkiel*, the "Visions of Ezekiel," and dated to the fourth or fifth century C.E., the reader is guided upward through seven superimposed heavens. Each contains its own throne room with an angelic host gathered around it and archangels appointed to carry out the specific divine functions appropriate to each level of heavenly authority. Even more vivid are the texts known as the *Hekhalot Rabbati* and the *Hekhalot Zutrati*—the "Greater" and "Lesser Palaces." In these texts, the famous rabbinic sages Rabbi Akiva and Rabbi Ishmael—both pupils of the revered mystical teacher Nehuniah ben ha-Kanah—report in great detail about their own heavenly ascents to obtain mystical secrets or prophetic knowledge to be used in the struggle against the enemies of Israel.

Seven palaces now replaced the seven heavens of earlier literature, each guarded by detachments of threatening heavenly guardians and each entered by a single gate. In heaven as on earth, the guardians were hostile to outsiders, and the gate to each palace could be entered only through the correct pronunciation of the secret name of the appropriate guardian angel or the appropriate form of God's name. If the mystical adventurer was successful in his upward quest, he succeeded in reaching the presence of God's direct representative, the angel Metatron, whom many identified as the figure Ezekiel had seen enthroned on the Chariot. Yet success was far from assured in this perilous undertaking. A complex body of lore was presented in some of the Hekhalot texts listing the names that had to be pronounced at each stage of the journey and describing the fearful obstacle course of fire, ice, monsters, and zealous, sword-bearing angels that ultimately led to the source of all holiness.

It was a journey that was potentially fatal to even the most accomplished mystic. One of the most authoritative voices of early rabbinic Judaism, the *Tosefta*, a collection of important rabbinic opinions, underlined the dangers of such an otherworldly journey in the form of a historical parable. "Four sages entered Paradise," it reported, "Ben Azzai, Ben Zoma, Aher, and Rabbi Akiva. Ben Azzai looked and died. Ben Zoma looked and lost his mind. Aher cut himself off from his fathers and became an apostate. Only Rabbi Akiva entered and departed in peace." That famous parable represented a stern warning. The secret techniques of the ascent to the heavens—so vital in gaining divine help in redeeming Israel from its present bondage— were to be undertaken only with great caution and careful preparation by the special class of mystics known as "Descenders to the Chariot," *Yordei ha-Merkabah*.

This practice of direct, visionary communion with the heavenly powers was never wholeheartedly accepted by all rabbinic leaders, especially because there seemed to be other, less potentially heretical methods of ensuring the survival of Israel. For by the end of the second century C.E., the Roman Empire was already beginning to be wracked by internal chaos and was unable to put up the imperturbably regal front that it had maintained for more than two hundred years. Thus some leaders of the Jewish communities recognized that they might be able to take advantage of the political upheavals to gain official recognition for Judaism's autonomy without having to resort to mystical appeals. Thus after the assassination of the Emperor Commodus in 192, when Septimus Severus emerged victorious from a bitter struggle between Roman generals and began to establish a multi-ethnic empire, Jewish leaders in Palestine sought ways for Jews—as a distinct community, not individuals—to participate in the new imperial reality. Their offer of loyal participation in the empire was wholeheartedly accepted. The edicts of Septimus and his successor Caracalla officially recognized the religious office of *Nasi* or Patriarch—initially filled by Judah I (170–220 C.E.), his son Gamaliel III (220–230 C.E.), and his grandson Judah II (230–270 C.E.).

As spokesmen and protectors of their people, the Patriarchs resided in Tiberias and, later, Sepphoris, presiding over the codification of Jewish law into a definitive corpus known as the *Mishnah*. They also conscientiously preached the obligation of Jews to pay all applicable taxes and avoid displays of resistance to Rome at all costs. Ritual law and purity regulations were adapted to this political effort: Jews of priestly lineage were even allowed to contract ritual impurity in their obligation to pay homage to the images and person of the emperor. In this age of prosperity and assimilation, good citizenship was everything. Yet what of the old ideals of Israel's independence and the transcendent power of God? Dissident voices would not and could not be silenced by the opulent courts of the Patriarchs, with their close relations with the Roman rulers and specially hired bodyguards of Gallic mercenaries. But now disaffected voices, increasingly discredited and silenced in public by the national leadership, expressed renewed faith in the heavenly powers through the development of ever more complex mystical, even magical, rites.

To many Jewish mystics of the Roman period, the secrets of creation were hidden in the Torah and its symbols, and their true meaning could only be understood through divine illumination. In sharp contrast to the increasingly accepted principle of rabbinic culture, which relied on scholarship and institutionalized authority, the Descenders to the Chariot and their followers continued to believe in the powerful possibilities of direct divine contact, quite unconnected with Patriarchs or rabbinical academies. While the sages supported and honored by the Patriarchs relied on the authority of tradition and authorized legal interpretation, the mystics looked to the heavens. Refining the best techniques to fall into trances and the most effective charms to turn back the threats of the guardian angels, they crafted a method of esoteric spirituality that required no higher human sanction than the intensity of their own experiences. In that sense, the Descenders to the Chariot were spiritual rebels, contesting institutionalized religious authority and opposing the political rule of Rome. From this dissident movement came a wide variety of handbooks, guidebooks, and mystical manuals whose dates cannot be determined with precision, but all seem to have appeared during the centuries of Roman rule. Among them are works that would later become the building blocks of kabbalistic speculation, providing various systems of understanding the hidden workings of God.

Among the important works of *Merkabah* or "Chariot" mysticism is the *Shi'ur Komah*, the "Measure of Height," a grandiosely detailed description of astounding dimensions of the limbs, body, and facial features of the stunning figure enthroned on the Chariot. Its mathematical mythologies of ratios between various limbs and the symbolic numbers of the enumerated dimensions would later become a basis for the figure of the "Primordial Adam" in the later Kabbalah. The *Sar ha-Torah*, or "Prince of the Torah," text appended to some of the Hekhalot manuscripts offered techniques for private ascents to heaven to gain from the appropriate angel an instantaneous, effortless understanding of the complexities of the Torah. And finally there is a text without parallel for its importance and its almost impenetrably cryptic content that, when combined with the visions of the Chariot, formed the very core of the Kabbalah. It is the *Sefer Yetzirah*, the "Book of Creation," a compendium of secrets purportedly given by God to the Patriarch Abraham, containing the keys to the forces of life through the manipulation of "the Thirty-Two Paths of Wisdom." These consist of the first ten numbers and the twenty-two letters of the Hebrew alphabet. The Sefer Yetzirah offered would-be mystics and wonder-workers the raw material for spells, charms, and incantations — and the clues to understanding and perhaps even reproducing the process of creation itself.

In a highly cryptic description of God's projected powers, the Sefer Yetzirah lists a series of ten qualities called *sefirot* — apparently identified with the first ten numbers — that are also identified as the initial emanations of God. The text declares that creation began with a manifestation of divine will that then produced the principle of *Hokhmah*, or "Wisdom." And from that principle emerged *Binah*, or "Understanding," which in turn gave birth to the seven additional principles or sefirot of divine energy, from which all of creation was formed. Later mystics would devote great effort to identifying these sefirot with the later kabbalistic symbols, but it is already clear that the earlier understanding of God's angelic attendants was being transformed into a constellation of abstract powers. The letters of the Hebrew alphabet were likewise seen as powerful elements whose combinations could produce far-reaching effects. Thus by the end of the Roman period, the earlier warnings against the danger of heavenly visions went increasingly unheeded. The ancient faith of Israel slowly split into an official religion, accepted as legitimate by emperors and aristocrats, and another, occult tradition — conveyed in whispers and magical wishes — that kept the apocalyptic faith of the common People of Israel alive.

THE GREAT BETRAYAL

Could any other ancient people have maintained such an unshakable faith in God's power to intervene in history? Could any be persuaded that the traditions of Israel held the secret keys to gaining political and even economic freedom from the earthly powers that be? Throughout the Hellenistic and early Roman eras, large numbers of pagans had been attracted to the religion of Israel as a class of sympathizers called "Godfearers." In cities throughout the Mediterranean, they had crowded into weekly synagogue assemblies and celebrated the festivals of the Hebrew year. Yet the destruction of Jerusalem and the transformation of Judaism into a tolerated, if not warmly endorsed, minority religion — led by an officially recognized elite — served as a powerful public demonstration that the institution of world empire had come to stay. And even that level of toleration was not to last long. With the adoption of Christianity as the official faith of the Roman and soon-to-be Byzantine Empire, the Patriarchate was abolished and the scattered Jewish communities of the Mediterranean were left to fend for themselves. Little wonder then that apocalyptic prophecies regained their power, and Jewish hopes turned eastward. The Sassanian Dynasty of Persia, in its militant brand of Zoroastrianism, had shown no particular favor for the Jewish communities of Babylonia, but as committed foes of the Romans, they — like the Persian kings Cyrus and Darius a thousand years earlier — could perhaps be seen as unwitting agents of God.

By the fifth century C.E., new texts, written by anonymous seers and mystics, predicted imminent redemption. Works like *Otot ha-Mashiach,* "Signs of the Messiah," and *Agadat ha-Mashiach,* "Legend of the Messiah," described God's coming intervention in history through a great war led by warriors in Persian costume. A late saying ascribed to Rabbi Simeon Bar-Yohai warned that "if you see the horse of a Persian tied to a post in the Land of Israel, expect the footsteps of the Messiah." Yet these specific predictions, translated into prescriptions for political action, proved to be extremely dangerous. Enthusiastic Jewish support for the successful Persian invasion of Byzantine Palestine in 614 C.E. resulted in the return of Jews to the Holy City of Jerusalem and a release from their status as a despised minority. But when the Byzantine forces regrouped and defeated the Persians in 629, Jewish leaders were slaughtered as turncoats and Jewish communities reduced to pariah status again. The lesson should have been learned that one could never smash the power of empire by courting an emperor—even the enemy of one's enemy. But an even greater historical miscalculation was about to unfold with the rise of the Muslim Empire.

It is difficult to imagine today—after more than a century of bitter and focussed conflict between Jews and Arabs—how great were the hopes and apocalyptic expectations evoked in the early seventh century C.E. by the rising of the Arabian tribes against the power of Byzantium. The Emperor Heraclius might have turned back the Persian threat, yet far to the south in Arabia, at the starting points of the overland trade routes that brought incense and the exotic goods of the Indian Ocean through the deserts to the Mediterranean port cities, a widespread movement of militant resistance—based on a novel apocalyptic ideology—was gaining strength. Rumors began to circulate in Roman official circles about the unrest among the Arab tribes, but that people—despised for so long as shiftless nomads—was not taken as seriously as it should have been. Among the Jews, however, the signs of God's imminent judgment were clear—and obtained through the technique of a mystical ascent.

An anonymous Aramaic text, *Sitrei de-Simeon Bar-Yohai,* or the "Revelations of Simeon Bar-Yohai," whose origins may go back to the seventh century, describes the heavenly journey of the famous second-century rebel against the Romans. Making his way through the labyrinth of palaces, Rabbi Simeon finally arrives in the presence of the angel Metatron, who reassures him that the Arabs, the sons of Ishmael, will be God's chosen instrument for the obliteration of the Roman Empire, traditionally identified with the sons of Esau. "Do not fear," Metatron informed Rabbi Simeon, "for the Holy One, blessed be He, only brings the kingdom of Ishmael in order to save you from this wickedness. He raises up over them a Prophet according to his will and will conquer the land for them and they will come and restore it in greatness, and there will be great terror between them and the sons of Esau."

And indeed in the twelve years between the beginning of Muhammad's movement in 622 C.E. and the appearance of armed Arab forces in the Land of Israel in 634, the trajectory of history was decisively changed. Scholars now debate whether the initial Muslim conquests should be described as a sweeping invasion of desert warriors into the settled regions of the Middle East or as a combination of outside attacks and wholesale *internal* popular uprisings against the repressive Byzantine bureaucracy. Yet it surely must have seemed—at least briefly—that the time of the long-predicted downfall of empire had arrived and that a millennial age had begun. The hated emperors had lost their control of the Land of Israel in an era no less wondrous than the time of the fall of Babylon and the return of the exiles to Jerusalem, when the prophecies indeed had come true.

After almost five hundred years of persecution, exclusion, and theological denigration by the forces of Church and Empire, seventy Jewish families were allowed back into the Holy City of Jerusalem, to establish a permanent residential quarter from which to conduct their religious rituals and carry on their trade. The arrival in Jerusalem of the Muslim general Umar ibn al-Khattab marked the beginning of an entirely new earthly regime for Jerusalem. Now in political control of Palestine, Syria, Egypt, Mesopotamia, and Arabia, Muslim leaders began to create a composite civilization that merged the ancient heritage of Jews and Arabs into a new faith that aimed at establishing a kingless kingdom of God. Pointing to their common ancestor Abraham—who was, through Hagar, the patriarch of Ishmael and the Arabs and, through Sarah, the patriarch of Isaac and the Israelites—the Islamic tradition gradually adapted many of the most vivid Jewish mystical beliefs and symbols that had been developing for centuries under Roman rule. The historian David Halperin has pointed to the many suggestive references to heavenly "throne-bearers," guardian angels, and ascending levels of heaven in the Muslim tradition that almost certainly reflects the language of Merkabah mysticism.

The rebuilding of the site of the Temple in Jerusalem became a monument to a particular heavenly journey: Muhammad's reported nighttime flight on his miraculous steed *Burak,* "lightning," to the "further mosque, *Masjid al-Aqsa,* from which he made a heavenly ascension, or *mi'raj,* to the highest heaven — precisely in the manner of the Descenders to the Chariot. Yet the ideal soon lost its mystical passion. As Umar's successors, the Umayyad caliphs of Damascus, embellished the Temple Mount with monumental buildings and the religious center of their own royal rule and power, the imagined grandeur of the heavenly realm symbolized the power and grandeur of the Umayyad leadership. Little wonder, then, that new visions arose in Jewish mystical circles to amend the original predictions. The Revelations of Rabbi Simeon Bar-Yohai was expanded in the eighth century to include a prophecy that linked the Umayyad Dynasty to previous evil empires and declared that redemption would come only after the last of *its* kings was deposed.

Yet off to the east in Mesopotamia, where the Jewish presence had been extensive and well established since the time of Ezekiel, there was a greater hope—and greater reason to hope—that a new age could dawn. Unlike the situation in the Land of Israel, where centuries of Byzantine rule had reduced the institutions of Jewish communal life to a few small Galilean academies, the Jewish institutions of Mesopotamia remained vibrant and visible. Their sages produced the single greatest compendium of Jewish law, legend, and literature in the Babylonian Talmud. The great rabbinic academies of Sura and Pumbedita drew eager students from all over the Near East and were presided over by the *gaonim,* religious authorities who oversaw the enactment and enforcement of Jewish ritual law. There was, in addition, an officially recognized *Resh Galuta,* or Exilarch, who served as the political leader of the Jewish community. During the rule of the Umayyad caliphs of Damascus, Babylonia remained a peripheral province. But with the rise to power of a coalition of political and religious dissidents from among the Umayyads' subject peoples under the leadership of Abu al-Abbas, the ideal of a new civilization much more in line—at least initially—with the Muslim vision of a heavenly kingdom on earth was revived.

In place of a select group of Arab aristocrats who had adopted the trappings of Byzantine grandees, political and religious factions from Persia, Mesopotamia, and Arabia now began to come together, establishing a new, composite culture and a brand-new capital city at Baghdad. A significant segment of the leadership of the Jewish communities in Mesopotamia joined in this new movement, with the Exilarch and some of the wealthiest members of the community shifting their residences to the new city. The fortunes of the new Abbasid Dynasty soared to unprecedented levels. Baghdad became the bustling centerpoint of a long highway of exchange that stretched from Spain in the west all the way to the Far East. And as some Jewish merchants grew rich and intoxicated by the Thousand-and-One-Nights atmosphere of Baghdad, the leadership of the Jewish community in Abbasid Iraq became increasingly linked to the interests of the caliphal court. Out in the rural districts of the great Tigris and Euphrates Valley, the vast majority of the Jewish population continued to struggle for existence as farmers and craftspeople. And the pattern of imperial life that had arisen so many times before now materialized again. The solidarity of the House of Israel was severely tested by the seductive grandeur of earthly kings. And once again, a movement arose within Judaism that turned away from complete reliance on rabbinical authority, preferring to direct their appeals for support and sustenance to the heavenly powers of the Chariot.

How shocked the prophet Ezekiel would have been to see how his original vision of the Chariot and its accompanying angels transformed from a symbol of God's transcendent glory to a solver of personal problems: debt, illness, neighbors' spats, lost loves, and lost prosperity. There had been a long tradition within Judaism of practical magic—known from such diverse sources as the biblical tales of the wonder-working prophets Elijah and Elisha; from the Talmudic stories of the great rainmaker Honi the Circle Drawer; and from the many historical references to divinely inspired healers and miracle workers in the first century C.E. But by the eighth century, the practice of popular magic merged with the texts and symbols of a developing mystical tradition. And in subsequent centuries of Islamic rule, the isolated, alienated Jewish population of Iraq's hinterland turned to the services of a class of professional amulet makers and magicians whose art was drawn directly from the mystical journeys and otherworldly visions of the Descenders to the Chariot. Even today there is clear archaeological evidence of this phenomenon: scattered throughout the ruins of medieval Jewish settlements in the Tigris and Euphrates Valley are remains of amulets and bowls inscribed with strange symbols, figures, and drawings of heavenly beings and monsters, bearing heartfelt private appeals from simple folk who found an easier access to the heavens than to the caliph's court or the elite circles of the rabbinical academies.

ANGELS AND AMULETS

Without an awareness of the earlier complex tradition of the Hekhalot literature, this widespread use of amulets and "magical bowls" could be considered just a folk superstition. Yet the powerful charms they bore included the names of angels and heavenly beings known from the Hekhalot traditions and mystical combinations of letters produced in accordance with the profound secrets of the Sefer Yetzirah. At the same time, new handbooks like *Harba de-Moshe*, the "Sword of Moses," and *Otiot de-Rabbi Akiva*, the "Alphabet of Rabbi Akiva," and the *Sefer ha-Razim*, the "Book of Mysteries," offered detailed instructions for divination, spell-casting, and treasure-hunting to a new class of professional sorcerers. At first this development of Jewish magical lore was restricted to the enclosed culture of the Tigris and Euphrates Valley. But as the years passed and the population pressure built up in Iraq's crowded riverside towns and thickly settled canal districts, increasing numbers of Jews sought new opportunities in the West—in the wide-open lands of North Africa that had been brought into the Islamic world through the force of conquest. And they could take a private new faith with them, one that might offer protection from the political and economic hazards that continued to confront the People of Israel. Thus the lore of the Chariot and the Names of God and of the angels would soon be adopted as the secret faith of the increasing numbers of Jewish merchants and travelers in an age that was characterized not by empire but by far-flung international trade.

By the mid 800s, the Golden Age of Abbasid Baghdad had given way to an era of economic collapse in the Mesopotamian heartland, brought about by the profligate spending and unceasing dynastic disputes of the later Abbasids. Yet this growing chaos in the Mesopotamian heartland offered an unprecedented opportunity. New networks of traders were now free to take over the lucrative commerce that Baghdad had once firmly controlled. One such group was the the class of long-distance merchants identified as Jews and known as the *Radhaniya,* most likely named after their place of origin in the region of Radhan in southern Iraq. Their travels were far-reaching, extending from southern Spain to Italy, across North Africa, through Syria and Mesopotamia, out to the Indian Ocean and China. Their trade goods were the most precious commodities known in the ninth century: exotic medicines, spices, gems, silks, and perfumes from the Orient, and furs, long swords, silver, and slaves brought from the barbarian countries of the north and west. And packed in the crates and camel bags of the Radhanites and other Jewish traders—along with their rich merchandise—was the secret knowledge of the power of the names of the angels and of God. In their magical spells and amulets addressed to the heavenly powers, they sought protection in an age when the former centers of political power and spiritual leadership had been effectively stilled.

Through the ninth century—as sectarian and religious disputes raged among rival exilarchs and the sages of the great academies back in Mesopotamia—the great emporium of al-Qayrawan in Tunisia gradually became a cosmopolitan center of culture, economy, and politics. It also became the site of one of the most innovative and independent-minded Jewish communities in the world. Deposed exilarchs, messianic pretenders, business messengers, philosophers, and mystics of various tradition made their way westward to al-Qayrawan, an obvious place of asylum ever since its takeover by a dynasty of local governors-turned-despots—known as the Aghlabids. Basing their power on the lucrative international trade that passed through their territory, the Aghlabids embarked on a campaign of conquest northward through Malta and Sicily and onward even to southern Italy. And in the court of the Aghlabid Dynasty, mystical speculation flowed powerfully, if seamlessly, into the disciplines of philosophy, astronomy, medicine, and alchemy. The involvement of Jews in the Aghlabid court was extensive, and the old esoteric traditions were eventually taught quite openly. In the early tenth century, the Egyptian-born philosopher Isaac ben Solomon Israeli served as the private physician of the emir and studied the Sefer Yetzirah as a valuable work of scientific and medical principles, as well as mystical lore. Al-Qayrawan also became the scene of independent Jewish learning, with the establishment of a great academy in the late tenth century by the refugee Babylonian scholar Hushiel ben Elhanan.

But perhaps an even more significant development was the influx to al-Qayrawan of Jewish mystics and magicians known as *Baalei Shem,* or "Masters of the Name." Utilizing the secret names of God and of the angels, they achieved great public acclaim in their reported feats of magic: making themselves invisible, tying the hands of robbers, stilling the stormy ocean, raising corpses to life, and accomplishing long journeys in seconds by psychically transporting themselves. Though we know of the practices of these North African Baalei Shem only from the accusations of their opponents, it is clear that their secret lore was placed in the service of commerce. Here in a community whose prosperity was intimately linked to trading and long-distance travel, they offered services that protected their clients against traders' fears of distance, robbery, weather, and mortality. And their ritual reportedly utilized papyrus amulets, leaves of olive trees to be thrown into the face of robbers, and inscribed potsherds to be tossed into the raging surf of an angry sea. The familiar traditions of invocation suggest a continuous elaboration and refinement from antiquity through medieval times. Yet the conspicuous prominence of mystical practices among the Jews of North Africa would not go uncontested for long. Back in Babylonia, new leaders had arisen in the famous Jewish academies and they sought to bring al-Qayrawan and the other independent centers of Jewish trade and magic back under their control.

After a long period of internal conflict among Babylonian sages, the leaders of the great academy of Pumbedita—Sherira Gaon and his son Hai Gaon—succeeded in establishing a certain degree of uniformity in the religious regulation of business practices among Babylonian Jewish merchants. And in an attempt to regain some of their lost power, they renewed direct contacts with North Africa, supporting the establishment of a new academy in al-Qayrawan under a faithful ally, Rabbi Jacob ben Nissim ibn Shahin. Not unexpectedly, Rabbi Jacob was among the first public figures in al-Qayrawan to call into question the popular religion of the Baalei Shem. Thus around 1010, the leaders of the congregation at al-Qayrawan dispatched a letter to Hai Gaon in Pumbedita, asking questions about these magical practices and requesting an official response.

Were the rituals and spells of these Jewish sorcerers part of the genuine tradition? Were they legitimate? If not, what was to be done about them? In light of the widespread popularity of these magical practices, Hai Gaon was not willing to risk an all-out conflict. His interest was more in reasserting control. As a skillful politician as well as religious leader, he acknowledged that there was a place for the Hekhalot literature and the Descent to the Chariot within the mainstream Jewish tradition — but only so long it was done under rabbinical supervision, in the proper scholarly way.

In his written responses to the al-Qayrawan community, Hai Gaon revealed his familiarity with works like the Sword of Moses, the Lesser and Greater Palaces, the Sar ha-Torah, and other texts. Yet he used a tone of authoritarian condescension to indicate that mystical speculation must be developed in an atmosphere of closely supervised scholarly training and be entirely separated from the affairs of the world. Hai set out the requirements for achieving a genuine mystical experience, insisting that anyone "who desires to behold the Merkavah and the hekhalot of the angels on high must follow certain procedures. He must fast a certain number of days, put his head between his knees and whisper many traditional songs and hymns toward the earth. Then he gazes into their inner rooms and chambers, as if seeing the seven palaces with his own eyes, and he sees, as if entering from one palace to another, and perceives what is in it." Such warnings and condemnations — in their goal of attempting to maintain discipline and control over the Jewish mystical movement — did not discourage further mystical developments. They had already become too basic to the day-to-day life of Jewish communities to be stopped. For at the heart of their power was that centuries-old belief in the vision of the prophet Ezekiel: God was not restricted to any land but manifested His power through a constellation of forces that could be studied and at least functionally understood.

Who knows what would have happened to the ancient mystical tradition had the Babylonian gaonim succeeded in reining in and closely controlling the movement. Yet there is no evidence that the unauthorized practice of magic condemned by Hai Gaon was in the least bit deterred. On the contrary, in the decades after the Christian millennial year 1000, a series of political and economic upheavals from Babylon to Western Europe fragmented the Mediterranean region into a patchwork of small, hostile political units, and the help of the heavenly powers was needed more desperately than ever. The traders who had once prospered from the ability to cross continents and exchange precious merchandise were now forced to utilize any available means to match sellers and buyers with valuable trade goods. The complex heavenly hierarchy of God's powers could be dependably appealed to for good weather, rapid journeys, and safety from physical danger in an ominous new era of religious warfare and ethnic enmity.

Just after the year 1000, the Fatimid caliph of Egypt al-Hakim embarked on a ruthless campaign against non-Muslims in his dominions. In 1055, the once great line of the gaonim of Sura and Pumbedita in Babylonia was extinguished with the invasion of the Seljuk Turks. Far to the west, in 1057 al-Qayrawan, so long a center of alternative ideas and independence, was sacked and its Jewish community was scattered. Within just a few more decades, the Jewish community in Palestine would be decimated in the bloodbath otherwise known as the First Crusade. Thus by around 1100, a new age was dawning, with the old centers destroyed and the Jews dispersed ever more widely in exile. The vision of Ezekiel seen so long before by the waters of Chebar as a realization of the transcendent power of God would now flare brightly in places where it had never appeared before. The potency of the old charms and incantations would never be far from the heart of the Jewish tradition, yet the key to the future would be the continual, systematic elaboration of the original celestial vision. In it, the experiences of heavenly journeys and the vision of God on His Chariot would be transformed into a far more abstract philosophy.

GOD'S MANY FACES
Chapter 2

I f the roots of the Kabbalah lie in the ancient mystical faith of Israel and Babylonia, its rising trunk and spreading branches soon offered unique spiritual shelter from the violence and intolerance of medieval European society. Until around 1000, the scattered Jewish communities of Europe, never numbering more than a few thousand and broken up into tiny colonies of traders, craftsmen, and farmers were the last survivors of the commercial life of the fallen Roman Empire, with its once-stable routes of communications and networks of trade. Along the great highways and waterways from the Euphrates to the Atlantic flowed merchandise, ideas, and rabbinical rulings, linking even the most distant congregations to the great academies and sages of the East. Yet after the middle of the ninth century, with the impoverishment of Palestine, the political upheavals in Baghdad, and the growing isolation of Europe, the Jews living in the villages and towns of southern Italy, Provence, and the

Rhineland were left to piece together a new society by themselves. Although we know little about the size and character of most Jewish communities in Western Europe in the so-called Dark Ages, the occasional references to Jews in church chronicles and fortuitously preserved snatches of Hebrew poetry and family chronicles offer suggestive indications of the depth of magical and mystical belief. As always, it meshed closely with the material needs and ambitions of its practitioners.

With the slow deterioration of economic activity throughout Western Europe, many Jewish communities fell back into traditional patterns of village life and small-scale regional trade. A few exceptionally ambitious individuals developed commercial connections with Jewish traders from the Islamic world and procured the spices, silks, and jewels that were so highly prized among the knights and kings of Christendom. As was the case with the Radhanite traders, heavenly protection was needed to ensure the precise confluence of the right winds, the right timing, and the well-being of such valuable shipments. And it is clear from the disdainful remarks of archbishop Agobard of Lyons in the 820s, in his polemical work *De judaicis superstitionibus*, "On the Superstitions of the Jews," that the old mystical contemplation of the Shi'ur Komah—the mystical use of the numbers drawn from the proportions of the divine figure enthroned in the Chariot—was a conspicuous part of their faith. In his attacks on the privileged position of Jewish traders in the courts of the local nobles, Agobard condemned the Jews for worshipping God as a gigantic heavenly figure, and for precisely calculating the most favorable prices, sailing dates, and markets from their mystical contemplation of the length of their "God's" nose, lips, cheeks, forehead, arms, and legs.

In another region of Europe—southern Italy—there is intriguing evidence of mystical innovation, with the merging of the ancient traditions of the Chariot and the divine names with the new strains of magical practice emanating from Abbasid Baghdad. The mixture proved to be potent, for it was from the communities of southern Italy that the new composite tradition would travel to Spain, North Africa, France, and the Rhineland and provide the common ground from which a distinctly European Jewish mysticism would grow. The Jewish communities in towns and villages along the hilly spine of the Italian peninsula had proved themselves to be unusually resilient. Through the centuries of political and social chaos that attended the disintegration of Roman civilization, they had adapted to the changing conditions, making the most of their geographic position at the crossroads of cultures and the fortunate mix of natural resources and commercial opportunities that came their way. From the hills and green valleys of Apulia came all the land's rich bounty: wine, olives, grain, and the thick wool of the grazing sheep to be spun into fine textiles. Towns like Venosa and Oria became centers of both commerce and learning. The small harbors along the southeast coast, like Bari, Brindisi, and Otranto, served as embarkation points for the yearly springtime traffic of traders to the Byzantine Empire and pilgrims to the shrines of the Holy Land. And on the annual return trips in late summer, the Italian ports welcomed the convoys of high-prowed ships bringing traders with their rich cargoes of spices and luxuries from the Orient, and returning pilgrims carrying relics, amulets, and mystical texts.

This was a time and a place where magic still seemed to possess invincible power; when the medical and metaphysical skill of the Hekhalot mystics was believed to move mountains and give life to the dead. We have a unique source of information about this period—preserved by chance in the library of the cathedral of Toledo in Spain—where later zealous examiners of the Inquisition collected and confiscated every "suspect" Jewish text they could find. The document in question is the eleventh-century *Megillat Yuḥasin,* the "Scroll of Genealogies," also known as the *"Chronicle of Aḥima'az."* Written in Hebrew in the southern Italian town of Oria, it traces in rhymed prose the family history of its author—Aḥima'az ben Paltiel—all the way back to the days of his great-great-great-great-great grandfather Rabbi Amittai, who served as the head of Oria's Jewish community and religious academy. As the dominating figure, Rabbi Amittai was remembered as having "a number of amiable and worthy sons, intelligent and learned men, scholars and poets zealously teaching, worthy disciples, men of merit and renown, masters of secret lore, grasping and applying the deeper truth of scriptures." Through the flowery praises of this founding father and his sons, we can recognize the clear references to the main texts of the mystical tradition—particularly as it had developed in Palestine through the Roman period. Amittai's sons are described as "adepts in the mysteries, fathoming the veiled principles of Hokhmah and Binah [mystical love and traditional wisdom] and of all abstruse learning; wise in the knowledge of the Book of Jashar, and familiar with the hidden meaning of the Merkaba." The prominent mention given to the family's mystical erudition offers a clear indication of the high regard in which it was held for generations to come. But it was also remembered that in the time of the fabled Rabbi Amittai, an even more powerful magical lore arrived in the harbors and hill towns of Apulia. It was borne on the winds of Islamic expansion and invasion—and fueled by the deep rifts growing within the leadership of Babylonian Jewry.

All we have to go on is a fable—about a mysterious rabbi and a sorcerer named Abu Aharon. "In the days of these good men," relates the chronicler Ahima'az son of Paltiel of his honored ancestors, "there came from Baghdad, from our beloved ones, an esteemed man of a distinguished family, an illustrious scholar, warding off wrath from the descendants of those that sleep in Hebron." Thus begins the medieval description of one of the greatest wonder-workers in the history of the Middle Ages, a figure who may provide a human link between the great age of the Descenders to the Chariot and the further development of European Jewish magic and mysticism. For once the legendary details are stripped away from his life story, its basic details dovetail neatly with the period's larger historical events. And in the tales of exorcisms, resuscitations, and miraculous escapes, we can begin to see that the arrival of Abu Aharon in southern

Italy marked the introduction of a far more activist kind of mystical practice. Its goal was not merely to gain divine blessing but to manipulate the forces of nature itself.

According to the Chronicle of Ahima'az, Abu Aharon was a scion of the House of David—the son of an exilarch in Baghdad. Yet he was banished from his native land for magical improprieties. One day, so the story went, he was tending his father's mill on the banks of the Tigris when a roaming lion entered the millhouse and killed the donkey who turned the heavy millstone. So enraged was Abu Aharon at this loss of a faithful draft animal that he pronounced certain holy names of God and appropriate incantations, thereby placing a spell on the lion and forcing him to continue the dead donkey's job. When Abu Aharon's father came to the mill and saw the harnessed lion turning the millstone, he declared that his son had sinned by using his magic to make something exalted serve a low purpose—and ordered that he be banished from the country for an extended period of time. The tale then describes Abu Aharon's magical peregrinations, from Babylonia to Jaffa and by ship across the Mediterranean Sea to the port of Gaeta south of Rome. In one colorful episode after another, Abu Aharon exhibits his extraordinary powers as he travels among the Italian Jewish communities. Confronting wicked sorceresses and bringing the dead to life—and the restless spirits of the deceased to final peace—he gains fame far and wide. He is eventually invited to the town of Oria, where Rabbi Amittai and his sons invite him to settle and serve as their spiritual leader—passing judgments on ritual and criminal matters and condemning sinners to death. Among the Jewish communities of southern Italy he rose to a position of unquestioned power, eclipsing the leadership of the individual communities. Although we can assume that the tales of his changing kidnapped boys from mules back to human form, raising the dead, and exorcising evil spirits are more imaginary than authentic, they are all connected with the tradition that Abu Aharon brought to the region a highly developed technique of magical power through the use of amulets and incantations bearing the secret names of God.

Up to this point, the story is filled with colorful wonders and cartoon-like situations, yet the inclusion of details of the invasion of southern Italy by the Aghlabid Dynasty of Tunisia offers a sudden touch of reality. It is well documented by both Muslim and Christian sources that in 841 the coastal city of Bari was captured by the Tunisian forces. The Muslim hold on southern Italy was, in fact, so strong that even Pope John VIII (872–882) reportedly had to pay tribute to the Aghlabids. The Chronicle of Ahima'az relates in detail how Abu Aharon became the chief advisor of the commander of the invasion force, lending his magical powers to their colonial rule. So valuable was he, according to the Chronicle, that the Aghlabid commander of Bari refused to allow Abu Aharon to return to Baghdad at the end of his imposed period of exile—and sent warships after him to bring him back to Bari when he attempted to flee. But using his powerful incantations to halt the pursuing fleet, Abu Aharon made good his escape, leaving behind him only a legend, and bequeathing to the Jews of southern Italy a new repertoire of mystical charms.

Of the subsequent events we have only a series of personal vignettes, extending for a century and more. Having learned new secrets from Abu Aharon, Rabbi Amittai's son Shephetiah, described as "zealous in the pursuit of wisdom," made the most of his powers. Against the background of the Byzantine reconquest of southern Italy (which began with the recapture of Bari in 871), Shephetiah of Oria worked his magical powers to overturn the edict of the emperor Basil I ordering a forcible conversion of the Jews. First arguing with skill and wit in a public debate on the relative merits of Judaism and Christianity, Shephetiah then cured the emperor's daughter of an evil spirit, thereby obtaining the emperor's consent to exempt the Jews of Oria from the decree. The sense of security was short-lived, for by the beginning of the tenth century, Muslim raids resumed along the coast of Calabria, and Oria was occupied, with many of its Jewish population killed or taken prisoner. In this unexpectedly violent way, the mystical tradition was dispersed far beyond Apulia. Among the Jewish captives taken from Oria was a young man named Shabbetai Donnolo, later famous as a physician and philosopher, whose commentary on the Sefer Yetzirah, the Book of Creation, detailed some of the practical techniques of manipulating sacred names for magic and divination.

Yet perhaps most telling of all, in respect to the gradual diffusion of these mystical secrets, is the legend of the "four captives" from the same period. The fable that circulated much later in Spain related that Muslim privateers had hijacked a group of four sages—all well versed in the secrets of the Merkabah and the use of divine names—who had set out by sea from Bari. Their mystical knowledge apparently did not help them gain freedom, for they remained in captivity until they were ransomed with money raised by Jewish communities across North Africa and along the Spanish coast. In gratitude for their rescue, each of the sages settled in one of the communities that had set them free. And in each of the communities, a distinctive mystical tradition was established, further spreading and deepening the ancient belief in the earthly power of the heavenly spheres.

MAGIC AND MARTYRDOM

The mysterious figure of Abu Aharon of Baghdad left its traces in another part of medieval Europe, and his dimly perceived footsteps offer an alternative route to the reconstruction of the history of the Kabbalah. While his brief appearance in Italy in a cloud of legend and miracle tales became the cherished memory of scattered mystics throughout Italy, North Africa, and Spain, a certain prominent family of sages, poets, and preachers from the Lombard town of Lucca transferred Abu Aharon's secret lore far to the north. They were the descendants of Rabbi Moses ben Kalonymus, a famous liturgical poet whom Abu Aharon chanced to meet in the course of his wanderings and reportedly "transmitted all his secrets to him." In centuries to come, Rabbi Moses' descendants would proudly trace their unique spiritual authority to this connection—in their knowledge of "the secret of the true version of the prayers." Yet while

Abu Aharon's other protégés—the Amittai family of Oria—remained in the central Mediterranean, the Kalonymus family left for the Rhineland, where they prospered through trade, skill in local political relations, and their mystical powers derived from their use of the Holy Name in amulets and in incantations. And their migration was tied to larger developments in European society and to an act of imperial patronage. According to the thirteenth-century account of Eleazar of Worms, one of the family's most famous descendants, "King Charles brought them with him from the country of Lombardy, and settled them in Mainz, and there they multiplied and flourished very much."

Historians have long debated the precise identification of the "King Charles" who invited the Kalonymus family to the Rhineland. Yet whether it was Charlemagne (who reigned 800–814), or—as most scholars now agree—his grandson Charles the Bald (who reigned 875–877), a new day was dawning in the river valleys and fertile plains of northern Europe that would have fateful consequences for the history of the Jews. Over the centuries since the disintegration of the Roman Empire, regional commercial centers had arisen as agricultural production intensified and long-distance trade accelerated—exchanging slaves, furs, and timber from the Baltic region and Russia for the spices, silks, and ornaments of the south. Although most towns of Dark Age Europe were merely villages huddled around the residence of a local leader, trade was essential to seal bonds of loyalty between political leaders through the exchange of valuable goods. By the late eighth century, the great lords of medieval Europe carefully controlled access to specialized craftsmen and the kinds of products, delicacies, and precious items that could cement alliances or make life at court conspicuously grand.

Archaeological excavations of the walled trade-and-crafts compound of Dorestad in the Netherlands has revealed the extent to which foreign traders were carefully controlled and segregated from the rest of the population during the reign of Charlemagne, in order to maintain complete royal control over their goods. Yet within a few decades, with the breakdown of the unity of Charlemagne's kingdom, centralized control of trade crumbled and every regional king—and many local nobles—sought to gain access to trade goods for themselves. The Jews of Italy were in a perfect position to become involved in this northern commerce, both as craftsmen, weavers, and as bearers of contacts with the East. Thus, under the watchful eye of a *Magister Iudaeorum,* or "Supervisor of Jews," Jewish traders flocked northward to the major river valleys, obtaining slaves, furs, and swords (all highly prized in the Islamic world) for the artworks, jewelry, and spices of the East. The story of "King Charles's" invitation to the Kalonymus family of Lucca to come northward is only one incident in a far wider historical trend of officially encouraged immigration. Legend has it that Charlemagne himself granted a group of Jews—led by a certain Rabbi Machir who was reportedly of Davidic lineage—the rights of settlement and commerce in the Provençal town of Narbonne. It is likely that the various Jewish communities in Europe during this period were linked by complex family relationships and religious connections that enabled them to maintain valuable trading contacts in the East.

Certainly the Jews were an alien element in the river valleys and ports of northwest Europe, not only for their strange language, customs, and cosmopolitan outlook, but for the bizarre magical beliefs that some of their religious leaders practiced with such devotion. In the legendary stories of the chain of tradition brought by Abu Aharon, in repeated references to esoteric learning and rituals, we can understand how, in gross and ignorant caricature, the Jews of Europe gained a reputation for sorcery. At the core was the continuing belief in the Chariot and creation. Texts from the East were preserved and avidly studied, perhaps no one more than the complex number-mysticism of the Shi'ur Komah. And for the prominence of the image of the enthroned figure on the Chariot, we have already mentioned the angry testimony of Archbishop Agobard of Lyons—the great opponent of the Jews and their influence in encouraging trade throughout the Rhône Valley—who bitterly condemned the vile "Jewish superstitions" that encouraged them to worship a gigantic heavenly figure of a man with arms and legs. The reality of Jewish mystical speculations on the figure in the divine Chariot was far more sophisticated—and far less idolatrous—than Agobard suggested. But it mattered little to most European princes and rulers. With Europe's growing economy, diversity could be tolerated in the name of prosperity. The attraction of trade goods and the clink of gold and silver coins was more than enough—at least for the time being—for medieval Christian sensibilities to look the other way.

An intense period of anti-Jewish agitation spread through France around 1000, the millennial year with its apocalyptic hopes for the return of Christ and punishment for all heretics and non-believers. But the persecution of Jews and their expulsion from various cities merely hurt those cities' economies. The lesson was learned, and before long the active recruitment of Jews in new communities throughout the Rhineland signaled an end to the repression, and the church, recognizing the economic consequences for their own prosperity, reined in the fomenters of anti-Semitic persecution. By the beginning of the eleventh century, the members of the Kalonymus family were settled in towns along the west bank of the Rhine, in Lorraine, and in the ancient episcopal seats and trade centers of Cologne, Mainz, Speyer, Worms, and Trier. They were also to be found farther eastward in the religious and political centers of Regensburg and Prague. Their expansion seems in large measure to have been encouraged by local officials. Bishop Rüdiger of Speyer, seeking a boost to the economy of his city, encouraged Jews to settled in order "to increase the honor of the town a thousandfold." Yet threatening storm clouds were building that would put an end to the Jews' protected status. Their very success in promoting trade and their growing prosperity marked them as tempting targets in the eyes of poverty-stricken peasants and unemployed townspeople when the old feudal system began to deteriorate.

A widespread religious movement gathered force in the 1090s throughout Western Europe, closely tying together the goals of Christian unification, the recovery of the holy places, and control of the eastern trade routes. Beneath the rhetoric of the crusading movement lay the economic ambitions of European traders and merchant cities. They would benefit to a far greater extent from the coming bloodshed than the peasants in search of absolution or the leading knights of France, the Low Countries, Germany, and England, who sought landed estates in the Middle East. Yet the knights and the peasants were the strike force. Roused to action by the preaching of Pope Urban II at the Council of Clermont and by the fiery sermons of Peter the Hermit, they were persuaded to leave their homes and farms and join the great enterprise to liberate Christ's Tomb in Jerusalem from the grip of the Infidel. In their minds danced visions of glory, divine blessing, and the wealth of the Orient that they had only seen from a distance—in the warehouses of the great merchants and in the glittering courts of their own nobility. But now their nobility were leading them onward, and the Infidel at home and abroad became the prime enemy.

In the spring of 1096, as the crusading knights and peasants of Flanders and Lorraine passed through the Rhine Valley on their way southward, the close-knit communities of Jews in each of the towns of the Rhineland offered tempting targets for immediate plunder. The Jews of Mainz were not prepared for the violence; they assumed that their offer to provide food and shelter for the traveling Crusader armies would pacify them until they resumed their march. Yet the hordes of peasants following the armies—far from home and inflamed by the ideology of Holy War—exploded in a frenzy of killing, raping, and looting all those they perceived as Infidels in the towns along the Rhine. In May 1096, the Jewish communities of Speyer and Worms were attacked by arriving crusading contingents and, after their residential quarters were thoroughly ransacked and plundered by the mobs of peasant warriors, the few surviving Jews of those once-prosperous cities were given the choice of Christianity or death.

And here the Kalonymus family entered the picture in a capacity far different from their traditional role of a peaceful trading aristocracy. In Mainz, the Jewish leaders had sought the local bishop's protection, but finding his support to be luke-warm and evasive, they prepared an armed resistance under the leadership of Kalonymus ben Meshullam. Their defense was desperate but ultimately unsuccessful, with those few survivors who had escaped the Crusaders' massacre choosing to take their own lives. The carnage continued in Cologne and in the sur-rounding towns, and in Trier and Regensburg. By the time the Crusaders had passed on to the Danube Valley to bring their destruction to others, the role of the Jews as valued interna-tional traders in the Rhineland had been damaged beyond re-pair. The first great season of Crusader carnage had taken place at one of the holiest times of the Jewish year—between Passover and Shavuot. The congregations had gathered in fear for their lives, declaring public fasts and ordering that special prayers invoking the Name of God be said to save them from a terrible fate.

Yet divine intervention had not stopped the carnage nor would it in any way deter further outbreaks of violence in the decades to come. And with the establishment of the Crusader colonies along the eastern coast of the Mediterranean, the great Italian trading cities now claimed exclusive control of the Mid-dle Eastern trade. Not only had the Jews of the Rhineland lost their most prosperous livelihood and been restricted to the ever more dangerous and despised pursuits of pawnbroking and ped-dling, but they had also lost their faith in the saving power of their traditional appeals to God. The prayers, charms, and amulets of the mystics among them had not saved them from the fury of the Crusaders. And thus arose in the ashes of that dis-aster, a new movement of spiritual revival—led, almost natu-rally, by members of the Kalonymus clan. Shortly after the violence of the First Crusade had subsided, Rabbi Kalonymus ben Isaac ha-Zaken, of a branch of the family that was noted for its scholars, moved his family from the ruins of Mainz down river to Speyer, where the local bishop Rüdiger had granted protection. And in the course of the next century, Rabbi Kalonymus's descendants and followers would forge a new mystical movement to help the People of Israel deal with the intensifying violence and inhumanity of the medieval European world.

THE SECRET CULT OF
THE PIOUS ONES

In the fearful images of dybbuks, ghosts, demons, and succubi so vividly portrayed in the imaginary Eastern European landscapes of Isaac Bashevis Singer lie the distant aftereffects of a medieval heresy. In those same towns along the banks of the Rhine that served as the bloody marching ground of the Crusader knights and their hooligan followers, arose one of the most important mystical movements in the history of Judaism. As a direct response to the first great wave of violent attacks against them, the Jews of the Rhineland were forced to make a grim reevaluation of their position in European feudal society. As tiny, scattered communities of traders and craftsmen in the midst of a large and increasingly hostile peasant population, they were now openly branded as unwelcome aliens by many church leaders and members of the landed aristocracy. The Jewish responses to this ominous situation were several: Some members of the community drifted off and abandoned their ancestral traditions to find new identities in the dominant culture. Others clung tightly to Talmud and Torah, utilizing every possible scriptural contortion to reconcile Jewish religious law with the culture of Christendom. And yet others, who came to be known as the *Hasidei Ashkenaz*, "the Pietists of Germany," crafted a protective, if intensely pessimistic, vision of the *true* disposition of heavenly powers. Through it, they explained their own outcast status and strengthened their determination to survive.

Their visions of the heavenly realms, obtained from the pain-induced hallucinations of severe ascetic rituals and from the older texts of the divine Chariot and its accompanying angels, gave rise to a heretical distinction between divine forces: a cold and unchanging God who was the merciless Master of the universe and a compassionate figure known as the *Kavod*, or "divine" Glory, who was none other than the traditional figure enthroned on the Chariot. In their belief that self-induced pain through intense penitential rituals wiped away the sins of individuals and communities, dispelled demons, and won for them the protection of beneficent heavenly powers, the Hasidei Ashkenaz bequeathed to subsequent Jewish tradition a rich lore of angels, evil spirits, and monsters, which would form a folk religion within Judaism for centuries. And with it came a radical rejection of the crystallizing economic structures of Europe—in which profit, not piety or solidarity, had become the main priority.

The history of the Jewish communities of the Rhineland in the first decades of the twelfth century—following the first wave of crusading massacre and plunder—can be roughly reconstructed on the basis of poems of lamentation, resettlement records, and accounts of rights granted the surviving Jews by local authorities. In the main centers of the butchery—Mainz, Worms, and Speyer—the survivors attempted to put their lives back together, immortalizing the dead as the martyred victims of an unprecedented Holocaust and going about their business much as before. The emperor Henry IV recognized what harm could be done to the prosperity of his dominions with the loss of an entire class of experienced traders and craftspeople, and he offered a blanket order of protection to the Jews. In Worms, new Jewish settlers were encouraged to reoccupy the houses and workshops left empty by the victims, and in Speyer, whose community had survived through the intercession of the bishop, a dynamic new center of Jewish culture was formed. Sages and scholars from all over the Rhineland flocked there to piece together their shattered lives around an impressive new synagogue constructed (in an easily defensible position) in the upper town.

Prominent, of course, in this wave of rebuilding and community renewal were members of the Kalonymus clan. They resumed the study of the ancient scriptures and the codification of Talmudic lore that had been a hallmark of their family for hundreds of years. Other legal experts and religious poets joined them over the course of the twelfth century, supported by the slowly building prosperity of the Jewish merchants active in the grain trade. Yet in the wider Christian society around them, along the Rhine and across Europe, the clock could hardly be turned back. The networks of trade were growing ever more complex and thicker, and with the growth of the great Champagne Fairs in the Loire Valley, the role of the Jews in the Rhineland was gradually losing its importance, increasingly relegated to jewelry-selling, pawnbroking, and local marketplace trade. Among the immigrants to Speyer in the wake of the First Crusade was Kalonymus ben Isaac, a member of the clan particularly known for his mystical bent. And in the decades that followed, he, his son Samuel, and his grandson Judah (who were both both reverently called *ha-Hasid* or "the Pious") would rail against the complacent leadership of the Jews of the Rhineland and, becoming the most prominent leaders of the Hasidei Ashkenaz, would offer some radical alternatives.

Buried beneath an exuberant, sometimes macabre, thicket of myths and magical tales lie the authentic historical characters of Samuel, son of Kalonymus, and Judah the Hasid. But disentangling the facts from the myths is almost impossible. For generations, they were remembered as unparalleled miracle workers, faith healers, and dream travelers among the Jews of Germany and Poland. Indeed there is little in those folk fables that distinguishes the most famous members of the Kalonymus family from Abu Aharon three centuries before—or from the various Baalei Shem, or "Masters of the Name," centuries before that. But aside from their legends, their theology marks them apart from all earlier mystics in its profound pessimism about God and the nature of the world. Far from seeing God as the devoted protector and ultimate salvation of the People of Israel, *their* God is an unmovably cruel and transcendent force.

Their personal perspectives had been profoundly shaped by their own powerlessness at the hands of the Crusaders—and their utter helplessness in the midst of Christian society. Thus their vision of God was a post-Holocaust nightmare in which fervent prayers in the midst of unimaginable suffering had remained unanswered. Their numbed inner vision was of a God that had created and ruled over a world in which the wealthy and the wicked retained their earthly power. Though His power penetrated throughout the universe, from the highest heavens to the rocks, grass, and crawling creatures, his saving grace was nowhere to be found. This was a God of natural laws, time, space, and cold unconcern for His creation—a morally bankrupt deity who set people within the world to get along however they would.

But what of the Holy Scriptures venerated for centuries with their explicit references to God's covenant and His protection of Israel? For Samuel and his son Judah, the answer lay not in the highest heaven but in the awesome figure enthroned in the Chariot, described and identified for centuries by the prophets and sages as merely the divine Kavod or "Glory"—the outermost appearance of the power of God. They and the Hasidei Ashkenaz who followed them came to believe that the figure so long meditated upon by the Merkabah mystics was a special emanation of God, an independent entity that was God's first creation, far higher and more powerful than any of the angels or heavenly beings. It was almost as if the Hasidei Ashkenaz were abandoning God in favor of a more familiar—and more beneficent—protector, whose unique features were described in Judah's most famous work, *Sefer ha-Kavod*, the "Book of Glory." It was a work that stretched the Jewish commitment to monotheism almost to the breaking point, with its separation of distinct intentions and emotions within the Godhead. And even though the book, written in the Rhineland in the late twelfth century, did not survive, we can gain fragmentary glimpses of Judah's vision in the quotations preserved in his and his followers' writings.

In its blaze of indescribable brightness, surrounded by the countless angels and heavenly spirits, the Kavod was Israel's true intercessor. While God remained aloof and unmoved by the suffering of humanity, the Kavod—in its capacity as a "special cherub"—presided over myriads of demons, spirits, and wandering souls. It was a force that could alter the direction of events through the use of miraculous powers. And it was a heavenly energy that could bend the otherwise changeless course of creation, offering relief to those caught in the grip of tormenting demons, angry spirits, or oppressive overlords. In a world that was haunted by manifestations of evil—ghosts, evil eyes, and rampaging Crusaders—the Kavod showed its power through miraculous rescues from certain destruction. Pain and suffering had become such standard experiences of the life of the Jews of the Rhineland that the protector of Israel was perceived to be most powerful when he even briefly made the pain go away. His miracles were those rare events when someone was unexpectedly revived from a fatal accident or illness, when an enemy's attack was inexplicably averted, or good fortune and prosperity was suddenly bestowed upon the poor.

The clearest testimony to the profoundly pessimistic worldview of the Hasdei Ashkenaz is the fact that they did not consider spirit possession, ghosts, or evil eyes in any way out of the ordinary. They were part of the normal flora and fauna of a world in which misfortune was the normal fate for all but the saintliest individuals—those who had transcended the ebb and flow of daily life by clinging absolutely to the scriptural and Talmudic precepts of righteousness. And indeed the Hasidei Ashkenaz were particularly fascinated by the strange and eerie happenings they saw in the dark forests, graveyards, and isolated places around them, for it was there—in the midst of the forces of darkness—that the power of the Kavod could be most clearly seen.

The Hasidei Ashkenaz insisted that the misfortunes of the People of Israel in the distant past—and in the continuing horrors of Christian violence and persecution—may have been the result of their failure to keep all of the commandments. In that sense their punishment could be seen as a manifestation of God's justifiable wrath. But here is where the followers of Samuel and Judah offered their greatest innovation. God, the remote and transcendent, was too distant to answer any prayers. It was only the Kavod, hovering above the earth in the throne of the fiery Chariot, who had the power to offer rare tokens of heavenly loving-kindness. And it would respond to the prayers of Israel only if a direct appeal through prayer and commitment to meticulous observance of all the commandments was sincerely and humbly made.

The Hasidei Ashkenaz, passionately committed to learning more about the Kavod and its inner workings, zealously collected manuscripts of old texts of the Merkabah mystics and the other esoteric descriptions of the heavenly powers. They seem to have assiduously combed study houses throughout Europe and established long-distance contacts to obtain more mystical tracts from the Jewish communities of the East. In fact, most of the ancient Merkabah texts that have survived the centuries have come down to us through the collection and preservation efforts of the Hasidei Ashkenaz. But the intense study of the texts and further speculation on the nature of the Kavod was not a mere intellectual undertaking. It was restricted to the small core of the followers of Samuel and Judah, who were willing to undergo exacting rituals of penitence and self-imposed suffering to atone for their own and their community's sins.

The painful rituals of the Hasidei Ashkenaz are legendary; in their constant attempts to redress personal weaknesses and ritual transgressions, they regularly subjected themselves to immersion in freezing water, long fasts, excruciating physical contortions, and scourging of the flesh. Their belief was—again uncannily similar to that of medieval Christianity, in its monastic preoccupation with rooting out evil thoughts and sexual desires—that each sin had to be counterbalanced by the infliction of pain on the sinner. Like the penitential texts of the Irish, Frankish, and German churches, the *Sefer Hasidim,* or the "Book of the Pious," prescribed particular ordeals for every sin. They ranged from prayer and self-reflection to bizarre forms of self-discipline, like lying naked in snow in the winter or remaining impassive while ants and bees crawled over them in the summer. The object was both self-discipline and abject humility.

The modern scholar Gershom Scholem has quoted, as an example of this penitential state of mind, a medieval account of a

Hasid who once unintentionally "washed away the ink from a strip of parchment on which were written prayers which included the name of God. When he learned that he had sinned against the honor of God's name, he said: 'I have despised God's honor, therefore I shall not think higher of my own.' What did he do? Every day during the hour of prayer, when the congregation entered and left the synagogue, he lay down on the doorstep and the old and young passed over him; and if one trod on him, whether deliberately or by accident, he rejoiced and thanked God. Thus he did for an entire year, taking as his guide the saying of the Mishnah: 'the wicked will be judged in hell for twelve months.' "

As self-appointed moral leaders of the people, the Hasidei Ashkenaz tirelessly sought to educate the Jews of the Rhineland and surrounding regions in the particular ethical behavior that would most effectively evoke the sympathy of the Kavod for the beleaguered People of Israel. To that end, they ceaselessly campaigned in synagogues and at community meetings to gain a larger and more important role in leading the prayers and setting the moral tone of each community. Marked in their distinctive costumes of prayer shawls perpetually worn as their outer garments, they demanded of their fellow Jews only the highest standard of piety so as to evoke the power of the Kavod. And they became—at least to the wealthy and the powerful among the Rhineland Jewish communities—annoying puritans, ever battling devils and demons in bedrooms, workrooms, and synagogues.

For their part, the leaders of the Rhineland Jewish communities had little interest in esoteric theories of the "special cherub" or heretical whisperings that God the Creator had no particular interest in Israel. Their main preoccupation was the survival of their people and in the ongoing cultivation of the trade practices and vital political connections with local Christian rulers that they had depended on for generations. Under their patronage, the Talmudic scholars continued to codify and discuss the laws of the tradition. And due to their influence, communal privileges and favors could be extracted from local bishops and kings. But by the beginning of the thirteenth century, when a massive wave of knights and peasants prepared to set out for the south of France to massacre the Cathar heretics, Judah the Hasid could clearly see that the old ways were not working. He believed that a great part of the misfortune of Israel lay within their own hearts—and in their own involvement in the heartless medieval economy.

It was not that the Hasidei Ashkenaz loathed money or wealth as the source of all evil—as the holy poor of the contemporary Franciscan order did. They recognized from their people's long experience with trade and craftsmanship in Europe that the exchange of goods and crops for easily convertible currency could produce positive achievements and support works of the spirit and the mind. It was rather that the increasingly monetarized trading networks discouraged the equitable exchange of crops and goods within individual communities. The new systems of speculation led to the hoarding or export of commodities that were locally needed until the price rose sufficiently. The new free market was free only to those with funds to set aside for long-range planning and who had no greater concern with the use of the money than the level of the profit that could be made.

Although the Hasidei Ashkenaz have long been pictured by scholars as otherworldly ascetics and visionaries who cared about nothing more than the shape and character of the Kavod and the menagerie of heavenly spirits around it, they also had passionate earthly concerns. As historian Ivan Marcus has pointed out, their visions of the Kavod and the behavior of Israel that would summon its blessings represented an implicit critique of the economic injustices of the day. According to the Sefer Hasidim, Judah the Hasid "ordered his children and students not to buy grain for profit. When it is sold at a higher price, (a profiteer) is happy that its price so sharply rose. But it is written, 'He that is glad at calamity shall not go unpunished' (Proverbs 17:5). Out of concern for his own gain, he is not concerned for the welfare of the majority."

Nowhere in Judah's writings is there any condemnation of

the wealthy if they are "pious"—and are righteous in their decisions about where their wealth should be applied. For Judah
and his followers, of course, that meant supporting the poor in
the community and encouraging others to cleave to the Law
through the strict observance of the commandments and separate themselves from the impure and violent aspects of Christian society. Not unexpectedly, these idealistic, even utopian,
goals made Judah and his followers marginal figures and even
outcasts within their own communities. Though revered among
the poor as the saints of a radical new vision of the heavenly
powers, they had to look away from the Rhineland for spiritual
allies in the great battle against the forces of evil and posses-
siveness in the world.

TREE OF LIFE, BOOK
OF BRILLIANCE

Far to the south, along the seacoast and river valleys of southern France—at about the same time that the Hasidei Ashkenaz
were first formulating their theories—another stunning development in the history of Jewish mysticism took place. It took
place in an entirely different cultural and economic milieu, for
Provence was a distinctive region of Europe, preserving the
urban-based civilization of the Roman Empire long after it had
crumbled almost everywhere else in the West. Along the coast,
Mediterranean trade continued, with the ports of Marseilles
and Toulon prospering from the continuing flow of Middle
Eastern luxury goods and spices along routes of commerce that
remained largely unimpeded by the Muslim-Christian conflicts
farther east. Inland, in the rich valleys and wine-growing country of Languedoc, the counts of Toulouse, ruling more like independent Roman aristocrats than feudal vassals, managed to
keep the Capetian kings of France at bay. The lesser nobility of
the region was no less independent of their own overlords, and
even the Jewish communities of the region enjoyed nearly unprecedented autonomy—surely in comparison to the Jews of

the Rhine River towns, where the desperate mysticism of the Hasidim offered the only hope. Had Languedoc been less prosperous, its independence and distinctive culture may have been tolerated more easily by the French king and the pope. But along with the elegant tradition of troubadour poetry, Romanesque architecture, and codes of chivalrous manners came a far more daring theological development.

By all accounts it was Western Christendom's most dangerous medieval heresy. Arising in the mountain town of Albi and spreading throughout the region, groups known as Albigenses and Cathars developed—or perhaps inherited from other underground heretics—a radical dualistic view of the world. In their eyes, the universe was ruled not by one but by *two* rival powers: God, the Creator of the heavens and all pure spirits, and Satan, the fallen angel who had created the material world. Through deception, however, Satan had imprisoned human souls in earthly bodies and had subjected them to lives of pain, misery, and sin. This Satan, they believed, was none other than the God of Israel and the Old Testament, the Church of Rome, and all earthly kings. Their goal was to break Satan's grip on humanity by renouncing all worldly pleasures, avoiding procreation, and willingly rejoining the true God by cultivating the purity of spirit in which each soul was originally born. For them, death was a release, life on earth was a punishment. And during the course of their earthly lives they would have nothing to do with the Catholic Church and its sacraments—and if need be they were prepared to fight its priests and its armies as the satanic hosts they believed they were.

The Jews, for their part, were seen by the Cathars as agents of Satan, worshippers of the Satan-god of their Hebrew Bible, and accomplices in the same earthly realm that gave authority to both king and church. Yet as Catharism spread and grew more pervasive, its challenge to orthodoxy created a uniquely permissive atmosphere for theological speculation and polemics. And this atmosphere of exhilarating ideological diversity seems to have aroused a strong response from the more mystically minded among the Jews of Provence. Without fear of a campaign of church persecution, certain Jewish groups, of whose precise identity or social standing we know almost nothing, began to collect a wide range of ancient and contemporary Jewish mystical sources about the nature of God, heaven, and the material world. And with these materials for reflection, they produced a unique text that offered a potent counterargument to the contention that the universe was profoundly split between the world of the spirit and the world of earthly affairs.

That text, the *Sefer Bahir*, the "Book of Brilliance," provides a key to understanding the intimate and complex *connection* between an Unknowable God and His creation. It has also been regarded as the first and perhaps the single most important work of kabbalistic knowledge, since it was woven together from dozens of fragments of spells, philosophy, folktales, tradition, and magical lore. The book's title—drawn from the Book of Job 37:21: "And now men cannot look on the light when it is bright [*bahir*] in the skies, when the wind has passed and cleared them"—bespeaks a time of great religious turmoil and illumination. It combines many earlier, distinct systems of symbols to show that varieties of trees, the organs of the human body, the heavenly constellations, colors, sounds, and biblical heroes are all variations of a *single* pattern from which the world and everything in it is made. Like the sublime symmetry of the vortexes and whirls of modern fractal geometry, the creators of the Sefer Bahir saw a single master pattern endlessly reproduced. More than that: in assigning a particular role in creation to each of the ten potencies mentioned centuries before in the Sefer Yetzirah, the Bahir described the continuous process by which earthly, material reality is indeed produced by an ineffable God. While earlier mystical works had described the ten potencies of God as an indivisible unity, the Bahir reserves this special function to the three highest sefirot as a sublime trinity of qualities that translates the timelessness and placelessness of divine energy into a finite, perceivable world.

The impact of the Sefer Bahir was to last into the distant future as the first work in which the basic scheme of heavenly powers, reincarnation, and human involvement in the repair of the divine forces was set out in great—if admittedly cryptic—detail. Its genre is hard to pin down precisely. At first glance it seems to be a traditional midrash, in which ancient rabbis explain the meaning of particularly difficult scriptural passages. Though the book details no heavenly journeys, it seems to be identified by its editors as a book of Hekhalot literature through the mention of Rabbi Nehuniah ben ha-Kanah, prominent in Hekhalot Rabbati as the teacher of Rabbi Ishmael. Yet that too is puzzling, for with the exception of Rabbi Nehuniah and a few other well-known rabbinic figures, the "authorities" quoted throughout the Bahir are either clearly fictitious or otherwise unknown. Scattered through the midrashic discussions are unique—and unattributed—parables about kings, princesses, farmers, and traders.

These colorful parables and uniquely mystical rabbinic interpretations—completely unknown in either medieval or more ancient Jewish literature—offer tantalizing clues about a secret body of knowledge that had lain beneath the surface, perhaps for centuries. Some of the sources of the Bahir are obviously ancient and Near Eastern, with specific references to the plants, animals, and customs of the region. Certain turns of phrase are distinctive to the Hebrew style adopted by Jewish sages in France in the Middle Ages, and other concepts seem to be drawn from the work of Jewish philosophers working in Spain at the same time. Yet this text of not more than 12,000 words (less than a hundred pages) is not merely an eclectic collage of old and new sources. It represents the creation—or at least the formal declaration—of the existence of a mystical religion lying beneath the traditional scriptural faith of Judaism. For the principal intention of the Book of Brilliance—dated by distinctive linguistic and literary clues to its final composition somewhere among the vineyards, market cities, and whitewashed, red-tiled Mediterranean houses of Provence between 1150 and 1175—was to disseminate a new explanation for the movement of history and the structure of the universe.

The Sefer Bahir goes far beyond the fabulous mythic imagery of God's Chariot of the Hekhalot mystics or the dry, an-

alytical principles of the numbers and letters of the Sefer Yetzirah. It offers images far more abstract and multi-layered than
those being formulated far to the north in the Rhineland by the
Hasidei Ashkenaz. Utilizing biblical quotations, rabbinical comments, stories, and even observations on the shape of the Hebrew letters and their vowel marks, the Bahir reveals the
existence of a great "Tree of Life," composed of the ten sefirot,
which are the channels by which God's power reaches the
world. Although this vivid image is never systematically described in the book, it is skillfully delineated by comparisons
with other systems of mystical symbols and understandings of
the heavens. The Tree of Life emerges for the first time in the
Sefer Bahir as an image that would remain forever central to
the Kabbalah.

The first manifestation of God's power, according to the
Sefer Bahir, is the *sefirah Keter*, or "Crown," that symbolizes
God's pure thought, spreading endlessly in all directions and at-
taching to no particular object. It is the symbol and the medium
by which a transcendent God expresses His existence. It is the
still, peaceful, hovering consciousness sought by every true
mystic — pure energy, untouched and untainted by worldly concerns. Yet this energy does not remain inert once it is expressed
by the Unknowable God. The act of creation, according to
Proverbs 8:22, began with the creation of Hokhmah, or Wisdom. And thus, the Bahir recognizes this as the second sefirah,
a heavenly filter and transformer that channels God's pure
thought into the channels of transmission of letters, numbers,
concepts, and ideas that had been described by the Sefer Yetzirah. Yet still the energy remained abstract and formless, requiring a third potency and a completion of the highest triad of
heavenly powers. It came with the third sefirah, Binah, or Understanding, which, as the created world's supreme mother,
molds abstraction into recognizable forms in the depth of her
cosmic womb. Binah is mother. She is the Torah. She is the root
and the flowing spring from which the cosmic Tree of Life
grows.

Beneath that upper triad lie seven more sefirot, arranged in two contiguous triangles with two more individual sefirot extending below. In their configuration, if not their initial appearance, they represent the trunk and spreading branches of the Tree of Life—from which all forms of life and matter blossom forth. Their number calls to mind the seven days of creation; the seven daily praises of God mentioned in Psalm 119:164; the seven major parts of the human body (head, torso, two arms, two legs, and genitalia); the seven pillars of wisdom (Proverbs 9:1); and the seven planetary stars. Yet these lower seven sefirot have more than a symbolic significance as a further differentiation of God's descending and transforming power. The relationship and balance among them will influence the quality and quantity of divine emanations reaching the world. In subsequent commentaries on the Bahir and on the countless kabbalistic expansions to follow, kabbalists enumerated the names and distinctive qualities of these sefirot. The mystics and scholars distinguished between the forces of the Right (which express divine mercy and loving-kindness), those on the Left (which bear the fiery vengeance of God's justice), and those in the Center (which embody a harmonious combination of the two). We will examine each of the seven lower sefirot in greater detail in subsequent chapters, but already in the Bahir arose a distinctive and intriguing characterization of the last and lowest of sefirot.

Symbolically described as the "bride," the "daughter," the "queen"—or even the "congregation of Israel"—the final link in the network of the sefirot is the decidedly feminine power that gives birth to all the variety and vitality of the world. Unlike the third sefirah Binah, which brings forth the mechanism of creation, the tenth sefirah is a direct link between humanity and the heavenly powers above. Significantly named *Shekhinah*, or "Presence," which was a term traditionally used in Judaism to describe the generalized divine Glory, it now took on a far more personal aspect. And in light of its historical environment it presents a strange counterpart to the adoration of the figure of the princess in the ballads of the troubadours—and in the parallel cult of the Virgin Mary in the religious poetry and visual arts of the time. Again, we have no reason to believe that this cultural similarity was a conscious borrowing from Christianity but rather the expression in Jewish mystical terms of a powerful concept in the contemporary milieu. Thus the tradition of the Chariot was transformed from the image of an extraterrestrial vehicle to a sophisticated conduit of God's life-giving energy into the world. And through its unique biblical interpretations, mystical parables, and vivid juxtaposition of images, the Sefer Bahir offers a powerful, Jewish alternative to the mystical speculations of the Cathari. Its image of the Tree of Life extending between earth and the heavens showed that the material and spiritual worlds—the realm of the here and the realm of the hereafter—were not opposites or opponents but were both part of the unity of God.

That is not to say that evil was an illusion, for over centuries of exile, persecution, and ostracism, the Jews of Europe had tasted their share. Yet while the Cathari had condemned the God of the church (and for that matter, of the Hebrew Bible) as the earth-bound Satan—in direct opposition to their own spiritual God—the Bahir located the personification of evil within the forces of God Himself. In associating the source of evil with the fifth sefirah of *Gevurah*, or "Harsh Judgment," the Bahir strengthened and emphasized the role of Satan in Jewish tradition as a prosecuting angel, who aggressively seeks to evoke God's vengeance on those who have transgressed the Law. But here the Bahir once more transformed a mythological image into a structural principle of the created world. Evil is due to an excess of God's harsh judgment untempered by mercy. The ultimate cause of misfortune therefore did not lie only in ourselves but in an imbalance in the configuration of the sefirot.

And yet perhaps the most unexpected feature of the Sefer Bahir is its fervent belief in reincarnation—a concept that is not only not discussed but never even mentioned in earlier Jewish tradition. But here it is taken for granted as the only logical way to explain why sometimes "things go well for an evildoer and badly for a righteous man." The Cathars believed that Satan did his best to keep pure souls in enslavement, going so far as to reincarnate them generation after generation, sometimes as humans and sometimes as various insects, birds, and beasts. Yet expectably, the Bahir has an entirely different attitude. It saw the process of reincarnation as one of a necessary circulation of divine energy and a simple form of the administration of divine justice. The book offered several cryptic parables about vineyards repeatedly replanted until the fruit was acceptable; about soiled garments washed and donned by new people; and about moldy bread in the king's storehouse that must be dried and made fit for eating. And although the kabbalistic doctrine of reincarnation would become far more complex in the coming centuries, it already stood in sharp contrast to the pessimistic view of earthly life held by the Cathars. For the circle responsible for the production of the Sefer Bahir, earthly life and earthly events were *parallel* to, not in any sense *opposed* to, the happenings in the heavenly spheres.

Now that the hidden system of the sefirot had been openly discussed, Jewish mystics were able to envision and even influence the transfer of divine energy from the heavenly sphere to earth—and then back again. They no longer needed merely to sing hymns of praise to the Chariot of God or the heavenly throne for passive dispensation. With special techniques of meditation, they could focus their own energy on maintaining a balance of heavenly powers. The Sefer Bahir therefore offered an entirely unique description of God's relationship to the world. And according to its mystical precepts, humanity had an important role to play.

ELIJAH AND ISAAC
THE BLIND

The strange mysticism of the Sefer Bahir was only one of the elements in the creation of a vast mystical movement. In the highly charged atmosphere of open heresy and independence— unique for the theological orthodoxy of the Middle Ages— Jewish sages of many kinds flocked to southern France for the openness and experimentation it allowed. The followers of the German Hasidim established contacts in the south and they were responsible for the rise of a special class of full-time mystics—ascetic "Nazirites" who responded by their dedication and behavior to the *perfecti* or *bonhommes* of the Cathars. At the same time, immigrants from Muslim Spain, now being slowly overrun by the rough-and-tumble Christian forces, made their way northward. They brought with them the tenets and texts of neoplatonic philosophy, in which God's energy was seen as a series of light emanations, cascading down to earth and becoming more material as it descended through the heavenly spheres.

All this made for a lively period of experimentation and mystical reflection in which one thing alone was clear: the God of Israel was beyond all reckoning or understanding but had transmitted some of His energy to the world through a complex constellation of forces that were only now beginning to be fully understood. The ancient traditions of the figure on the Chariot, the Kavod of the Hasidim, and the network of the sefirot were all separate faces of the same divine phenomenon, studied in distinctive ways by the various Jewish mystical schools. We have only scattered hints here and there in the texts of communication between the mystics of Germany, Provence, and the Middle East. They sometimes shared texts and were occasionally influenced by each other's theories, but the distances between the groups were too great and the solidarity of each too intense to permit a regular interchange.

Earthly affairs played the primary role in determining the fate of the various schools of the Jewish mystics. By the end of the twelfth century the Cathars had gained control of most of Provence, and even though they considered the Jews to be little more than Devil-worshippers, they effectively shielded them from persecution by the church by the fact of their own patent heresy. And precisely at this time, during the simultaneous mystical revival within the Jewish community, a number of prominent Jewish scholars in southern France claimed to have received miraculous visits from the prophet Elijah—a sure sign of the revelation of a profound new mystery. Indeed, the appearance of the Bahir was just the beginning of a period of experimentation and speculation on the nature of God. For depending on the influences that each of the leaders absorbed, a distinct brand of mysticism emerged. Yet each of the sages to whom Elijah reportedly appeared seems to have shared a basic and highly heretical question: If the Supreme God of the universe was beyond all reckoning, shouldn't the prayers of the faithful be directed to the collective or individual sefirot? The respected Abraham ben Isaac, chief of the rabbinical court in Narbonne—by no stretch of the imagination a radical—carefully and circumspectly acknowledged that there might indeed be a profound truth to this vision of God's emanated powers, accessible and understandable, in contrast to the Ineffable God. His son-in-law Rabbi Abraham ben David of Posquières, who after having received his own vision of Elijah, retired from commerce to devote himself entirely to the pursuit of mystical studies, went much farther in his mystical course. He began to speculate on which of the ten sefirot each of the prayers in the daily liturgy should be addressed to—a practice that was greeted as outright polytheism by some of his less mystically minded contemporaries.

The last person in medieval Provence who claimed to have been a recipient of a visit of Elijah was Jacob "the Nazirite" of Lunel. He alone was a member of the class of ascetics that appeared in this period, partly under the influence of the Hasidim of Germany, and partly as a response to the *perfecti* of the Cathars. Jacob's mystical speculations centered on the identity of certain angels with the basic sefirotic qualities mentioned in the Bahir. Yet the element that linked all three mystical scholars was their adoption of a distinctly modern and strangely rationalistic approach to prayer. Since there could be no direct prayer to a completely transcendent God, it was the duty of the righteous to use human intellect to understand the heavenly powers and address them directly. An older approach to God through the intermediary of rabbinical authority, law codes, and ritualized supplication to a Supreme God now seemed to be fading. Merging in prayerful meditation with the various divine potentialities and powers, the Jewish mystics of Provence dared to imagine that if their study continued and they gradually understood more about the mysteries of the heavenly powers, they might have access to those powers themselves.

So long as the Cathars retained their influence in the region and enjoyed the support of the counts of Toulouse in the maintenance of their independence from both the king of France and the Church of Rome, the mystical speculations and polemics between Jews and Cathars continued. And it was the apparent good fortune of the first generation of Provençal Jewish mystics—Rabbi Abraham ben Isaac of Narbonne, Rabbi Abraham ben David of Posquières, and Jacob "the Nazirite" of Lunel—to go to their graves before the accession of the aggressive young pope Innocent III in 1198. Earlier attempts at a campaign of persistent missionizing by Cistercian monks had proved fruitless. Worse yet, Raymond VI, the count of Toulouse, refused to give more than lip service to the goal of restoring the authority of the Catholic Church. The Cathars were not his enemies but potential supporters in a quest for regional autonomy. Forming an alliance with King Pedro II of nearby Aragon, Raymond was ready to mount a defense, but in 1208 Pope Innocent persuaded King Philip Augustus of France to assemble a great host of northern knights and nobles to mount a Crusade against the heretics of Languedoc.

Transported down the Rhône and marching westward through Nîmes and Montpellier toward Béziers, the crusading army acted with its by-now predictable savagery in a quest for booty and forgiveness for sin. The siege and storm of Béziers was horrifyingly bloody, and after the sack of Carcassonne the Crusader force proceeded to the city of Toulouse, the stronghold of the Cathars, here known as the Albigenses, after the nearby town of Albi. The siege of Toulouse continued until 1213, when the local population, suddenly abandoned by Pedro II of Aragon, lost all hope of maintaining resistance and suffered one of the most thorough genocidal campaigns ever witnessed in Europe—at least until modern times. The unique security and prosperity of Provence—and its openly proclaimed heresies—were now all things of the past. Here and there through the region the fires of rebellion still smoldered—once again resulting in a siege of Toulouse in 1217—but with the final surrender of Count Raymond in 1229, the stage was set for an era of repression. From now on the Church of Rome would dominate theology and be the sole arbiter of orthodoxy. The wealth and property of those accused of heresy would be expropriated by church officials and used to establish theological departments in the university of Toulouse.

The fate of the Jews of the region was only slightly better. Always scorned by the church as unbelievers and deicides, they were simply stripped of their right to hold public office—which had been one of the many unconventional features of Cathar rule. Yet retreating into the inner life of the community, the insights and speculations that had percolated through Jewish thinking over the past few decades was impossible to stop. On the contrary: the son of Rabbi Abraham ben David—one of the noted mystics of the previous generation—now emerged as a leader of a secret esoteric movement that would have enormous influence. He was Isaac "the Blind," the first medieval kabbalist whose personality and mystical power comes through clearly in his surviving writings and in the frequent references to his words and techniques of meditation by the countless later mystics who claimed him as their greatest teacher. His public qualities were not unlike the legendary Abu Aharon four hundred years before—performing miraculous healings and peering into the aura of those he conversed with, to determine if or how often they had been reincarnated over the centuries. His blindness (which apparently struck him as an adult) did not prevent him from expressing the most vivid and brilliant imagery of light and flame in his quest to clarify the concepts of the sefirot.

Yet Isaac the Blind was unlike Abu Aharon in that he was not a solitary magician, a solitary leader working his power for the good of the community and then departing as suddenly as he came. He viewed the heavenly world not as a secret but a science. And in the study and teaching of that science and its practical application in the focused concentration of prayer, he showed his followers how it might be possible to ascend along the path of the energy, up to the highest sefirah—of God's limitless and non-articulated thought.

His commentary on the Book of Creation was the first to attempt to regularize and describe the seven lower sefirot and to understand how their qualities effected the flow of divine energy into the world. At the heart of his belief—and at the culmination of this first great transition of Jewish mysticism in Europe from Chariot worship and incantation to a philosophical discipline—was Isaac's conviction that just as divine energy flows outward along the trunk and branches of the Tree of Life to every object, thought, and creature, so it has the potential of flowing back. There is no necessary dualism between spirit and matter. All has its roots in the emanations of the Ineffable God, and that rootedness forms a potential connection by which energy can return to its source. Thus in his technique of meditation, Isaac taught his students how they might ascend into the worlds of the sefirot and, in their thought, merge with the highest levels. Yet it was not to be an escape from the world or a complete merging with God. The object of this mysticism was the establishment of a powerful, energized connection between heaven and earth.

Isaac the Blind died in 1235, just a few years after a new pope, Gregory IX, decided that punitive measures against the people of Provence and Languedoc would have to be supplemented by a continual investigation of the most ruthless kind—to make sure that heresy would be entirely rooted out. Thus the Dominican Order were given their instructions, and they fanned out in the city streets and in the countryside, beginning in every place with a strident public sermon about the danger of heresy. Then they proceeded to establish an office of special investigations—an Inquisition—to bring in a respectable number of heretics, whether the facts justified their accusations or not. And even among the Jewish leaders there was a renewed effort to root out deviant beliefs that might lead to social resistance to the newly imposed order.

Rabbi Meir ben Simon, one of the leaders of the Narbonne community in the terrible days after the Crusade, was anxious to prove to the church leaders that Judaism was entirely respectable and that its heretics were few. Ironically, in his polemical tract, *Milkhemeth Mitzvah*, "War of the Commandments," written around 1235, he offered eloquent evidence of just how widespread mystical speculations and prayer techniques had become. He reported that he had found "in one of the books of errors, a book which they call the Bahir," an injunction to "pray, at daytime, to one created god, and at night to another, who is above him, but who is created like him, and on holidays to yet another . . . for they have chosen many gods and they say in their unreason that they are all connected with one another and all is one." He further raged that "the book which they call Bahir, means 'bright,' but no light shines through it . . . the language and content of the book show that it is the work of someone lacking command of either literary language or good style, and in many passages it contains words that are out-and-out heresy."

That "heresy" was growing all across Europe. In the towns of the Rhineland, a new leader of the Hasidei Ashkenaz, Rabbi Eleazar of Worms, had taken the place of the sainted, and departed, Judah, to fashion an ethical movement far less militant and separatist than before. In Provence—Rabbi Meir's invective notwithstanding—anonymous groups and Isaac the Blind's students continued to devote themselves to the study of the Bahir, while others carried his teachings of the sefirot and the techniques for heavenly communion to the farthest corners of Aragon, Catalonia, Italy, Provence, and Castile. By the mid-thirteenth century, in retrospect at least, we can see that the scattered kabbalists of Provence, northern France, Spain, and Germany were coalescing into a coherent movement—even if there were still many mystical beliefs and rituals that each group considered to be their own. For most, the days of angels and amulets were over. The goal of this new Kabbalah was to raise the consciousness of the entire people and regain control of their destiny. As a model of behavior for everyone—rather than a technique for individual salvation or profit—the new Kabbalah now offered the raw materials for a mystical defense of the People of Israel by linking the heavenly powers with an earthly reality.

Chapter 3

LIGHT AGAINST DARKNESS

Concealed between the lines of the Kabbalah's most powerful scriptures are the echoes of a forgotten and fateful epic of power that swept over the dry plains and winding river valleys of central Spain in the thirteenth century. Its main characters were a Castilian king who coveted the mantle of world empire; a circle of Jewish courtiers who hoped to share in their patron's riches; and a secret movement of kabbalists who eagerly looked forward to the destruction of Christendom and the end of the world. The first steps toward a new understanding of the cosmic destiny of the Jews had been taken in Provence under the shadow of the Cathar heresy, and it had been driven underground with the bloody climax of the anti-Cathar Crusade. But as the students of Isaac the Blind and other Provençal mystics scattered to the nearby kingdoms of Castile and Aragon to avoid new waves of repression, they encountered political and religious struggles hardly less dangerous than those they had left behind.

Even though their mystical terminology was still far from uniform, they shared a conviction that the true message of the Bible and of Jewish tradition was the tangible link between the People of Israel and an Unknowable God. And their contemplation of the intermediate heavenly powers—variously described as angels, divine potencies, or sefirot—were to become objects of intense fascination among not only scholars but a growing sector of the Jewish population at large. In fact, by the mid-thirteenth century, the word "Kabbalah," which had heretofore been used to describe almost any kind of inherited—and venerated—Jewish tradition began to take on the mystical meaning it still possesses today. In the wake of the mystical innovations of the first generation of Provençal sages, "Kabbalah" came to describe the detailed study of the constellation of heavenly powers through which a transcendent and Unknowable God had created the world. By the fourteenth century, it had become commonplace to refer to Jewish mystics as *mequbbalim,* "kabbalists," and according to the Spanish mystic Meir ben Solomon ibn Sahula, "they call the science of the sefirot and some of the reasons for the commandments by the name Kabbalah." This way of knowledge had become Judaism's science of creation—a kind of biblical astrophysics that sought to understand and even manipulate the forces of good and evil, sin, righteousness, and redemption, to obtain personal and communal freedom from tyranny of every kind.

The small Catalonian town of Gerona, perched in the hills overlooking the sea just a few miles north of Barcelona, became an important new center of kabbalistic learning. And its influence in shaping the emerging doctrines of the Kabbalah and inspiring new groups of kabbalistic scholars can hardly be exaggerated. By around 1215, at the height of the Crusade against the Cathars, a number of students of Isaac the Blind had fled across the Pyrenees to Catalonia, a region long linked by culture, language, and economy with the Mediterranean coast of France. The group that settled in Gerona included some of the most dynamic and forceful kabbalistic scholars of the time. And in the very different political climate of Catalonia, their modes of expression were far less restrained than those of the Provençal kabbalists had been. Even before the official renunciation by Aragon to its claims in Provence in 1258, the kabbalists there, shielded from the Inquisition, began to produce an astounding quantity of mystical literature in an effort to transform the very nature of medieval Judaism.

The gathering of such mystics as Moses ben Nachman (later famous in Jewish lore as the "Ramban," or Nachmanides), Yehudah ben Yaqar, Abraham ben Isaac, Jacob ben Sheshet, and Ezra ben Solomon and his associate Azriel among others produced what the great modern scholar of Jewish mysticism Gershon Scholem has called an "epochal moment" in the history of the Kabbalah. For unbridled by the cautious circumspection of the earlier generation in Provence, the strong personalities who led the school at Gerona felt no need to make do with mere hints or compose texts in the name of ancient scholars. Speaking freely and openly, they attempted no less than the construction of a coherent ideology that could interpret the deepest mysteries of heaven and earth. They were convinced that they had been granted the rare privilege of transmitting the true Kabbalah in their generation and saw their responsibility as watching over the universe and protecting the fate of individual Jewish souls. To that end, their literary output was prodigious, producing a wide range of works on law, scripture, ritual, and ethics in which traditional Jewish motifs were reinterpreted kabbalistically. Their aim was to demonstrate how the system of the sefirot and the network of powers emanated by the Unknowable God were a fact of nature—they were the forces that determined the character of life on earth. And they insisted that more than merely being compatible with Jewish tradition, this configuration of heavenly powers *underlay* the scriptures, the laws, and even the letters of the Hebrew alphabet.

Back in Provence, the carping of Meir ben Simon of Narbonne against what he considered to be the heretical kabbalistic doctrine continued. Yet the sages of Gerona were unfazed. Each attempted to reinterpret and make accessible the obscure, abstract teachings of Isaac the Blind to a wide cross section of the Jewish public. Thus the cantor of the community, Abraham ben Isaac, offered poems and tunes that expressed the concepts of the ascension of the soul through the network of sefirot. Ezra ben Solomon wrote, among many other works, a kabbalistic commentary on the Song of Songs, showing that its ostensible description of the passion of King Solomon for the Queen of Sheba was really about the ideal union between the creative energy of God in the upper sefirot with the feminine principle of the Shekhinah below. Ezra's close colleague Azriel produced a detailed commentary on the daily liturgy of Jewish worship, showing how the particular prayers were relevant for the communion of the individual worshipper with certain combinations of the sefirot.

In their active preaching and teaching they conveyed the new vision of creation in which heaven and earth were intimately linked. And in their belief that even a simple person could recognize his or her own role in the maintenance of creation, the sages of Gerona extended their influence to communities hundreds of miles away. This outreach to the masses was soon to become a source of discord between kabbalists and mainstream community leaders — and indeed among kabbalists themselves. Those with misgivings about the radical theological movement were outraged by reports that kabbalistic subjects — once held as the deepest and most precious of secrets — were now being openly discussed by shopkeepers and workers in the public plazas and gathering places of many Spanish towns.

In fact, shortly before his death in Provence in 1235, Isaac the Blind received reports of the extent to which his own students were incautiously spreading powerful secrets among the unlettered Jewish masses throughout Castile and Aragon. He demanded that the practice stop at once. Isaac the Blind had always considered the mystical lore to be the preserve of a tiny elite that had dedicated themselves to study and meditation. And it was only because of their exacting training and profound knowledge of the mystical meanings of difficult texts like the Sefer Yetzirah and the Sefer Bahir that they were successful in making fruitful contact with the creative powers of God. The Middle Ages was a time for heresy and bizarre theologies, as the Cathar experience had proved. Jewish townspeople were no less susceptible to novel ideas and seductive images. And now, with the secrets of the Kabbalah written down and published, who was to say that they would not be misused?

"What is written cannot be kept in the closet," Rabbi Isaac wrote to his former students in Gerona. "Often these things are lost or the owners die and the writings fall into the hands of fools or scoffers, and the name of heaven is thus profaned." In particular, he noted that in a casual appeal to the heavenly powers by those not fully trained in the mystical traditions could lead not only to a failure to pray correctly—but to natural catastrophes. "I have also heard from the regions where you dwell and concerning the men of Burgos that they openly hold forth on these matters, in the marketplaces and in the streets, in confused and hasty discourses, and from their words it is clearly perceptible that their heart has been turned from the All-Highest and they cause the devastations of the plants." Rabbi Isaac's plea was for discretion. And to make sure that the dangerous and irresponsible spread of kabbalistic secrets would cease as soon as possible, the aged scholar dispatched his nephew Rabbi Asher ben David to Gerona. He could only hope that the sages there might "follow every counsel that he gives you, for I will let you know my will through him."

Yet the effort proved to be a failure, for like it or not, the movement of kabbalists was gaining a recognizable center and connection, changing from the isolated speculations of closeted scholars to a popular pietistic movement. And while Rabbi Asher ben David understood his uncle's concerns, he quickly immersed himself in the work of the Gerona circle, expressing kabbalistic secrets in a slightly more innocuous format as popular sermons and homilies. Even he understood that the age of the closeted scholar was over; he and many of his fellow kabbalists were concerned that critical developments in the heavenly realms would soon become manifest in human history. In an anonymous work apparently produced by a member of the Gerona community, called *Sefer Temunah,* or the "Book of the Figure," the history of creation was divided into seven cosmic epochs, each linked to one of the biblical days of creation—and symbolically linked to one of the seven lower sefirot. Each of epochs was said to last seven thousand years and bear the mark of its dominating heavenly quality according to the sefirah with which it was linked. At the conclusion of the seven successive epochs, the world was believed to return to its origins in the sefirah Binah, and the peace and harmony of the time before creation would be restored. In the eyes of the author of the Sefer Temunah—and presumably among the members of the Gerona school—the time for that great event was growing closer. The diffusion of the knowledge of the Kabbalah, as a key to understand the unfolding events, was crucial. And in the middle of the thirteenth century, the students of Isaac the Blind, now on their own in Aragon, became the first to throw off the solitary airs of their teachers in order to convey their deep sense of mystical urgency to the entire People of Israel.

RISE OF THE FRONTIER MYSTICS

Far inland from the Mediterranean culture of Aragon and Provence with their academies and bustling markets lay a completely different world—of farmers, herders, and knights-errant—where a radically different interpratation of the Kabbalah arose. In the citadels and dry, dusty plains of Old Castile, the Kabbalah burst through its passive, almost scientific, contemplation of the interlocking balance of divine powers. For the leading kabbalists of Castile had little confidence that the proper understanding of the relationships among the sefirot, combined with a precise targeting of prayers, could alone restore harmony and peacefulness to the world. The hard facts of power, conquest, and imperial ambition convinced the small but influential circles of Castilian mystics that suffering and persecutions were not the result of a passing celestial imbalance. They came to believe that evil was a very real and independent network of demonic powers—formed at the creation of the world. And they further believed that those powers, which long reigned supreme in human history, would soon be defeated, leading to the redemption of Israel.

The birthplace of this new kabbalistic preoccupation with evil was—not coincidentally—also the cradle of a distinctively aggressive imperialist mentality. Under the reigns of a succession of crusading Christian kings, the vast—and expanding— Kingdom of Castile-León, stretching southward from the northern coast of the Iberian peninsula to the great plains and river valleys of the interior, was changed beyond recognition by its victory over the Muslim kingdoms of al-Andalusia and its acquisition of their substantial resources and collected wealth. The Christian kings of Castile and León were at first no more than bandit leaders in the mountain fastnesses of Asturias, high in the narrow mountainous ridge between the plains and the sea, yet they gradually styled themselves as successors to the long departed Visigothic rulers of all Iberia. Their rise to power was made possible by the raids of their mounted knights southward in full armor. Appearing at the city walls of the various Islamic cities, they demanded handsome yearly tribute payments—known as *parias*—simply to leave the cities and their inhabitants alone. From the eleventh century to the twelfth, this widespread practice of extortion produced a small but wealthy Christian warrior elite skilled in the arts of terror and intimidation.

In time, the Age of the Parias gave rise to the Age of the *Reconquista,* with the kings of the Christian north pressing farther southward to conquer and rule the major Islamic principalities. By 1085, the ancient city of Toledo on the Tagus River had been conquered. By the middle of the thirteenth century, the most important centers of ancient civilization and culture had lost their independence. The former Roman provincial center of Seville and the Islamic city of Córdoba both passed from merely paying yearly tribute to being permanently ruled and taxed by Christian kings.

With the Reconquista came great population movements: large numbers of Muslims fled south to the remaining enclave of Muslim rule in Granada or escaped across the straits of Gibraltar to the Muslim principalities of North Africa. A select few of the remaining Muslim aristocracy—those with property to protect and who were skilled in the courtly arts of administration, public finance, and sycophantic praise of the reigning rulers—remained behind to facilitate the rule of the rustic Crusader-kings. It is important to keep in mind this difference of status and relation to the new ruling powers when considering the so-called Age of *Convivéncia*—that supposed period of Edenic and exemplary harmony between Christians, Muslims, and Jews. For among the conquered population were also a small number of Jewish aristocrats noted for their skill as diplomats, translators, and court officials. They were granted new urban properties, dues, and agricultural estates in return for their service as loyal administrators for the king. Despite the disapproval of the church, the Crown of Castile always protected its own interests, if necessary, through the services of infidels. In the thirteenth century, King Ferdinand III and his son Alfonso X entrusted Solomon Ibn Zadok of Toledo (known as Don Culema in Spanish documents) to be ambassador, chief tax collector, and supervisor of tribute from the kingdom of Granada, the last Muslim enclave in the south.

Yet while a few Muslim and Jewish nabobs enjoyed the fruits of Christian conquest, the simpler craftsmen, farmers, and workers who remained in the conquered territories found that the world they had known for generations was no more. Ancient mosques, synagogues, and cultural monuments were destroyed or reused with Philistine impunity—in an unwitting rehearsal for the far vaster conquests of Spanish adventurers and explorers in the Western Hemisphere. And more important than the individual acts of desecration and appropriation was the rise of an aggressive frontier ethos of conquistadors, cowboys, and land barons that would create an entirely new world.

For the vast expanses of central Iberia—formerly cultivated only in the river valleys and around the towns and cities—were gradually transformed into range land, with enormous herds of cattle and sheep providing great wealth for the few. The traditional agricultural practices of the conquered cities now had to bear the burden of increased taxes, and subsistence farming gave way to the production of cash crops. And with the gradual assimilation of the scattered regions into a single royal economy based largely on stock raising, many former farmers and craftsmen from the south immigrated north to the towns of Old Castile on the edge of the vast range land. There they sought—in unprecedented numbers—to survive under the new conditions by tanning, weaving, or trading in raw hides and raw wool.

The Jews of Castile, both rich and poor, were therefore faced with a far more focussed historical transformation than any that had confronted the communities of Provence or Aragon. And before long, new interpretations of the kabbalistic texts were produced to reflect the particular conditions they faced. In the fabled city of Toledo—long a center of Jewish learning and culture, even after it had become the official residence of the Castilian monarchs—the prominent Jewish philosopher Isaac ben Abraham Ibn Latif engaged in innovative kabbalistic speculations. In an attempt to understand the unique nature of the epoch in which he lived, he combined the subtleties of neoplatonic theories of emanation with the system of the sefirot of the kabbalists of Gerona, to suggest that the current configuration of the heavenly powers was a particular, time-bound creation of an unchanging, eternal divine will.

The determination of precisely *what* was unique about the current configuration of heavenly powers was left to a circle of mystics from the small town of Soria in Old Castile. It seems likely that students from the towns of Castile had long come across the mountains to Aragon to study in the academies of Gerona. Yet two brothers from Soria, Isaac and Jacob, sons of Jacob ha-Cohen, were not content merely to study the standard texts under the acknowledged mystic masters. They were anxious to find and locate new sources of kabbalistic insight that might help them better understand the unique changes taking place in Castile. To that end, they left their hometown and traveled widely through the cities of Provence where the Kabbalah had first crystallized, seeking out solitary mystics to talk to—and searching for collections of texts that had not become generally known. Their mystical wanderings took place at a time when the great age of the early kabbalah had already passed into legend; Isaac the Blind himself had been dead for twenty-five years. But here and there were elderly sages who had experienced that first flush of excitement at discovering the complexity of God's projected powers. And in their musty old libraries, there were still many secrets to be found.

"When I was in the great city of Arles," Rabbi Isaac of Soria later reported of the unexpected high point of his journey, "masters of the tradition showed me a booklet, a very old one, the writing in it being rough and different from our writing." After explaining that it had originally come to Arles from Jerusalem, Rabbi Isaac reported that this text was "brought by a great scholar and Hasid called Rabbi Gershom of Damascus. He was from the city of Damascus and lived in Arles about two years, and people there told stories about his great wisdom and wealth. He showed that booklet to the great sages of that age, and I copied some things from it." That text itself is now lost, but its impact on the development of the Castilian Kabbalah was profound, for it revealed a story of the emanation of evil at the time of creation that sharply diverged in its details and outcome from any Jewish mystical tradition known to that time.

In later years, after returning from his travels around 1260, Rabbi Isaac produced a wide range of mystical documents, in which the story he discovered in Arles is always implicit but never written as a single, continuous narrative. Like the other kabbalists of his time, Rabbi Isaac sought to interpret every facet of Jewish tradition in the light of the hidden knowledge of the heavenly powers. Other sages—particularly those in Gerona—had explained the deeper meaning of the prayers, the laws, and the prophets in terms of the relationship of the sefirot to each other and to the Unknowable God from whom they emanated. In terms of literary genre, therefore, Rabbi Isaac's *Te'ame ha-Te'amin,* or "Commentary on the Te'amim," was a remarkable attempt to offer a mystical interpretation for the various cantillation marks placed above and below the lines of the Torah, to be used for public chanting of the biblical text. There was, he argued, a deeper significance to those musical notations than just melody. What they revealed in their tones and in their very names, according to Rabbi Isaac, was a great drama of good and evil, of light and darkness, subliminally conveyed every time the Torah was read before a congregation of Israel.

Most other kabbalists of this era concentrated on meditative methods by which a mystic could ascend through the sefirot to eventual union with the divine will, thereby returning to the primeval source of eternal harmony and balance. Yet Rabbi Isaac looked to the future, where he believed the divine harmony and balance would be manifested again. He did this by identifying each of the cantillation marks with one of the many "princes of evil" or one of the celestial powers of good. The names of each offered further clues to the unfolding drama, as each name was seen to be composed of the initial letters of the words of a suggestive scriptural verse. Like a chanted Homeric epic of great heroes and bloody battles, the melody of the Torah could be seen to tell the story of the expulsion from heaven of Samael, the chief of the demons, who subsequently gained the support of a vast army of lesser fallen angels to keep the world under his control. Some of the cantillation marks referred to the acts of evil they committed; others voiced great lamentations over the length of the misfortunes that humanity would have to suffer under their rule. Of course the apocalyptic struggle between light and darkness had long been a feature of Jewish mystical belief, going back to the malicious fallen angels of the Book of Enoch. In their bizarre names and descriptions, they were a primary focus of the amulets and incantations of the Descenders to the Chariot and the Hasidei Ashkenaz.

Yet in the messianic outcome of Rabbi Isaac's story—with the destruction of the power of Samael and his cohorts and the restoration of the People of Israel to Zion—Rabbi Isaac made an astounding connection between the current plight of his people, on the one hand, and, on the other, with the internal relationships of the sefirot. For one of the main outcomes of the preordained battle between light and darkness was not only political liberation but a material change in the position of both the sixth sefirah, *Tiferet*, or God's Glory, depicted as a royal figure associated with kingship, and the tenth and lowest sefirah, *Malchut*, associated with the Shekhinah and the feminine principles of queenship, motherhood, womanhood, and the moon. With the defeat of the forces of darkness, Rabbi Isaac noted— relying on Isaiah 30:26—"the light of the moon will be as the light of the sun, and the light of the sun will be sevenfold, as the light of seven days, in the day when the Lord binds up the hurt of his people, and heals the wounds inflicted by his blow." The "king" and "queen" would thus ascend to higher levels in the heavens. And in their union and enhanced power would come a time for divine revenge against the forces of evil both in heaven and on earth.

A far more detailed exposition of this myth came in Rabbi Isaac's *Torat ha-Atzilut ha-Smalit*, or "Treatise on the Emanations of the Left," which would become the foundation for the subsequent important developments in the Kabbalah. Earlier mystics had attributed evil to a single, excessive emanation of divine judgment, yet Rabbi Isaac attempted to show that the complex reality of evil—with its many well-known "princes" and demonic figures—precisely paralleled the sefirotic structure of good. Thus, just as the emanations from the Right Side manifested the aspects of God's loving-kindness and positive energy, so the emanations from the Left Side manifested all that was destructive and negative. More than that: the emanations of the Left were a mirror-image of the sefirot, a sort of medieval bizzaro-world in which every positive attribute of balance was precisely matched by a negative attribute of chaos. And the familial relationships of male and female giving birth to secondary powers were the same on both sides.

Because the names and attributes of the sefirot had still not been completely standardized in this period, it is difficult to be precise about evil's genealogy. So many demons and evil spirits were known from earlier tradition that it is difficult to know in Rabbi Isaac's writings precisely how he fitted them into a sefirotic tree. Yet just as the pairs of male and female principles of Hokhmah and Binah and *Hesed*, or "Loving-Kindness," and Gevurah, or Harsh Judgment, were emanated by God and gave "birth" to the lower pair of Tiferet and Shekhinah, Rabbi Isaac saw a similar phenomenon in the emanation of Samael, the prince of evil, and his wife Lilith, the ancient killer of infants, from the Left Side. For they gave birth to another lower pair known as "Asmodeus, king of the demons" and his wife "Lilith the Younger," whose appearance was described as "that of a beautiful woman from the head to the navel, and from the navel downwards—burning fire."

In this entirely novel kabbalistic myth, the ancient hobgoblins of personal and public misfortune were drawn together in a family portrait that offered a strange counterpart to the ideology of the Church and of the Crown of Castile. Precisely at the time of the intensified Reconquista, Rabbi Isaac recognized that the main characteristic of the forces of evil was their ambition to conquer the world. "These are the worst of all," he explained in the Treatise on the Emanations of the Left. "It is their wish and ambition to be on top of the divine, to distort and cut the divine tree with all its branches." And this Tree of Death was also an evocative metaphor to describe the particular forces of power and oppression in Castile in the mid-thirteenth century.

"It is said that from Asmodeus and his wife Lilith, that a great prince was born in heaven, the ruler of eighty thousand destructive demons, and he is called *Harba de-Ashmedai Malka*, 'The Sword of King Asmodeus,' and his name is *Alpafonias*, and his face burns like fire. He is also called *Gorigor.*" It is impossible to know how closely Rabbi Isaac followed current events in addition to his mystical concerns. Yet it might be argued that as a perceptive scholar and observer of the world in which he lived, he was well aware that the guiding vision of Christian power in this very period was the theory of the "two swords" of the Crown and the Papacy. And it can hardly be merely a coincidence that the rival candidates for control of Christendom — or "Edom" in the traditional biblical image — were a Castilian king named Alphonso and a pope named Gregory.

The brilliance of redemption seemed to be dawning just at the moment of greatest pain. For Rabbi Isaac envisioned that at the very moment when this last generation of demons was emerging, God had mandated the rise of a counterforce that was destined to destroy the minions of evil and redeem the world. "And in the same form from which the destroyer was born," Rabbi Isaac continued, "another prince was born in heaven, from the source of Malchut, who is called *Harba ∂i-Meshiha,* 'Sword of the Messiah,' and he too has two names, *Meshihiel,* 'God's Messiah,' and *Kokhviel,* 'God's Star.' When the time comes, and God wishes it, this sword will come out of its sheath, and the prophecies will come true." And he concluded with a portentous quotation from Isaiah 34:5 that would fire the imagination of would-be Jewish Messiahs for generations to come: "For my sword has drunk its fill in the heavens; behold it descends for judgment upon Edom, upon the people I have doomed."

THE MESSAGE OF
THE ZOHAR

The work of Rabbi Isaac ben Jacob ha-Cohen of Soria was just the beginning. An incomparably greater composition — the *Zohar,* or "Book of Splendor" — would soon be established on the foundations he had laid. In its five massive, and often impenetrable, volumes of mixed Hebrew and Aramaic biblical commentaries, fables, anecdotes, and biographical portraits, the Zohar is not an easy path to mystical wisdom for outsiders. And yet it is unquestionably the single most important kabbalistic work ever written. In midnight study sessions, in amulet texts and mysterious symbols, in the superstitions and private appeals of generations of Jewish men and women, the influence of the Zohar is unparalleled. It combines all the earlier genres of Jewish mystical writing—prophecy, heavenly journeys, mystical symbolism, and mystical commentary on the scriptures—into a single body of knowledge, with an overall (if not entirely consistent) ideology. Whereas most of the earlier kabbalistic works were mystical interpretations of basic Jewish tradition, the Zohar shares—perhaps only with the Sefer Yetzirah and the Sefer Bahir—the authority of sacred scripture among the sages and students of the Kabbalah.

Like the Bahir, it takes the form of rabbinic dialogues—in this case of Simeon Bar-Yohai, the heroic rabbi who struggled under the Roman domination in the second century C.E. Bar-Yohai (known over the centuries by the reverent Hebrew acronym for Rabbi Simeon Bar-Yohai, Rashby) lived at the time of the most intense Roman persecution, and legends about him relate how he braved almost certain execution to convene secret assemblies with his nine faithful followers. The Zohar contains some of the mystical secrets revealed in these assemblies, yet its order is far more obvious than the fragmented, convoluted dialogues contained in the Bahir. Its first three volumes arrange the dialogues of Bar-Yohai according to subject, in biblical order, thereby constituting a massive commentary on selected weekly portions from the Torah. And interspersed with those scriptural interpretations are anecdotes about the life of the Rashby, parables, and detailed descriptions of the two most important mystical conclaves he held with his followers: the *Iḏḏra Rabbah,* the "Greater Assembly," in which the mystery of the sefirot was expounded, and the *Iḏḏra Zutah,* the "Lesser Assembly," convened by the Rashby at the time of his death. In addition, the Zohar includes mythic tales of wonder-workers, accounts of heavenly journeys, and a number of short mystical treatises on the significance of the Hebrew letters, the mysteries of divine emanation, the Song of Songs, the Book of Ruth, and Ezekiel's vision of the Chariot.

The main challenge of kabbalists over the centuries has been to extract a coherent system of symbolism and cosmology from this mass of literary forms and traditions. And most of the modern how-to books on the Kabbalah proclaim their success in that theological quest, making order of the unique scheme of the sefirot, the form of the Primordial Adam, and the principles of good and evil, where the Zohar itself is far from uniform in its treatment of these subjects in various places in the enormous five-volume text. It is now quite clear to scholars that the Zohar is not a single continuous composition, but is, rather, a collection of earlier sources skillfully woven together and embellished by Castilian kabbalists sometime late in the thirteenth century. This issue was first fully explored by the greatest modern scholar of the history of the Kabbalah, Gershom Scholem, who persuasively demonstrated some fifty years ago that the Zohar's text contains a number of quotations and paraphrases of the work of medieval Jewish commentators. And he noted that the Zohar's literary style and subject matter was strikingly similar to the writings of the great Castilian kabbalist Rabbi Moses ben Shem Tov de Leon of Guadalajara (c. 1240–1305). But the question of precise place, date, and authorship—which we will discuss shortly—should in no way undermine our appreciation of the Zohar as a brilliant and breathtakingly massive attempt to weave all earlier mystical traditions into a powerful expression of both protest and faith.

What was the Zohar protesting against and what was the basis of its faith? Since many of the Zohar's apocalyptic predictions identify the year 1300 as the time of redemption, it is reasonable to assume that at the time of its composition, this day lay in the not-too-distant future. And other hints suggest that the Zohar's likely date and place of final composition must be somewhere in the Kingdom of Castile-León, during the reign of King Alfonso X (1252–1284), an energetic monarch popularly known as Alfonso "the Learned" or "the Wise." Indeed, the historical context of Alfonso's reign offers an extraordinarily vivid background for some of the Zohar's main themes.

Even more than during the rule of his father, Alfonso advanced the Reconquista through an aggressive and expansive imperial ideology. With the territorial conquest of the central peninsula almost completed, Alfonso set to work to unify and centralize the territories and fiefdoms that had come under his control. To that end, he sponsored the formulation of a uniquely vivid cult of the king. From the time of his accession in the old Visigothic capital of Toledo in 1252, Alfonso and his courtiers effected a sweeping glorification of the person of the king in Castilian society. His own description of the kingdom — as a human figure with the people of Castile as the body and the king as the head — is suggestive of a realm of political ideology that is almost indistinguishable from theology. The great Alfonsine law code, the *Siete Partidas*, "Seven Parts," emphasized that just "as the soul resides in man's heart and the body lives and is sustained by it, so justice, which is the life and sustenance of the people, resides in the king."

In drawing down the blessings of the Blessed Virgin upon his people (a perennial subject for the king's own literary creations), Alfonso insisted that the king had a particularly crucial role to play. His role was that of unifier of cities, ethnic groups, territories, and classes; his personal example was meant to convince his subjects of the divine power that had been invested in the Crown. And Alfonso's ambitions extended beyond Castile, indeed even beyond the unification of the Iberian Peninsula. As the great-grandson of the Holy Roman Emperor Frederick Barbarossa through his granddaughter Beatriz of Swabia, he had truly imperial pretensions. After the death of the imperial pretender William of Holland in 1256, Alfonso lobbied, cajoled, bribed, and bullied his way across Europe to claim the imperial Crown for himself. But back in the Kingdom of Castile, as problems mounted, visions of worldwide dominion lost their luster. Taxes rose, and the nobility grew restless, and many suffering, hungry Castilians began to wonder if Alfonso the Learned was really so wise after all.

What a stroke of literary brilliance it was in this time and place to marshal the resistance and solidarity of the scattered Jewish communities of Old Castile through the formulation of a perfect antitype to Alfonso's royal ideology. It is true that the Zohar adopted and adapted mystical themes that had been crystallizing over centuries, such as the structure of the sefirot and the emergence of evil. Yet what makes this vast compendium so coherent and compelling is the focus on the character and personality of Rabbi Simeon Bar-Yohai. As one of the sages known for his resolute opposition to the tyrannical decrees of the Romans ("Slay the best of the Gentiles" was his most famous epigram), the Rashby and his followers offered an idealized model for later resisters of royal arrogance.

As already mentioned, Scholem had identified Rabbi Moses ben Shem Tov de Leon as the likely author of the Zohar, basing his theory on early reports of de Leon's possession of a manuscript copy of the Zohar and the striking similarity of some of its passages with Rabbi Moses' own work. In recent years, however, the theory of single authorship has come under attack. Judah Liebes has forcefully argued that the vast compendium of the Zohar was compiled over a number of years — by collection of sources as much as original composition — by Rabbi Moses de Leon and a close-knit circle of followers who elaborated on the earlier anti-royal ideology of the Castilian Kabbalah. These mystics saw themselves as the true heirs of the Rashby and his associates, meeting in secret conclaves far from the centers of royal power, connecting with the divine forces and envisioning a radical change in the order of things. As radical opponents of the ideology of the Reconquista, they shaped the earlier kabbalistic traditions into a far more politically focussed myth. In place of the Tree of Life came the figure of the Primordial Adam, containing within him all the sefirotic components of divine power, a far more potent image in Jewish eyes than the figure of the Alfonsine king.

The arrangement of the ten sefirot was seen to be formed in the main outlines of a human figure with the uppermost sefirah of Keter, hovering literally as a crown above the two guiding forces of divine thought: Hokhmah, Wisdom, and Binah, Understanding. Beneath these three uppermost sefirot, the lower seven were seen as symmetrically arranged organs and limbs. Hesed, or "Mercy," was the right arm of loving-kindness; Gevurah, also know as Din, "Judgment," was the fearful left arm of divine rage. Tiferet, or "Glory," below and between them was the heart of divine balance. Netzah, "Stability," and Hod, "Splendor,"were the right and left legs of the Primordial Adam, while Yesod, or "Foundation," was the phallus that focussed all of the divine energy—through the body of Malchut, "Kingdom" (or Shekhinah), into the lower worlds. The sheer anthropomorphism and blatantly sexual imagery of this configuration of the sefirot and their organic existence has scandalized countless religious authorities from the time of its composition to the present. It is certainly an understatement to say that its ascribed roles to male and female within the constellation of divine forces are, by today's standards, exceedingly politically incorrect.

Yet the political point made in the ideal of the "marriage" of Tiferet and Malchut or the Shekhinah was a direct repudiation of the royal ideology of the Castilian king. For where Alfonso sang as a troubadour of his love and attachment to the Virgin, the Zohar described the great, painful rift that had been forced on the heavenly king and queen. As already expressed by the earlier Castilian kabbalists, the Shekhinah—the regal, motherly guardian of Israel—had been abducted by the forces of darkness, who were now even more explicitly parallel to the Alfonsine ideal. Only the restoration of the power of the ten sefirot and the defeat of evil could restore the harmony between the true heavenly king and queen. And in its description of the passionate commitment of Rabbi Simeon Bar-Yohai to the *rescue* of the holy Shekhinah, the Zohar highlighted its radical critique of Alfonso's royal troubadour ideology.

In fact, by 1274, Alfonso's dreams had begun to crumble after two decades of costly and tireless efforts to gain temporal reign over Christendom. He had never gained more than a handful of supporters in Germany for his campaign to become emperor—which was pursued through a combination of arm-twisting and bribery financed by Castilian tax revenues. Desperate to gain support for his candidacy, he gradually emptied the treasury in courting allies in the unlikeliest of places— northern Italy, Sicily, and Norway. He even offered to pay ransom to the Byzantine Greeks to free the son of the defeated

Latin emperor Baldwin — in order to garner papal support for himself. All of those strategems and operations were expensive; even the respectful official chronicle of the Castilian court reported that over the first twenty years of Alfonso's rule the booming frontier economy of Castile and León had been taxed to the breaking point. Revolts soon broke out in conquered Muslim territory, which had to be put down with great difficulty and at great expense.

The depletion of the wealth of the realm for unnecessary wars and for Alfonso's life-long obsession, known as *el fecho del imperio,* "the affair of the empire," only made the Castilian nobles increasingly upset. And papal support never came for his candidacy, no matter how assiduously he courted Rome or how convincing he believed his career-long public relations campaign to be. In 1273, Pope Gregory X (Gorigor, that other satanic figure?) threw his weight behind Rudolf of Hapsburg in return for Rudolf's promise to lead a crusade to the Holy Land. Alfonso grew increasingly desperate, and there has never been anything more dangerous in history than a despot who suddenly feels that his grip on power is slipping away.

Yet the worldview of the Kabbalah has always been that events in heaven are closely mirrored by unfolding historical events on earth. Could Alfonso's humiliation mean that the forces of darkness were being weakened? Could this mean that the dawn of redemption so long awaited by the House of Israel was not far away? Thus, under the gathering clouds of even greater oppression in Castile, Rabbi Moses ben Shem Tov de León and his colleagues began to put their writings, speculations, and collected traditions into coherent manuscript form. The process undoubtedly took many years of collection, compilation, and revision. And naturally enough, as a palimpsest of mystical opposition to earthly kingship, it included a wide diversity of forms.

Indeed what makes the Zohar unique among all kabbalistic writings is that it skillfully combines earlier sources to create something entirely new. Modern scholars have stressed the legendary character of the Zohar's accounts of the Rashby's secret assemblies and the description of the countryside and lifeways of Roman Palestine in terms that were much more appropriate to medieval Castile. Yet these mythic themes and historical anachronisms may have offered the Zohar a greater persuasive power than mere historical exactitude. Up to the 1270s, kabbalistic texts were essentially esoteric speculations produced by a few specialist scholars who were lost in deep contemplation of the destiny of Israel. They lived in the rarified atmosphere of mystical reflection, far from the bustle of the markets, far away from the clicking of the looms, or the bleating of Castile's huge flocks of thick-coated Merino sheep. In an earlier stage of the Reconquista, the brothers Isaac and Jacob ha-Cohen in Soria had only dreamed of the down-to-earth historical effects. But now with the cooperative work of a much larger circle of scholars—and the creation of a literary form with an outstanding hero—the Kabbalah could become a movement for a far wider public than ever before. The earliest manuscripts of the Zohar seem to have been known to Spanish kabbalists by 1280, and their impact was immediately profound. The close connection between current events and the unfolding cosmic drama of the reunion of Tiferet with the Shekhinah would be perceived in the coming years in Italy, France, and Palestine—as well as the original homeland in the plains of Castile.

ROYAL COURTIERS AND COURTLY WISDOM

If the reign of Alfonso X has often been depicted by historians as a "Golden Age" of Spanish Jewry, it was certainly a Golden Age for only a few. The royal court at Toledo was graced by some of the most brilliant minds and sparkling intellects that Jewish history has ever known. But in the villages of Castile, in the regional markets, in the weavers' rooms, and in the dye factories, the royal regime was a constant source of political interference and financial demands. This is not, of course, meant to minimize the unique status of the court Jews of the kingdom of

Castile-León. At a time when most Jewish leaders in Europe restricted their activities to rather narrow religious study or closely circumscribed economic activity, the courtiers of Castile were entrusted with the oversight of the kingdom's burgeoning financial institutions and played a major role in the kingdom's intellectual life. Working closely with Muslim and Christian scholars assembled at court in the ancient Visigothic capital of Toledo, a number of Jewish scholars and men of letters embarked on a massive project of literary collection and publication under royal patronage.

In their search for sources of ancient wisdom, philosophy, science, and legislation, they combed the libraries of the former Muslim kingdoms of Andalusia, acquiring a wealth of Greek scientific and philosophical treatises that had been translated in Arabic. Seldom before had there ever been such a single-minded massive project of intellectual appropriation. And in their facility with languages—and personal connections to the Muslim-Jewish society that had flourished before the Reconquista—Jewish courtiers played an especially important role. The names of some were among the most well known of Castilian Jewry: Rabbi Isaac ben Sid of Toledo, who had served as the *hazzan*, or cantor, in the city's main synagogue; Moses ha-Kohen; son of the great leader of Catalonian Jewry; and Abraham Ibn Waqar, a prominent physician and member of a family of Jewish leaders and community activists. Yet others were drawn from other Jewish communities in Europe to participate in the intellectual renaissance. Among them was Rabbi Abraham of Cologne, a disciple of Eleazar of Worms, who was known as an outstanding kabbalist.

This was truly a gathering of wise men, though the goal of their wisdom was perhaps not identical to that sought by the visionaries of the Kabbalah. For the work of the royal scholars was not merely one of academic research and translation but was profoundly connected with King Alfonso's centralizing ideology. In undertaking the difficult task of uniting a fractured realm, conciliating his rivals in Portugal and Aragon, and attempting to gain for himself the Crown of the Holy Roman

Empire, no source of knowledge—practical, scientific, or theoretical—that could help in the efficient running of the government or the exploitation of its resources could be overlooked. Even before he ascended to his father's throne in 1252, Alfonso was distinguished by his practical-minded intellectual curiosity. The first of the foreign works for which he commissioned a translation from Arabic into Castilian, done by the Jewish physician Yehuda Mosca, was the *Lapidario*. It was a convenient and useful handbook for any royal of the Middle Ages, detailing the techniques for the appraisal of precious stones. Later, when he ascended the throne, Alfonso recognized the importance of efficient navigation for both trade and warfare, and he commissioned translations of works on seamanship and cartography, such as the *Astrolabio redonodo, Lamina universal,* and *Libro del quadrante,* translated and even expanded upon by Rabbi Isaac ben Sid. These works eventually proved crucial to the success of Spain's explorations and conquests in the New World.

No less significant were the works of astrology and astronomy that Alfonso assiduously sought out, better to be able to anticipate the vagaries of international politics. Through the efforts of his Jewish translator Yehuda ben Moshe, the *Libro conplido de los judizos de las estrellas,* "The Comprehensive Book of the Jews about the Stars," was available in Castilian at the beginning of his reign. And in the midst of this massive intellectual effort, Alfonso's translators did not neglect the mystical works of Jewish tradition. The king's nephew Juan Manuel noted with particular interest that, in addition to commissioning the translations of important Islamic texts, Alfonso had "ordered translated the whole law of the Jews, and even their Talmud, and other knowledge which is called *qabbalah* and which the Jews keep closely secret. And he did this so it might be manifest through their own law that all is a [mere] representation of the Law which we Christians have."

The specific mention of "qabbalah" is significant, for the use of this term just decades after the mystics of Provence and Gerona had begun to use it, indicates how widespread the fame of this esoteric lore had become. And it is ironic that this tradition was seen as so potentially useful for the Castilian monarch—how the image of the Primordial Adam and his role as a personification of the forces of goodness could have been used to demonstrate the universality of imperial ideology. As we have seen, that image was meant to be a hostile reaction to kingship, a culmination of hundreds of years of Jewish mystical creation of *antitypes* to the powerful symbols of earthly kings. From the time of Ezekiel's vision of the mighty Chariot over Babylon—to the radical messianic response to the cult of the Roman emperors—to the imaginings of heavenly palaces more splendid than any earthly court, the point of the tradition was a *rejection* of monarchy. And yet the superficial similarity of the images could lead the naïve or the devious to assert that they were the same. That is presumably what happened among the Jewish courtiers of King Alfonso. They were anxious to prove their loyalty to the Crown and eager to show that their own Jewish tradition validated its ideology. They mistook the superficial similarity between the Zohar's ideology and Alfonso's for agreement and mistakenly believed that the Kabbalah could be used to support the Crown.

Few scholars have paid enough attention to the sharp social differences among various groups of Spanish kabbalists. It is certainly not the case—as Gershom Scholem once asserted—that the Castilian kabbalists were an elitist group with little interest in social reform. Some were community leaders in the outlying districts; others were laypeople who had been profoundly influenced by the mystical ethics of the Gerona circle earlier in the century. And even though the courtly kabbalists close to the center of power in the kingdom may have initially shown no interest in social issues, they were soon to find to their own great misfortune that the ancient mystical wisdom of the People of Israel was not ultimately compatible with the "divinely" mandated kingship of Castile. The faith of the Jewish courtier had been badly misplaced, for by the 1270s, with the repeated humiliating setbacks to Alfonso's imperial ambitions, the dreamlike visions of a peaceful, world-conquering kingdom began to crumble. Under the pressure of the unsuccessful foreign adventures and internal opposition, Alfonso began to turn on the leaders of the Jewish community who had invested so much energy and faith in the ideological justification for his rule. Some now hedged their bets and sided with the Crown Prince Sancho, but that only endangered their position even more. Fearing that the Jewish courtiers had all turned against him, Alfonso ordered dozens to be imprisoned, and in 1279 he issued a sentence of death for treason against Castile's most prominent Jewish courtier — Don Cag de la Maleha, the former chief tax officer of Castile-León.

This was only the start of a campaign meant to wring out of the Jewish communities of Spain the wealth that they had managed to acquire in their wholehearted participation in Alfonso's Golden Age. In 1281, communities all over Castile were confronted with detachments of soldiers sent to collect the payment of a special tribute — twice the sum of their usual taxes — to support the faltering regime of the king. The arrest and torture of Jewish nobles, now for the first time accompanied by demands that they abandon their ancestral religion, revealed the basic brutality of the regime that had masqueraded as enlightened for so long. Yet with the passage of time, Alfonso's son and successor, Sancho, had no choice but to rely once again on Jewish officers and financial planners in the operations of the realm. And they, for their part, still had not learned the lesson of power. They were far more concerned with personal wealth and status than the inevitable misfortune that their vulnerable position in Castilian society would bring. And they still clung to the sweet seductions of the imperial ideology.

Only the acknowledged spiritual leader of Castilian Jewry, Todros ben Joseph Abulafia, an aristocrat who once maintained close ties with the court of Alfonso, arose to marshal Jewish resistance to the course of events in Castile. Recognized as one of the foremost kabbalists of his time, Don Todros severed forever the connection between Kabbalah and royal ideology. Preaching to Castile's Jewish congregations, he insisted that the laws of the Torah must be strictly observed and that the

People of Israel must maintain their way of life apart from the dominant society. His emergence as a leader of Jewish renewal precisely at the time that the Zohar was reaching its final form has led a number of scholars to see in Don Todros the contemporary model for the Zohar's central hero, Rabbi Simeon Bar-Yohai.

It is significant that in his public expositions, Don Todros only hinted at the kabbalistic vision that lay behind his words. The message of the necessary separation of light and darkness—good and evil, sacred and wicked—as expressed in the works of the Gerona circle and the Castilian kabbalists lay behind the practical reforms he instituted among the Jews of Toledo in the wake of official persecution. Complete separation from the cosmopolitan culture seemed to be the only political solution, and in the years to come the Jewish courtier class utterly failed in its attempt to reconcile the tradition of Israel with the self-serving royal ideologies of Castile. Yet even in the face of ever-greater repression, they continued to try. A turning point came in the last decade of the thirteenth century, when King Sancho once again felt it necessary to resort to financial exploitation of Jewish leaders, and the officials of the church imposed graver restrictions on Jewish life in the realm. The vast majority of Jews in Castile no longer felt that their destiny was tied with that of the Jewish courtiers, who had chosen the Kingdom of the Other Side for themselves. The eternal struggle between light and darkness, between the People of Israel and the foreign nations, went on, but it now included an economic distinction. The passionate struggle for freedom and redemption was now to be waged against the wealthy wicked by the forces of the righteous poor.

THE BIRTH OF A RADICAL IDEOLOGY

As a vast compendium of stories, parables, commentaries, and prophecies, written in a wide variety of styles over a period of decades, the Zohar expresses a cacophony of voices and mystical trends. While its central imagery of the Primordial Adam could have—at least for a while—been used by Jewish courtiers to support the royal ideology of Alfonso, there are other works whose attitude toward the present state of the world leaves no room for mistaking their radical—even revolutionary tendencies. Rage against the inequalities of earthly empire was, of course, not unique to the Kabbalah in the High Middle Ages, and an intense brand of apocalyptic agitation had been particularly powerful in certain Christian circles since the early thirteenth century. The vow of the Franciscans to lead a life of pious poverty and good works was but the first step in an intensifying struggle against wealth and unjust earthly power. After the death of St. Francis in 1226, the radical wing of his followers, calling themselves "Spiritual Franciscans," were drawn to the apocalyptic prophecies of an Italian abbot named Joachim of Fiore. Wandering and preaching to all who would listen, they saw themselves as the true bearers of God's message, destined to overthrow the sinful materiality and soaring edifices of the Church of Rome. At the heart of their apocalyptic belief was Joachim's sequence of successive epochs in the history of the world. According to his mystical reading of biblical passages, an Age of the Father (dominated by the Law of the Old Testament) had been succeeded by an Age of the Son (embodied in the Incarnation of Jesus and the New Testament). That age would, in turn, be succeeded by an Age of the Spirit, in which millennial bliss and harmony would reign.

Needless to say, Joachim—and the Spiritual Franciscans who studied and expanded his theories—were, like all true apocalyptics, convinced that the Age of the Spirit was at hand, and that they were destined to inherit a renewed and purified world. In a distinctive symbolic interpretation of the biblical image of Noah's Ark, they portrayed the true faith as a precious cargo hidden away and protected by God from the storms and turbulent waves of history. The wicked and the sinful would surely perish in the great flood—and the Joachimites saw in the wealthy prelates and nobles of their own era the modern embodiment of the *Anakim*, or "Giants," who would soon be destroyed by God's command. For those at the bottom of the social heap, such an image of the mighty brought low offered obvious psychic satisfaction. And as early as the 1930s, the great scholar of Spanish Jewry, Yitzhak Baer, attempted to show how this powerful movement of social criticism and apocalyptic expectation that spread widely in Castile must have exerted its effects among the Jews. For even if a barrier of suspicion and fear separated the two religions—and the Kabbalah already possessed clear schemes of successive ages—the day-to-day encounters of neighbors, shoppers, and traders in the busy markets of the cities of Castile would have communicated a shared feeling of millennial excitement. And poor Christians and poor Jews alike could share the same vivid turns of phrase and biblical images of the great events to come.

Precisely that "Joachimite" language is found in two of the most widely quoted books of the Zohar, the *Ra'aya Mehemna,* or "Faithful Shepherd," and the *Tikkunei Zohar,* or "Corrections to the Zohar," both of which are dated (by their explicit references to the main body of the Zohar) to the last decade or so of the thirteenth century. In the Ra'aya Mehemna, Moses returns to instruct Simeon Bar-Yohai and his companions on the secret meaning of the commandments, and the importance of maintaining the basic elements of social equality between all the members of the People of Israel. The Tikkunei Zohar is devoted entirely to a radical rereading of the beginning of the Book of Genesis. Yet despite their different literary genres and subjects, these books are closely linked by the vivid and almost identical terms of attack that they use against nobles and courtiers *within* the Jewish community.

Earlier kabbalistic treatises on evil had concentrated on identifying the demonic aspects of the gentile nations. Yet the anonymous authors of these later works identify their sinful opponents by the names of the doomed biblical monsters—Amelekites, Nephilim, Gibborim, Rephaim, and Anakim—precisely the kind of symbolic comparison that the Joachimites made. Though it is now impossible to match particular allusions with classes of Castilian court functionaries, an important ideological breakthrough is made in these texts. Instead of seeing the kings of Edom—or the sins of the entire House of Israel—as responsible for the nation's misfortunes, a certain apocalyptic class-consciousness emerged in the highly stratified society of medieval Castile. Those courtiers and fawners among both Israel and the nations are the real cause of the great misfortune that history has brought to bear. And even in the subsequent centuries when these two works circulated widely with the Zohar—and the specific historical figures condemned in their fiery rhetoric were forgotten—the power of the "political" analysis remained. At least one branch of the kabbalistic movement took a resolute stand in condemning any who would collaborate with the kingdom—even among the leaders of the People of Israel—as a sworn and eternal enemy of the forces of light.

But if the Ra'aya Mehemna and the Tikkunei Zohar offered a radical literary critique of the standing order of privilege and favor, actions still spoke louder than words. By the end of the thirteenth century, the omens of historical change were many and the time was propitious for mystics to predict that the long epoch of medieval Christian civilization was at last coming to an end. The Crusader Kingdom, progressively shrunken by Muslim advances, had lost control of Jerusalem. Restricted to a few coastal enclaves, it seemed to be tottering on the edge of total defeat. And if the Crusades had been shown to be a historical failure—not a divinely ordained movement—what of the pretensions of the kings of Castile in their hope to gain rule over the Holy Roman Empire? In 1295, Alfonso's son Sancho IV died in Toledo, plunging the Castilian royal family into yet another period of internecine warfare and uncertainty. Could these events indicate that a great epoch was ending and the dawn of redemption was at hand as suggested by the Gerona sages earlier in the century?

Word came to Toledo in the late spring of 1295 of excitement spreading among the Jews in the outlying towns of the dry plains of the Extramedura. A prophet had arisen among them in the town of Avila, predicting redemption for the entire House of Israel within a month's time. Though a simple Jewish laborer with no formal education, he reportedly received visions from an angel of the events soon to unfold. Though illiterate, he copied them down in a work he called "The Book of Wondrous Wisdom," with fifty chapters of detailed commentary explaining how certain biblical passages offered precise allusions to personalities and events of Castile in the thirteenth century. Word of this folk prophet spread quickly throughout Castile and Aragon, and while the great sages pored over the dense, enigmatic texts, the people moved to action. In a growing hysteria, the Jews of Avila and the surrounding towns abandoned their normal pursuits and professions. Following the instructions of the prophet, they embarked on severe penitential rituals, gave away most of their earthly possessions, and prepared festive garments with which to meet the call of the shofar, which was to sound on the last day of the Hebrew month of Tammuz.

The only surviving account of the sad denouement of this messianic outbreak comes from the pen of a clearly hostile witness—a Jewish apostate named Abner of Burgos—who dismissed the credulity of the masses with cruel glee. He claimed that on the appointed day of the redemption, the followers of the prophet of Avila gathered in their synagogue, wearing their white garments and miraculously—inexplicably—black crosses suddenly appeared on them. This sudden disruption of their messianic expectations (and the failure of God to intervene in history, as predicted) caused great consternation and—at least according to Abner—many of the prophet's followers converted to Christianity. The prophet from Avila was never heard from again, and the Jews of the district (perhaps fewer in number as the result of conversions) prepared to weather the storms of violence and persecution that would now certainly shower down upon them.

As we will see, this pattern of messianic excitement followed by intense disappointment was to characterize several more episodes in the history of kabbalistic speculation, with disheartened disciples disappearing in humiliation and despair into the mass of the Jewish communities to resume their lives and sufferings. Yet the lessons of the radical apocalyptic theories exerted a continuing impact, even if a particular prediction of the coming of redemption was wrong. In a sense, the popular ethical teachings of the Gerona kabbalists and the vivid preoccupation with the reality of evil of the Castilian mystics had come together in the Zohar, preaching a secret ideology of resistance against privilege and royal power. As manuscript copies of the Zohar began to circulate among Jewish communities throughout the Mediterranean, it became a handbook and a scripture for a pervasive underground faith. Even if the precise date of Redemption was uncertain, many came to believe that the forces of evil were doomed. And before long, the Zohar would be used again by Jewish mystics — in quite different historical circumstances — to show how potent the proper summoning of the heavenly powers could be.

Chapter 4

CONFRONTING THE DEMONS

I n the glittering age of the European Renaissance, in the wonder of novel ideas, artistic styles, musical forms, and New Worlds discovered, the Kabbalah was slowly transformed from an ancient apocalyptic faith into a modern quest for personal liberation. During the fourteenth and fifteenth centuries, the constellation of powers and cultures across the globe was dramatically shifting as Spanish and Portuguese ships claimed new colonies in uncharted continents, Italian merchant cities bustled with exotic merchandise from Far Eastern kingdoms, and the Ottoman Turks established a far-flung empire from the Balkans to Afghanistan. Individual navigators, bankers, diplomats, and mapmakers were now given credit for these world-changing breakthroughs. And in every society—at least at its highest levels—the concept and importance of the Individual began to take on increasing force. Freed from the burden of medieval conformity, dynamic personalities began to believe that through their own efforts the world could be changed. They could see it happening all around them, in the public squares, in the court-houses, and along the docksides.

Kabbalistic thinking was also deeply affected in this increas-ingly fluid economic and cultural epoch. The mystical traditions that had crystallized in specific situations—in response to par-ticular political crises—in Castile, Catalonia, and Provence—were now prized as universally applicable knowledge by individual mystics in Italy, Germany, and the Land of Israel. The small, scattered groups of followers of the tradition—study-ing the impenetrable text of the Zohar and techniques of mys-tical prayer—eventually formed links that were far more regular and sustained than ever before. Through symbol and parable, they preached economic and political warfare against the forces of darkness as tangible elements in the unfolding his-tory of their times. New peoples, new continents, and new so-cieties were emerging. In this drama, the Jews would become active players. And an increasing number of Jewish mystics was coming to believe that God's long-awaited intervention in history would never come without their own concerted efforts, both as a nation and as individuals.

Cautiously, yet methodically—like explorers in search of great, golden treasure—kabbalists from the various places throughout the Mediterranean made their way to the earliest centers of kabbalistic learning to speak with the masters and to collect new texts. The sporadic contact of previous generations of mystics became a more general undertaking, with the former regional schools losing their distinctiveness through the shared study of the Zohar. And there was considerable urgency in this study, especially in light of the dramatic events now taking place. In 1291, the last Crusader stronghold in the Holy Land—the fortified seaport of St. Jean d'Acre—fell to Muslim forces, ending nearly two centuries of European occupation in the Middle East. That great historical turning point was naturally regarded in kabbalistic circles as evidence that the forces of the Other Side had suffered a stunning reversal. And a kabbalist from Palestine, Rabbi Isaac ben Samuel of Acre, himself now a refugee, embarked on a personal journey to speak with the masters of the Kabbalah in Castile and discover what great historical events still lay in store for the People of Israel. And in 1305, he had the good fortune to meet Rabbi Moses de Leon in the town of Valladolid and spoke briefly with him about the Zohar, its message, and the mystical secrets that Rabbi Simeon Bar-Yohai had possessed.

By this time, there was already a group of outspoken anti-mystical skeptics who declared that the Zohar was nothing more than a recent forgery, masterminded by de Leon. Rabbi Isaac eventually reached the hometown of de Leon in Avila, but the old man had died in the meantime and his widow had only bitter memories. She claimed that Rabbi Moses had admitted the forgery to her, explaining that "if I told people that I am the author, they would pay no attention nor spend a farthing on the book, for they would say that these are but the workings of my own imagination. But now that they hear that I am copying from the book Zohar, which Simeon Bar Yohai wrote under the inspiration of the Holy Spirit, they are paying a high price for it, as you know." This cynical hearsay may have been the result of bad family feelings or influenced by the Kabbalah's critics, but it is significant that Rabbi Isaac was not in the least bit deterred by it. He went on to become one of the leading kabbalistic figures of his time, apparently unconcerned with the Zohar's precise historical source. The Rashby—according to his legendary image—*could* have said and written things like this, and probably would have had he been alive in the present age. The message of the Zohar was timeless and soon became the core of a continually embroidered ideology throughout the Diaspora, giving rise to countless commentaries, rituals, and mystical beliefs.

Through the 1300s, a wealth of new texts appeared in many Jewish communities throughout the Mediterranean and they were avidly circulated, leaving the question of the historical origin of the Zohar unanswered—and almost always unasked. It mattered little that the Book of Splendor appeared first in second-century Palestine or thirteenth-century Castile, for its powerful message of resistance to imperial pretensions offered hope and action throughout the Jewish world. Commentaries were written to adapt the Zohar's message to the differing conditions in the various areas. In addition to the kabbalistic anthologies of the widely traveled Rabbi Isaac of Acre, works like the anonymous *Ma'arekhet Elohut*, the "System of Divinity," appeared among the Italian Jewish communities together with the work of great Italian Jewish mystics, like Menachem Recanati and Reuben Zarfati, while in Germany, the still potent mystical traditions of the Hasidei Ashkenaz of the previous two centuries regarding the splendor of the divine Kavod were now integrated with the fully crystallized system of the sefirot set out in the Zohar.

Even as far afield as North Africa and Persia, the basic ideology of the Spanish Kabbalah began to affect regional mystical traditions, themselves derived from the literature of the Descenders to the Chariot and the literature of the Hekhalot. The basic message of the Zohar transcended the specific situation of any particular Jewish community in the region, for almost everywhere in the High Middle Ages, various aggressive forms of royal ideology had spread. Though the languages and costumes were different, there was much that the Hapsburgs, Bourbons, Byzantines, Persian Ilkhans, and Egyptian Mamluks shared. In its anti-royal symbolism of the heavenly powers, the Zohar offered a means of spiritual resistance to the contemporary imperial powers. And before long, as the early hopes for the destruction of the Other Side proved tragically premature, the spreading lore of the Kabbalah would gradually generate an independent mystical lifestyle for the People of Israel.

Yet the fall of Acre and the scattering of the surviving Crusader knights to Cyprus and the islands of the Aegean proved to be just the beginning of a new and even more intense period of repression against "Infidels" found closer to home. While a handful of wealthy Jewish courtiers continued to serve kings and princes throughout Europe, the vast majority of the Jewish population became subject to systematic harassment and violence. Conversion of the Jews to Christianity was the desired outcome; the continued existence of independent communities of Jews—with their academies, leaders, and mystical doctrines—were seen as deadly foes. Through the fourteenth century, formal legislation increasingly restricted Jews to formalized quarters, with prohibitions against practicing certain trades and professions, and the mandatory code of discriminatory dress. Several streams of self-interest flowed into the movement to demonize the Jews of all classes: the fears of urban merchants and craftsmen of stiff competition; the misdirected frustrations of an overtaxed and abused population; and the cynical "traditional values" of a self-serving aristocracy that sought the submission of all their social inferiors. Failing that, expulsion was always an option. In 1306, the king of France took a fateful step in that direction, expelling all Jews from the territories under his control.

The Iberian Peninsula still contained perhaps the single most important Jewish population in Europe, and the demonization of Jews on a spiritual level led to their becoming physical pariahs when the entire society was thrown into chaos by the Black Death. And there arose Christian leaders who aimed at nothing less than the extermination of all Jews who would not bow to the power of the church. Thus in the summer of 1378, an ambitious young cleric, Archdeacon Ferrand Martinez, began preaching from the pulpit of the Seville cathedral, calling for nothing less than a Holy War against the Jews. King Juan I could do little but mutter some muffled protests, and his successor, King Enrique III, being a minor, was entirely overawed by the self-righteous pronouncements of the extremists and the destructive potential of the mob.

By June of 1391, Martinez was above the law and acclaimed among the people as a self-appointed spokesman for God. His preaching led to popular riots in Seville that quickly spread across the country, to Toledo, and as far north as Burgos in Old Castile. Ancient synagogues were plundered, property looted, and Jewish women raped and beaten, while the respectable aristocrats and clerics silently turned their heads. The grim climax of the violent frenzy was the systematic murder of thousands of Jews who resisted or stood in the way of the rampage. Those who begged for their lives and the lives of their children were forcibly baptized and compelled to give up their ancestral faith. The long yearned for day of redemption did not arrive to save them. Injustice and evil had seemingly triumphed again.

For more than five hundred years, the Jews had contributed to the development of Castilian society on every level of politics and the economy from the most basic trades to grave matters of state. Yet the dominating, oppressive ethos of purification, of absolute homogeneity of thought, allegience, and action, would eventually transform the country into new spheres of economic conquest as an aggressive, predatory state. Indeed, the effects on the economy and daily life of Castile after the 1391 riots were substantial and shifted the focus from domestic development to a continued Reconquista—or Conquista—across the sea. Beyond the considerable loss of property and the disruption of normal trade and craft production, even the most basic feeling of security had vanished in the fear that the preaching, the rioting, and the pillage could happen again. Martinez was briefly imprisoned and died shortly thereafter, but his memory was cherished by his otherwise downtrodden followers who still felt empowered by anti-Jewish hate. They represented a dangerous, unpredictable element, and even though the kings of Castile and Aragon attempted to resurrect Jewish communities within the main centers (under ever more intense scrutiny), Jewish life in the Iberian Peninsula had irreversibly changed. Urban communities scattered to outlying rural towns for greater safety, while ever-increasing numbers of forced converts adopted a new mode of living that exchanged open observance of the Covenant for an underground, cultural solidarity.

These were the *conversos,* or New Christians, who, in their significant numbers and high visibility, began to take the places—and suffer the discrimination—formerly accorded to observance of Jewish religious law. Also known as Marranos, from the Castilian slang word for "swine," they formed a substantial segment of the population trapped between a Judaic heritage and the unwelcoming surroundings of Catholic Spain. And even though these forced converts are relegated in most accounts of the history of Jewish Spain to tragic footnotes, it is important to recognize how pervasive a phenomenon "marranism" had become. By the fifteenth century, with a total Iberian population of about eight million, no fewer than 700,000 or 8 percent were forcibly converted Jews. And despite the continual pressure—and constant surveillance—of the authorities to make sure that they remained loyal to Church and Crown, the New Christians maintained a secret life. Sabbath, festivals, and dietary laws were maintained behind the closed doors of the family residence. Marriage connections were restricted to other New Christian families. As we will see, there is also evidence that the message of the Kabbalah was preserved among the New Christians, serving as a reassurance that their present surrender to the forces of power was not really a fatal sin. For just as events on earth—and the world itself—were but the outermost veneer of a heavenly reality, so too was their ostensible conversion and daily demeanor as believing Christians a conscious concealment of a far more profound reality. The time would come when this sham would no longer be needed. And in maintaining their faith in the symbols of the Kabbalah, if not the full observance of the laws of the Torah, they looked forward to the day when they would be redeemed from their present "hidden" state.

VOICES FROM HEAVEN

Sometime between the horrible arrival of the Black Death across Europe in the 1340s and the decimation of Castile's Jewish community a half century later, widespread reports of angelic visitation and divine instructions—miraculously delivered to inspired individuals in suffering Jewish communities—assumed an extraordinarily prominent place in kabbalistic belief. Where focussed prayer and incantations were formerly the main avenues of access to the heavenly powers, the gift of the spirit now came to be the most powerful link to the realm of the divine. Increasing emphasis was also placed on the fulfillment of deeper mystical teachings, rather than the explicit law codes of the Torah, which undoubtedly offered solace to the New Christians who still clung secretly to Judaism. This message is powerfully conveyed in the anonymous kabbalistic texts known as the *Sefer ha-Kanah,* the "Book of Kanah" (ascribed to a relative of Rabbi Nehuniah ben ha-Kanah, the putative author of the Sefer Bahir,) and the *Sefer ha-Pli'ah,* the "Book of Wonder," a mystical commentary on Genesis, both written sometime in the fourteenth century. In the Sefer ha-Kanah, the three-year-old son of the narrator receives miraculous visions—described in detail in the body of the text—in which he is made to understand that Samael and his demonic forces on earth are directing the current course of affairs.

Following the lead of the Ra'aya Mehemna and the Tikkunei Zohar, with their suggestive allusions about the demonic connections of Israel's enemies, the Book of Wonder went even further. It explained that of the seventy demons placed in command of the Gentile nations, thirty-five "leaned toward the religion of Ishmael" and thirty-five "leaned toward the religion of Esau, father of Edom." Those forces of evil—Muslims and Christians—were the link to the negative heavenly powers and in that recognition a major shift in kabbalistic thinking occurred. Before, the mystics had prayed to the appropriate sefirot to lessen the influence of the Other Side and—by association—to defang the demonic powers on earth. But now that the intimate link between heavenly and earthly realms was established, a reverse tactic might also bring on redemption. To attack the earthly demons would be to undermine the power of Samael and his heavenly hosts as well. The Sefer ha-Pli'ah conveyed the same message, seeing the story of creation as just the opening of a cosmic war. And the time was quickly approaching for a showdown between the demons and the angels, the forces of darkness and light. By a complicated series of mathematical manipulations of the numerical values of the Hebrew letters, the authors of the Sefer ha-Kanah and the Sefer ha-Pli'ah determined that the Hebrew year 5250 (equivalent to the Christian year 1490–1) would be a time of great changes. That part of the prophecy, at least, was surprisingly accurate, though surely not in the way anyone could have imagined at the time.

Whatever beliefs may have been held in private about the imminence of redemption, the campaign throughout Castile for Jewish conversion became a tiresome substitute for the real business of Church and State. Discriminatory laws (like the infamous Laws of Valladolid of 1412) were instituted to keep the practicing Jews a tiny minority—by maintaining economic and social pressure on them through segregated residential quarters, special dress, and exclusion from certain professions and trades. The pressure increased with the famous "Disputation of Tortosa," in which Jewish sages were summoned to a months-long public harangue about how Jesus had fulfilled all the biblical prophecies regarding the Messiah. It was presided over by the papal pretender Benedict XIII and a strident Jewish apostate, Joshua Lorki, who had adopted the name Gerónimo de Santa Fé. Yet, as always, along with the royal sticks came the royal carrots, to those Jews who agreed to kneel at the baptismal font. By the middle of the fifteenth century, the majority of conversos were not great courtiers anxious to maintain their high social status but urban middle classes simply desiring a fair chance to survive and raise their families in the growing Spanish economy.

The widespread rural livelihood age of stock raising on the open plains of Castile was now integrated into a more industrial process. The raw wool of the vast Spanish flocks that had formerly been sold in bales to the weavers of France and Flanders was now diverted to a significant textile industry in Castile itself. The finished bolts of cloth that were produced on the looms of Castilian craftsmen were highly prized for their quality and value throughout Europe—and garnered considerable foreign exchange revenue for the crown. Jews played a significant role in all levels of this industry, though by the mid-fifteenth century, it was not always easy to determine with absolute precision who or what was a Jew. For the boundary between Jew and converso often meandered through the same family, with some members honestly converting to Christianity, some merely paying lip service to their conversion, and some remaining adamantly faithful to Jewish Law and tradition, no matter what the cost. Thus the dogmatic rages of the early anti-Jewish preachers had achieved precisely the opposite of their intentions. By forcing the conversion of the Jews under the direst penalties and pressures they had debased the very principles of genuine personal faith. And with the growing acceptance of religious hypocrisy as a substitute for heartfelt belief, many conversos continued to practice Judaism in private, despite their public profession of Christianity. And thus few genuine conversions were effected; the religious boundaries remained almost precisely where they were before the campaign for forcible Jewish conversion got underway.

Jews-turned-New Christians, having been freed from the discriminatory legislation, now prospered. And their very success in commerce and craftsmanship forced the officials of Church and State to change the rules again. As power struggles between contending candidates for the crown of Castile intensified through the 1460s, demagogues arose to demand that all conversos be subject to intensive and continuing surveillance to make sure that they were remaining true to the faith. This was, of course, just a new form of harassment, a conveniently "patriotic" issue. It was also a pretext for rival royal candidates to look the other way when their supporters fomented sporadic anti-Jewish riots. These were opportunities for urban mobs to loot, pillage, and let off a little steam. Thus—ironically, in retrospect—many Jews and conversos warmly greeted the marriage of the seventeen-year-old Queen Isabella of Castile to the fifteen-year-old Ferdinand of Aragon in 1469. The union of the two kingdoms might help restore some order. Jews and New Christians might gain protection from the prestige of a powerful and respected king and queen.

For the kabbalists, of course, this fawning support of Ferdinand and Isabella was regarded as both an idolatrous act and a disastrous political strategy. Any increase of the power of the earthly "Edom" would only reinforce the dominion of evil. And instead of submitting to Samael and his demonic forces, it would be far better to confront them directly and undermine their power through the help of the heavenly powers of God. There is some evidence that a popular messianic movement arose in Castile and spread quickly through the remaining Jewish communities during this period—though its nature was so totally obliterated by subsequent events that only a few scattered descriptions remain of Jewish children being miraculously possessed by the divine spirit, and would-be Messiahs arising in various Castilian towns.

Far more suggestive is a text from this period known as the *Sefer ha-Meshiv*, or the "Book of the Answering Angel," that contained specific rituals and incantations to be used against the minions of Samael. Written in the form of a direct revelation to its anonymous author, the Sefer ha-Meshiv did not advocate passive expectation of God's intervention on earth. It provided a wide range of secrets in astronomy, alchemy, and exorcism that could empower its readers to overcome the forces of oppression. Through a carefully prescribed curse cast against Samael and his lieutenant "Amon of No," an individual kabbalist might be able to weaken and even dominate the forces of Christianity.

"By virtue of the Great Name of forty-two letters," went the words of the incantation, "I adjure you even against your will to have not the power to fly or do anything or make any further accusation against the Israelite nation than you have done until now. I bind you and adjure you that you will have no more power to accuse Israel for all time. Rather, from this day forward you will defend the Israelite nation." And it is hardly surprising that with such an assurance individual kabbalists tried their own hand at confronting the demons directly and personally. The most famous was a Castilian kabbalist named Rabbi Joseph della Reina—an exceptionally pious and observant mystic—who was remembered for centuries. The precise details of his life and career have been lost in the mists of later mythmaking, for Rabbi Joseph became less of a historical personality than a literary creation—the central actor in a kabbalistic fable that offered a dire warning against doing battle with the forces of evil. According to the popular fable, Rabbi Joseph was determined to bind both Samael and Amon of No and force them to do his will. In the various versions of the story, told and retold for generations, Rabbi Joseph and a small group of his followers entered a church where they intoned the appropriate words, summoning and capturing the demonic spirits precisely as planned. Yet when the demons pleaded with Rabbi Joseph that they were too weak to be of assistance to the People of Israel without just a tiny whiff of sacred incense, the hope of redemption was lost. Having pity on the weakened, starving demons, Rabbi Joseph lit the incense on the altar and immediately Samael and Amon regained their size and strength and flew away.

For decades, even centuries, afterward, Rabbi Joseph's legendary willingness to perform idolatrous rituals—even in an attempt to defeat the forces of darkness—was seen as a grievous sin that caused redemption's painful delay. Perhaps the story was a cautionary tale against the continuing kabbalistic faith of the conversos, who willingly performed Christian rituals in the hope that secret spells and kabbalistic symbols would bring about their freedom some day. As things turned out, neither spells nor obsequious support for the king and queen proved to be effective. Hatred of the Jews and suspicion of the conversos was far too popular a cause for the Spanish rulers to abandon. And in the midst of a bitter war to conquer the last Muslim state on the Iberian peninsula—the mountain kingdom of Grenada—the internal campaign against all Infidels was brought to a higher key. In the 1480s, as Spanish armies advanced inexorably toward the Muslim city, a wide-ranging Inquisition (authorized by Pope Sixtus IV in 1478) began a ruthless campaign of insinuation, innuendo, and intimidation against any conversos who were even suspected of practicing their ancestral faith. Headed by the ambitious Dominican prior, Fray Tomas de Torquemada, the Inquisition utilized enforcers, paid informers, and a wide-ranging reign of terror, sweeping up into its net all who had enemies or business rivals (willing to testify against them) or those who were not skillful enough in concealing their loathing for such an evil and tyrannical regime.

The list of horrors—ranging from ruined careers, to the loss of children, to public humiliation, to martyrdom at the stake—that met those unfortunate enough to fall into the clutches of Torquemada and his minions is too grisly to bear repeating here. Yet by the late 1480s, Castile and Aragon were gripped by a wave of panic, horror, and recrimination as the machinery of spiritual purification ground on. The stench of burnt human flesh, the screams and prayers of the victims, and the frightening faces of the church Inquisitors offered a grotesque foretaste of what was still to come. For despite handsome bribes to drop certain investigations and desperate plots to assassinate its officers, the reign of terror continued, fueled by blood libels and a cynical demonization of the Jews. In their robes, masks, and cone-shaped hoods—later copied in caricature as the garb of the self-styled "knights" of the Ku Klux Klan—the men of the Inquisition swung into action. And their frenzy would not be satisfied until all conversos were reduced to frightened helplessness and all Jews were driven away.

In March 1492, only three months after the conquest of Grenada by the forces of the united Kingdom of Castile-Aragon, Isabella and Ferdinand gave their blessing to an edict of expulsion. It required the remaining Jews of the kingdom the choice of conversion or forced exile by July 31. After a millennium and a half of Jewish contributions to the evolving civilizations of the Iberian Peninsula, a vindictive young king and queen and a cabal of arrogant Inquisitors presided over the destruction of an important bridge between East and West. The peoples of the New World were soon also to experience the brutality of the Spanish regime. But through the spring of 1492, all attempts to overturn or delay the edict were fruitless. By July, most Jews had left, many had converted, and some sought shelter in the neighboring kingdom of Portugal whose king John II had not yet succumbed to the purifying urge. The open existence of Jews in Spain was over, and a momentous new epoch had begun.

I AM DAVID, SON
OF SOLOMON

They scattered to the four winds in that year of Christopher Columbus, rekindling the messianic faith that the end of days was near. Over the centuries the People of Israel had always expected a sharp and painful increase in their sufferings just before the advent of the Messiah, and surely their current, unprecedented crisis could be nothing other than the "birth pangs of the Messiah" that tradition had always warned them to expect. Though it is difficult to trace the development of the kabbalistic tradition through the upheaval of the expulsion, it is clear from the manuscripts preserved by the refugees that the Bahir and the Zohar remained cherished keys to understanding both heavenly and earthly reality. New kabbalistic works like the *Kaf ha-Ketoret*, "Shovelful of Incense," interpreted the Book of Psalms as the battle hymns of the Messiah, and the writings of the former courtier Isaac Abrabanel saw in the liquidation of Jewish life in Spain an epoch-making change. Yet the messianic hopes that redemption was nearing offered little comfort to the men, women, and children who faced robbery, harassment, and violence as they began their forced exodus from the ancient towns and cities they had occupied for a thousand years. Some boarded rickety ships bound for ports and havens in Jewish communities they had only heard of. And on arrival, they were not always greeted with familial hospitality. Indeed, the vast scope of this human tragedy has been forgotten in comparison to modern genocidal persecutions—and in the seemingly limitless historical attention paid to Columbus's voyage in the same year.

Yet by the scale of the late Middle Ages, the impact was enormous, with as many as 100,000 refugees shifting the balance of Jewish population and economic connections. Most moved eastward toward North Africa and Italy, some even going as far as the eastern end of the Mediterranean, to Egypt and the Ottoman Empire. There were others—perhaps numbering as many as 30,000 or 40,000—who turned westward, across the dry plains and hill country, finding asylum in the small kingdom of Portugal. There in the small Atlantic enclave of the Iberian Peninsula, they might be protected from the fires of the Inquisition and the rage of the mobs. Yet they would be close enough to their own homeland to return to the familiar streets of Seville, Toledo, and Córdoba should this current storm of hatred and violence subside.

There had always been a small Jewish community in Portugal, yet now King John II (1481–1495) took advantage of a uniquely profitable opportunity. He demanded—and received—large payments from any Jew who requested admission. And while the wealthy could purchase permission for permanent residence, many of the poor could afford only an eight-month visa, requiring many of them to work on the Portuguese plantations off the coast of West Africa. Yet rich or poor, refugees from Spain soon overwhelmed the small Jewish community of Portugal, creating a new kind of Jewish culture, forged in the fear of extermination and motivated by the hope that they could survive until the evil passed away.

It was also a time of sweeping global changes. New horizons opened for European explorers and conquerors just as the gates to the East were closed to Christendom by the inexorable advance of the Ottoman Empire. The fall of the Byzantine capital of Constantinople in 1453 to the siege engines of the Ottoman armies of Mehmet the Conqueror had profoundly disrupted time-honored patterns of Mediterranean trade. But new routes were being opened that circumvented Near Eastern caravan cities and harbors—as every school child learns in picture books and textbooks about the great Age of Discovery. The relentless expansion of the Spanish across the Atlantic and the advance of the Portuguese down the western coast of Africa and into the vast expanses of the Indian Ocean marked the beginning of an age in which armed battleships, not merchants' caravans, would carry the day. And it was probably only a matter of time until the old unity of Christendom was shattered. The passion of the Reformation was about to tear much of northern Europe away from the authority of the Roman Church. And the church would soon also be beleaguered by the imperial aspirations of the various rival Christian kings. Thus all seemed to be in flux at the time of the Spanish Expulsion, and it was in this unique historical context that the various strands of kabbalistic tradition were woven together by widely scattered groups of Jewish refugees into a mass movement for change.

Of course long-term trends like these can only be recognized and understood from the distance of historical reflection. At the time they are unfolding, they manifest themselves in the form of uniquely magnetic personalities. And so it was in the autumn of 1523, among the docks and the markets of Venice, there arrived a colorful—if largely forgotten—character who would change the course of Jewish history. Calling himself "David the Reubenite" and claiming to be the son of a King Solomon and the brother of a King Joseph who "sits on the throne of his kingdom in the wilderness of Habur and rules over thirty myriads of the tribe of Gad and of the tribe of Reuben, and the half-tribe of Manasseh," he arrived in Venice with an astounding request. He described how he had been dispatched by his brother and by the seventy elders of the Lost Tribes of Israel to meet with the pope and propose a secret plan "for the good of Israel." The Jews of Venice were understandably leery of the claims of this odd, if charismatic, stranger. Dressed in exotic Oriental costume, he was tight-lipped about the nature of his mission but eager to regale his listeners with tales of his many hair-raising adventures in Arabia, Egypt, and the Holy Land. Yet he apparently had a highly persuasive manner, for by early 1524, he had persuaded some prominent members of Venice's Jewish community to help him. In February he arrived in Rome and proceeded directly to the papal palace at Castel Sant'Angelo, mounted on a white stallion and accompanied by his faithful servant and an entourage of local Jews.

Historians have long debated David Reubeni's origins—the strongest evidence suggesting that he was from Ethiopia, while other theories connect him with Yemen, and yet others insist that he was merely an ambitious Ashkenazi Jew. Yet whatever his origins, it is clear that he had a daring vision—of solving the plight of the People of Israel by a concrete political and military plan. His intention was to ask the pope's help in what can only be called an uncanny precursor of the Zionist movement of our own times. With the military and financial assistance of the Christian powers of Europe, he hoped to lead a mass movement of Jews from their present scattered and persecuted status back to the Land of Israel—defeating the armies of the Ottoman Empire with battleships and cannons, and reclaiming a land of their own. Reubeni's stories of his origins and royal heritage among the Lost Tribes of Israel may have been complete fabrications, but they served the important purpose of giving his plan prophetic urgency. For the sudden appearance of a representative of the Ten Lost Tribes was long considered to be a sure sign of the imminence of redemption—and the fulfillment of God's promise that "behold, I will take the people of Israel from the nations among which they have gone, and will gather them from all sides, and will bring them to their own land" (Ezekiel 37:21).

Reubeni was skillful in his sense of drama and fortunate in obtaining sympathetic contacts at the highest levels of the papal Curia. His regal entrance to Rome immediately attracted the attention of Cardinal Egidio da Viterbo, a confidant of Pope Clement VII and a longtime student of biblical prophecy. In fact, the cardinal was closely linked to a small circle of Christian scholars who had taken an interest in the kabbalistic tradition, believing that it validated the messianic theology of Christianity. This group of Christian kabbalists followed the lead taken by the late fifteenth-century Florentine intellectual Giovanni Pico della Mirandola, who believed that close study of kabbalistic texts offered new insight into the power and divinity of Jesus—as a heavenly being connected directly with God. The earlier speculations of the Hasidei Ashkenaz and of the compilers of the Zohar on the body and figure of the Primordial Adam had always unwittingly suggested parallels with the figure of Christ. Of course that was never their intention, but by the time of the Renaissance, with the spread of translated kabbalistic texts to Christian intellectual circles, the Kabbalah had gained enormous cachet in Italy. Cardinal Viterbo had himself written a mystical treatise on the hidden meaning of the letters of the Hebrew alphabet that was based on passages from the Zohar and the Sefer Temunah, the apocalyptic treatise written in Gerona in the thirteenth century.

So intrigued was Cardinal Viterbo by David Reubeni's appearance, eloquence, and apparent fulfillment of prophecy, that he cleared the way for a private audience with the pope. And in his discussions with Pope Clement, David Reubeni offered more than scriptural quotations. He promised the pope that the conquest of the Holy Land by the Jewish people would offer strategic and economic advantages to the nations of Europe—both in lessening the direct threat of the forces of Islam and in opening a new overland trade route from the Orient. Reubeni spent nearly a year in Rome waiting for the pope's response to his proposal, and eventually received a papal letter of introduction to King John of Portugal, whose nation was most deeply involved in the struggle with the Ottomans in the Red Sea and the Indian Ocean—and with international trade. The plan of the colorful Jewish adventurer was succeeding beyond anyone's wildest expectations. And as a sign that his mission had the enthusiastic support of at least some of the most prominent Jews of Italy, Reubeni was given a richly embroidered silk banner by Benvenida Abrabanel—the daughter-in-law of the famous Jewish statesman and apocalyptic writer. Bearing a Hebrew inscription and messianic symbols, it was meant to confer royal dignity on his entourage as he set out for Portugal.

In Lisbon, in the meantime, there were no longer any Jews—at least not officially. Nearly a generation before, in 1497, the Jews who had paid so dearly for shelter had been converted en masse by royal edict. Yet their continued cultural distinctiveness—and their continued, clandestine adherence to the basic tenets of Judaism—was among the worst-kept secrets in the Christian world. And in their success in participating and facilitating the ever-expanding Portuguese Empire, they aroused local enemies who were pressing King John to approve the establishment of an Inquisition in Portugal. Thus in arriving in Portugal with his papal letter in the fall of 1525, Reubeni entered a potentially explosive situation, and he could not possibly have anticipated the reaction he aroused. For although he had come to Portugal to ask the king for military aid in a Jewish campaign against the Ottomans, he was hailed as the Messiah by the Portuguese New Christians, who now threw off all restraint about their true feelings, believing the redemption of Israel was at hand. And when word reached royal circles that high-ranking New Christians in the kingdom had abandoned even lip service to Christian practice, Reubeni was placed under house arrest and expelled from the country for fomenting both sedition and heresy.

Suddenly becoming little more than a pawn in the struggles of the various Christian powers, Reubeni was now ironically seen as a partisan of the pope—and an implicit rival of both the Holy Roman Emperor Charles V and Francis I of France. He was threatened with arrest when his ship called at a Spanish port, now under the control of Charles V. Then making his way out of Spain, he was arrested on the authority of King Francis by officials in Provence. Though he was later freed upon payment of a large ransom by the Jews of southern France, the wave of messianic excitement that he aroused had now, for all practical purposes, ebbed. From the fall of 1528 until the fall of 1530, he remained out of sight, until he reappeared again in Venice to propose yet another alliance between Jewish forces under his command and the seaborne Republic to strike a blow against the Ottoman Turks. But by that time a new element had arisen that would have a much greater effect on the fate of the Jews. For back in Portugal, Reubeni had changed the life of an extraordinary New Christian, and his own meteoric career of preaching, traveling, and prophesying would exert its own explosive political and spiritual effects.

COURTIER, MESSIAH,
AND MARTYR

His Excellency Diogo Pires was born under such auspicious circumstances that one might almost have said that from the moment of his birth in Lisbon in 1500 he seemed fated to be a leading figure in the most spectacular kingdom of the time. Though his parents were New Christians and bore the stigma of a Jewish background, the child's exceptional intelligence earned him a proper Catholic education, and his brilliance was unmistakable as he gained training in the law of the realm. Quick-witted, diplomatic, and ambitious, he rose quickly through the ranks of the royal bureaucracy, reaching by age twenty-one the influential and powerful post of "secretary to the king's council"—the noble conclave where the most sensitive matters of the kingdom were addressed. If his Jewish background was even mentioned, it was noted as an example of how much the young man had successfully overcome.

In fact, Diogo Pires had everything to live for in Lisbon as a successful Christian gentleman. The Portuguese throne was now perched atop a mountain of the world's greatest treasures—Brazilian sugar, Indian silks, Sumatran coffee, and Malayan pepper—and the young Pires, elegantly dressed in his tight-fitting black corselet and stiff, starched honeycomb collar, found himself perched dizzyingly close to the top of the pile. Few young men in Portugal possessed such power. As a sign of the king's confidence, Pires was also appointed recorder at the royal court of appeals. And sitting there among the priests, judges, and nobles, he influenced the disposition of disputed profits from the vast trade of the East and West Indies as it was battled out in contentious lawsuits between Portuguese, Genoese, and Venetian maritime entrepreneurs.

Yet he could never completely put out of his mind the powerful apocalyptic expectations that were common among Portugal's New Christians—and that would change the course of his life. Something resonated deep inside Diogo Pires's mind in 1525, at the time of the arrival of David Reubeni in Lisbon. The appearance of the would-be liberator of Israel seemingly sparked a moment of stunning personal revelation—not unlike that experienced by Ezekiel, Rabbi Akiva, Isaac the Blind, or even the Christian apostle Paul. A heavenly figure—in this case the apparition of an elderly man—appeared to Pires, confirming the imminence of redemption and commissioning him to bring the good news to the People of Israel. A single biblical metaphor conveyed in the revelation suddenly made sense of his seemingly charmed life: like Moses, Pires had been raised as a pampered prince in the household of a modern-day Pharaoh. Yet with skill and spirit he was now destined to confront the evil regime he had faithfully served and lead his own people out of exile.

This was apparently not an isolated conversion. The arrival of David Reubeni in Lisbon in 1525 had caused great excitement among the New Christians of Portugal who, in the privacy of their hearts and homes, still clung to the kabbalistic faith. Pires may have gained the confidence of some underground groups in the wake of his own illumination. For his later cryptic statement that "they revealed to me great secrets" suggests that his understanding of the intensifying battle between the forces of light and darkness did not come solely from supernatural sources. And despite the severe laws in effect for any New Christian who would return to the faith of his ancestors and seal that commitment with the rite of circumcision, Diogo Pires, the once-elegant courtier, performed it on himself. Henceforth he would exchange the finery of a Portuguese nobleman for the robes of a prophet—and be known to the world as "Solomon Molcho," a messianic sobriquet composed of the name of David's son and the Hebrew word for "king." He had made a decision to confront and defeat—not support—the forces of royal power. But when word of his conversion got out, Reubeni was summarily exiled and Molcho fled Lisbon in fear for his life.

Much later, legends would be woven to account for Reubeni and Molcho's movements, seeing in them calculated political objectives aimed at toppling the institutions of Christendom. But that is almost certainly to underestimate the genuine fear that must have gripped the two men as they made their way across a region where the Jews were a pariah people, and where the armed forces, fleets, and palace bodyguards of Christendom would have made short work of them. Neither had any illusions about the hostility of the Other Side to the forces of righteousness. And since Molcho's first worry was to escape arrest and execution as a New Christian who had returned to Judaism, he headed eastward across the Mediterranean to the world of Islam, and to the lands of the Ottoman Empire.

In that vast expanse of mountains, rivers, deserts, and fertile river valleys stretching from Greece to Afghanistan, a different principle of imperial power ruled. Though the fabled Sultan Suleiman resided in the splendor of his palaces and harems at the Golden Horn in the once-proud Christian capital of Constantinople and claimed for himself the title of caliph, he had never displayed an inquisitorial urge. Surely the theological self-assurance of Islam did not in any way deny that its faithful—and they alone—held the keys to the Kingdom of God. Yet Islam's now-dominant Ottoman Empire ruled over the vast patchwork of peoples and cultures with the recognition that the key to its own security and prosperity lay not in crusading genocide and enslavement. It lay rather in maintaining a delicate balance of competing interests and alliances, of trade routes, craft specialties, feudal holdings, and natural resources. Theologically deviant groups like Jews and Christians were not hounded by mobs and humiliated in great shows of ecclesiastical power. They were subject to classification as "tolerated minorities" with the daily indignities and communal autonomy which that status entitled them to. And so long as they contributed to the vast economic network that called itself an empire, they were allowed to observe their ancestral traditions and maintain themselves economically.

Already in 1492 there had been a significant migration of Spanish Jews into the confines of the Ottoman Empire. And at several major centers in the Balkans—Salonika, Nicopolis, and

Adrianople—they had established a surprising measure of prosperity in just a few years. In taking astute advantage of their own hard-won skills in the Iberian textile trade, they recognized the extent of the potential Near Eastern market for European-style woven goods—and the eagerness of the Ottoman government to take a sizeable cut from the proceeds of a profitable local industry. The components were all there in abundance: huge flocks of sheep in the nearby mountains of the Balkans, a ready supply of valuable Middle Eastern dyestuffs, and a workforce of Jewish men, women, and children who were anxious to start new lives.

When Solomon Molcho, the renegade Portuguese courtier and would-be Messiah, arrived in Salonika, he found an explosive mystical anticipation. In less than two decades, the booming Jewish textile industry provided the support for a wide range of spiritual institutions. One of the leaders of the community in Salonika was Rabbi Joseph Taitazak, a refugee kabbalist and charismatic preacher who was passionately engaged in both spiritualism and alchemy. An intense apocalyptic thinker, he saw in the persecutions and great expulsion from Spain the "birth pangs of the Messiah." And when he came face-to-face with the charismatic Solomon Molcho, Taitazak and his followers came to believe that Molcho's messianic claims were real. All their calculations based on mystical interpretations of the prophets suggested that the Messiah would be born in the Christian year 1500, as indeed Molcho was. And with his aristocratic background and bearing, Molcho acted the part of a New Moses—commissioned by God to bring the People of Israel out of exile and see to it that no new Pharaoh would attempt to stop them as they crossed the Red Sea. Even if the notorious Rabbi Joseph della Reina had been outsmarted in his attempt to subdue Samael and his minions, Molcho convinced the kabbalists in Salonika that the time was now right for him to confront the powers of darkness. He would break the grasp of the lower worlds of darkness on the People of Israel, allowing their souls to ascend upward to the realm of the sefirot.

In practical, political terms, this would mean the liberation and separation of the People of Israel from the Christian world, a physical parallel to the separation of the network of the sefirot from the clutches of the Other Side. Tirelessly preaching to Taitazak and his followers about the meaning of current events and Israel's growing independence — and how the expulsion from Spain was actually a blessing — Molcho compiled a book of his kabbalistic commentaries and modern prophecies that he proudly titled *Sefer ha-Mefoar*, the "Book of Magnificence." Yet his time in the Ottoman Empire was to be just a brief respite before returning to the field of metaphysical battle. In 1527, the forces of Emperor Charles V entered Rome and sacked the city to prevent its occupation by the French army, and when news of this most recent humiliation of "Edom" reached Molcho, he interpreted it as a sure sign of the imminence of redemption. He therefore resolved to return Italy — to the Land of Edom — and help bring about the final collapse of the forces of evil in the world.

Like Ezekiel or Jeremiah, Molcho communicated his divinely inspired message with a series of shocking public performances. Making his way from the port of Ancona to Rome, he dressed himself in rags and sat for thirty days among the lepers and the beggars on the Elian bridge beneath Castel Sant' Angelo, acting out the sufferings that — according to a Talmudic legend — the Messiah of Israel would have to endure. Before long, Molcho came to the attention of Pope Clement VII, who was intrigued by the would-be Messiah's dire prophecies of the imminent demise of Christendom. And when, in the winter of 1530–1531, Molcho's prediction of the destruction of many churches, a devastating flood of the Tiber, and a severe earthquake in Lisbon came true, he was arrested and sentenced to be burned at the stake. Yet even though he was spared by the intervention of Pope Clement, Molcho did not tarry in Rome to witness the final destruction of Edom. Reestablishing contact with David Reubeni, now in Venice, the two visionaries proceeded northward across the Alps to Regensberg, where they sought to meet Christendom's most powerful leader — the Holy Roman Emperor Charles V. Events were moving quickly.

Apocalyptic expectations were high among the Jewish communities of Italy and Germany that Reubeni and Molcho would somehow obtain the emperor's consent to let their people go. And as Reubeni and Molcho approached the imperial capital, they were joined by an entourage of fervent supporters who carried Reubeni's distinctive silk banner embroidered with the Hebrew words "Who is Like Unto You, O Lord?"—the ancient battle cry of the Maccabees.

Yet the struggle was far from over. The Holy Roman Empire did not suddenly shatter, nor did the emperor look kindly on the mystical and political program of the Ethiopian adventurer and the Portuguese renegade. Reubeni was thrown in chains and deported to Spain, where he spent the few remaining years of his life in a royal dungeon. And Solomon Molcho, refusing to recant his belief and return to the tender spiritual embrace of the church, was martyred by burning—a fate that he had narrowly escaped just a year before. Yet neither was forgotten by the countless Jews across the Mediterranean whose hopes of redemption were buoyed at least briefly. Not in centuries had two Jewish figures so brazenly appeared on the international stage and contested the inevitability of persecution and exile. Copies of Molcho's spiritual autobiography, *Hayyat Kaneh*, "The Scepter Revived," were avidly read and supplemented by rumors that Solomon Molcho did not really die.

Reported sightings of the courtier-turned-Messiah sparked an underground folk movement that spread as far as central Europe, to Jewish communities who anxiously awaited his reappearance and the battle against the forces of evil to resume. The Jews of Prague obtained some of his personal belongings and displayed them in their synagogue as the relics of a kabbalistic saint. Yet Molcho's legacy proved to be even more powerful among the mystics in the great cities of the Ottoman Empire. Kabbalistic study and meditation in the closed study halls and synagogues would no longer be sufficient. Political and even economic action would not be needed to bring about the eradication of evil from the world. And unfolding events continued to lend themselves to the interpretation that their di-

rection lay not in the schemes of great empires but in the changing configuration of the heavenly sefirot.

THE PLAN OF THE
SECRET BROTHERHOODS

Time for action came within two years of the imprisonment of
Reubeni and the death of Molcho. The drama of these two un-
forgettable figures among the capitals and crowned heads of
Europe offered an unmistakable indication to a growing number of Jewish leaders and sages that the details and significance
of their divinely directed history were not to be found solely in
the lore of the Torah and Talmud. Over the centuries since the
destruction of Jerusalem, occasional apocalyptic preachers had
arisen to declare a great epoch of history was ending and a new
age about to dawn. But rarely had there been so many independent indications of a great change occurring: in the Jewish
communities of the Balkans, in particular, the growing prosperity and freedom from worry of rampaging mobs gave rise to
a general conviction that history had taken a decisive turn. Kabbalistic speculation on the length and character of the various
world epochs — first discussed by the sages of Gerona — was no
longer restricted to small circles of scholars. Watching for the
signs of the impending redemption became something of a public pastime.

In Salonika, gossip about the next season's wool prices and
the demand for fine textiles in Cairo and Damascus alternated
with rumors of stunning developments in Europe and Asia.
Word came that in the very same Rhine River towns where the
Hasidei Ashkenaz had suffered, been martyred, and developed
their mystical techniques of cleaving to God's Glory, Martin
Luther's revolt against the Church of Rome was spreading
widely and unsettling both emperor and pope. No less astounding was the word of great Ottoman victories in battlefields as distant — and far apart — as Hungary and Persia, which
would almost certainly strengthen the power of the sultan and

add many more lucrative markets for the sale of textiles. But the most avidly followed reports were coming from the Land of Israel, where Sultan Suleiman had embarked on an ambitious program of rebuilding and economic development. With the administrative reorganization of the former Mamluk province of Filastin a great opportunity arose for a massive migration of Jews back to the Land of Israel. And this time it would not be the result of countless individual decisions. It would be a coordinated effort inspired by the preaching of Molcho and the agitation of Reubeni to gather the People of Israel from their exile and thereby break the hold of the evil powers over the course of history.

By the mid-1530s, the leaders of this movement were centered in the Ottoman cities of Salonika, Nicopolis, and Adrianople, where tightly knit brotherhoods established under the guidance of Rabbi Joseph Taitazak still cherished the memory of Molcho's time among them. Yet the members maintained a sober and realistic view of the future, recognizing that the repair of the sefirot—and the parallel rebuilding of the Land of Israel—would not come through miraculous intervention alone. These brotherhoods developed and elaborated meditative techniques, speculated on the reincarnation of souls, and communicated with angelic intermediaries. And acknowledging that the close connection between earthly actions and heavenly blessings was essential, one of the most charismatic of Taitazak's disciples took a fateful step in transforming the movement from a mystical cult to a political action group. In 1534, the twenty-nine-year-old rabbi Solomon Alkabetz—highly respected for his gifts of the spirit—announced his intention to settle in the Land of Israel at a solemn Sabbath gathering of the brothers. And he explained why this was less a matter of personal decision than the start of a movement-wide campaign.

For centuries to come, Alkabetz would be remembered as a kabbalist who was extraordinarily devoted to the elevation of the exiled, suffering Shekhinah, which he pictured as a sorrowful, wandering bride. His Sabbath hymn, *Lekhah Dodi*, "Come My Beloved," would become a permanent feature of

Jewish worship in greeting the advent of the Sabbath, even though its kabbalistic significance—as the celebration of the return of the Shekhinah from exile and her reunion with her husband—was not always recognized. Alkabetz, the poet and the mystic, was always seeking new symbols to express the reality of human efforts in repairing the heavenly structures that lay beyond the power of any human words to describe. The exiled Jews, the wandering Shekhinah, and the seemingly desolate Land of Israel were all symbols and symptoms of the same cosmic flaw about to be repaired. And in his farewell sermon in Salonika, Alkabetz quoted from chapter 36 of the Book of Exodus which detailed the work of the craftsmen in building the wilderness Tabernacle. For at that time, they answered the call in their hundreds—"every able man in whose mind the Lord had put ability, every one whose heart stirred him up to come to do the work."

Salonika had been just a way station out of exile. Alkabetz now stressed that the timeless ideal of building up the Land of Israel had become something astoundingly real. Through the reign of Suleiman the Lawgiver, the face of Jerusalem had been transformed, with a new water system, new market areas, and an impressive encircling wall, thus ending the period of its desolation. The Land of Israel had always been an ideal and a symbol, but now in the reign of Sultan Suleiman its resettlement by Jews and rebuilding offered a unique opportunity to merge the heavenly and earthly spheres. This was a concept that did not require great erudition—or even an official rabbinical imprimatur. The time had come to make the centuries-old hope of the mystics of Gerona a reality by using the Kabbalah to change the world. There were, to be sure, many newly prosperous Jews in Salonika and the other Balkan cities who had invested too much in their new homes and industries to contemplate such a visionary project—even though they still dutifully prayed toward the east in their synagogues and unfailingly recited the ceremonial wish "Next Year in Jerusalem" at the Passover seder. Alkabetz was not interested in these people who had so interiorized their hopes for redemption that they had become almost meaningless. So Alkabetz' sermon in Salonika was just the first stage in a larger campaign addressed to those mystical craftsmen who would answer the call.

The straightest path toward the Land of Israel from northern Greece did not lead northward toward the Danube, yet Alkabetz followed an itinerary motivated far more by the spirit than by predictable overland routes. In search of receptive souls for his project, he arrived at the Danube town of Nicopolis (the site of the modern city of Nikopol in Bulgaria), where another kabbalistic brotherhood had been founded several years before. He arrived there just in time for the festival of Shavuot—that flood-time of the spirit celebrated with metaphysical pyrotechnics since the time of the Hekhalot mystics more than a thousand years before. Among the most prominent scholars in the city was Rabbi Joseph Caro, a boyhood refugee from Spain, who, now in his forties, had become acknowledged as one of the great experts on Jewish ritual law. Yet Caro also had a deeply mystical soul, privately keeping a diary of his visitations by a heavenly advisor—a graceful, woman-like apparition whom he identified as the spirit of the Mishnah, that most basic of Jewish legal texts.

As the Shavuot evening prayers began among the members of the brotherhood of Nicopolis, they began the ritual of heavenly ascent known since antiquity, with its combined meditation on the Sinai vision and Ezekiel's Chariot. Since the time of the Spanish kabbalists, the still of the night was considered the most propitious time for heavenly communication, with the souls of sleepers ascending to the upper realms and the interference of demons and negative spirits in the hustle and bustle of daily life at its lowest ebb. The evening of Shavuot was even more auspicious, for it was the time when the union of the Shekhinah and the Tiferet might be accomplished—at least briefly—by intense mystical exercise. And we have a unique first-person account of the extraordinary events of that particular Shavuot evening written by Solomon Alkabetz. Rarely are we permitted such a detailed account of the heavenly voices that directed the subsequent actions of the kabbalistic brother-hoods.

"Know that the saint and I," wrote Alkabetz, referring to his older companion Caro, "agreed to stay up all night in order to banish sleep from our eyes on Shavuot." And he went on to detail the long list of mystically significant passages from Genesis, Exodus, Deuteronomy, Ezekiel, Habakkuk, Psalms, Song of Songs, and the Book of Ruth, and the final verses of the Second Book of Chronicles, with its proclamation of return to the Land of Israel. "All this we did in dread and awe, with quite unbelievable melody and tunefulness," continued Alkabetz, as he described the next stage of the evening of study—moving on to the Mishnah and the more esoteric works of the Kabbalah. And at that moment, deep in the dark and silence of a Balkan spring evening, a heavenly power appeared.

"No sooner had we studied two tractates of the Mishnah than our Creator smote us so that we heard a voice speaking out of the mouth of the saint." Caro, the respected lawyer and leader, suddenly began speaking in tongues. "It was a loud voice with letters clearly enunciated. All the companions heard the voice but were unable to understand what was said. It was an exceedingly pleasant voice, becoming increasingly strong. We all fell upon our faces and none of us had any spirit left in him because of our great dread and awe." It is not clear how the message of this spirit was received and interpreted, but the indications are that Alkabetz served as stenographer for Caro's spirit-inspired utterances, which were subsequently deciphered and read.

The heavenly voice identified itself as both Mishnah and Shekhinah, confirming in terrifying directness that their mystical exercises had worked. "Friends, choicest of the choice, peace to you, beloved companions," the voice declared to the assembled brothers. "Happy are you and happy those that bore you. Happy are you in this world and happy in the next that you resolved to adorn Me on this night. For these many years had My head been fallen with none to comfort Me. I was cast down to the ground to embrace the dunghills, but now you have restored the crown to its former place. Be strong, My beloved ones. Be courageous, My friends. Rejoice and exult, for you belong among the chosen few. You have the merit of belonging to the king's palace. The sound of your Torah and the breath of your mouth have ascended to the Holy One, blessed be He, breaking through the many firmaments and many atmospheres until it rose upwards. The angels were silent, the seraphim still, the hayyot stood without speech and all the host of heaven heard, together with the Holy One, blessed be He, the sound of your voice."

Yet the purpose of the communication was not mere praise for pious behavior but a call to action that confirmed with indisputable authority what Alkabetz had already asked them to do. "Return to your studies, not interrupting them for one moment. Go up to the Land of Israel, for not all times are opportune. There is no hindrance to salvation, be it much or little. Let not your eyes have pity on your worldly goods, for you eat the goodness of the higher land. If you will but hearken, of the goodness of the land will you eat. Make haste, therefore, to go up to the land, for I sustain you here and I will sustain you there." This was a moment that would be repeated many times in the coming decades with the establishment of a new mystical society in Ottoman Palestine. And in fact, the very next morning, all those who had witnessed Caro's angelic possession, though still sleepless, went to the sages of the city and explained what had happened, hoping to gather an even greater group on the following night. Once again they gathered and as the evening hours passed into night, Caro expounded the Torah and suddenly the Voice again spoke through him. Alkabetz carefully copied down the strange syllables which were interpreted as a new covenant between God and the mystical elite of Israel as they entered a new era of sacred history.

"Let each help his neighbor and say unto his brother, be strong. Let the weak say, I am mighty, and let each be great in his own eyes since you belong to the king's palace and have the merit of entering the vestibule. Endeavor now to enter the great hall and do not leave the vestibule. For whoever leaves to go outside, blood be upon his head. Awake, My sons, and see that I speak to you. Awake, My beloved ones. Be firm and valiant in battle. Be strong and rejoice and a thread of mercy will be extended over you daily. Observe how intoxicated you are with worldly desires. Awake, O drunken ones, for the day comes when a man must cast away his gods of silver, worldly desires, and his gods of gold, lust for wealth. Go up to the Land of Israel, for so you are able to do it were not that you are trapped in the mud of worldly desires and vanities." The next morning, the brothers pledged to observe a long list of ethical and ritual regulations drawn up by Caro—and which was carried by Alkabetz as he departed from Nicopolis on his way southeastward to visit the brothers in Adrianople.

The instructions of the heavenly voice in Nicopolis marked the beginning of an unprecedented revival of the spirit, in which formerly independent mystical circles began to act in unison. For the next two years—until 1536—Alkabetz remained in Adrianople (today the large industrial city of Edirne in Turkey, once known as the "great metropolis of Israel," which had attracted thousands of Jewish immigrants and refugees from the Christian West in the early sixteenth century). Communications between the brotherhoods in Salonika, Nicopolis, and Adrianople grew closer, and word spread quickly of new visions and heavenly voices. Little by little, as growing numbers of the brothers packed up their belongings and booked passage to the Land of Israel, the focus of kabbalistic speculation and practice shifted. Yet as events would transpire, the new center of messianic expectation would not be Jerusalem, but *another* city whose recent history was as miraculous as the hopes soon to be invested in it.

Chapter 5

A MYSTICAL CITY

Visitors still come to Safed in the hundreds of thousands hoping to taste the forbidden fruit of the Tree of mystical knowledge, in the synagogues and cemeteries that have been hallowed by the footsteps of saints and sages for hundreds of years. Yet the modern city of Safed has become a caricature of its own sacred reputation, a religious tourist attraction for busloads of day-trippers and a lucrative market for souvenirs and ceremonial artifacts. Stall after stall in its main market and winding side alleys are filled with mezuzahs, tefillin, Sabbath candlesticks, prayer shawls, religious calendars, and mass-produced oil paintings of aged rabbis and prayers at the Western Wall.

The Lubavitch Hasidim have set up headquarters in the city, readily offering traveling teenagers free accommodations in their youth hostel and evening courses in mysticism that mask their deeper missionary aim. Here and there small groups of aging, former American and European hippies mix their devotion to mystical observance with an equal measure of their modern marketing of handmade candles and leather goods. Licensed tourist guides spend their days showing visitors the high points of the city—almost always spending a few minutes in the five-hundred-year-old Abuhav Synagogue, with its hanging lamps and rickety circular wooden bimah—and its blue-painted central dome ornamented with kabbalistic symbols of crowns, spherical vessels, and blossoming trees. And they unfailingly lead their groups down the steep, stepped walkway on the western slope of the city—to take snapshots and toss pebbles of remembrance on the humble graves of the famous sixteenth-century rabbis Joseph Caro, Solomon Alkabetz, Moses Cordovero, and Isaac Luria, the mystical master still revered as the "Holy Lion" of Safed.

In the crowded, narrow streets around the summit of modern Safed, filled with modern shops, open-air restaurants, and the constant, throaty exhaust fumes of the tourist buses, it is almost impossible to understand what took place here in what has come to be called Safed's Golden Age. It is a tale of how the separate threads of trade, textiles, and metaphysics were skillfully woven together to create an unexpected garment of splendor for the kabbalistic tradition. Through a miraculous confluence of technical know-how and business savvy, raw materials, trade routes, and unimagined profit, the tiny mountaintop town of Safed became one of the most dynamic economic centers in the world. From around 1535 to 1575, hardly more than two generations, Safed flourished as an independent center of learning, culture, and mysticism, eclipsing in prestige every other Jewish community in the world—including the Holy City of Jerusalem. And in its meteoric rise as a center for the manufacture and sale of woolen textiles, it rivaled—incredible as it may seem—the output and profitability of some of the greatest cities of the age.

Rising from the haze and fog of Upper Galilee's deepest ravines and valleys, Safed has no biblical pedigree, no deep roots in the scriptural or prophetic history of Israel. Scholars still debate the date of its establishment, but in no case was it ever anything more than an anonymous hilltop village until well into the Middle Ages. Bypassed by the main trade routes of commerce through the Roman and Byzantine periods, its rugged, heavily forested terrain became the hinterland of a rural Jewish culture. While rabbinical institutions flourished in the main Galilean cities of Sepphoris and Tiberias, the less formalized religious aura of legends, ruins, and ancient tombs sanctified the landscape of the Galilean highlands. Ironically, the Crusades, which had played such a bloody and formidable role in the crystallization of modern Jewish culture in Europe, were also responsible for Safed's sudden transformation from its traditional agricultural way of life. After the conquest of the Holy Land in 1099 by the massed Crusader armies, Galilee became a feudal fiefdom of a succession of European princes. The city and the surrounding region were eventually handed over to the Order of the Knights Templar—the highly skilled fighting force of Christian warriors that was responsible in large measure for rooting out and liquidating the Cathars in Provence.

It is an extraordinary historical coincidence that around 1170—precisely at the time when the first kabbalists of Provence and Aragon were responding to Cathar ideology and formulating their complex theories of the sefirotic powers—Templar knights in the Holy Land were clearing the summit of Mount Canaan in Galilee and unwittingly building a city that would become the Kabbalah's most famous home. Yet their motives, as usual, were not religious. In order to establish an effective system of border control for the Crusader kingdom and maintain the feudal order over the local peasantry, an impregnable fortress-castle was needed. Before long the clinking of masons' chisels, the creaking of wooden hoists, and the staccato of carpenters' hammers echoed throughout the surrounding valleys as a huge castle rose above the skyline, protected by three lines of fortification, with turreted towers and a central keep. And it was, ironically, that looming Crusader castle, meant to impose by intimidation European feudal control over the region, that provided the basic armature for the later Jewish "mystical" city of Upper Galilee.

In the shadow of the castle walls arose a European-style town, with markets and burgesses' court for the European settlers—and less rule-bound jurisdiction over the peasants in the surrounding Galilean villages, Christian, Muslim, and Jewish alike. Though the Jews in the large cities were massacred with the coming of the first wave of Crusaders, Jewish peasants remained part of the rural landscape, working the land and dutifully handing over their taxes to the increasingly dominant European feudal elite. In fact, outside the city, Jewish peasants lived a rural existence that was almost indistinguishable from the way of life of the Muslin and Christian villagers. They all shared the seasonal agricultural cycles of plowing, sowing, and reaping, and came together to celebrate annual pilgrimages at the very same ancient tombs and sacred places.

With its new administrative center, rich water sources, and abundance of good farmland, Safed was destined to become a major economic center. Within just a few decades, the fortress-castle at Safed (known as *castrum Saphet* in medieval Latin) effectively controlled the crops and produce from more than 260 villages, mills, and orchards throughout the Upper Galilee. With the military victory of Salah ed-Din over the Crusaders in 1187, the great fortress passed to Muslim control. And even though it reverted only briefly to Templar rule in the thirteenth century, its economic system did not really change. The Mamluk sultan Baybars conquered it in 1266, allowing Jews to settle in the attached market town and to participate as royal officials in the administration of the feudal hinterland. And it was in the thirteenth century—at the time when the Castilian kabbalists were shaping the Zohar at the other end of the Mediterranean—that the first yeshiva and Jewish communal institutions were established at Safed. Gradually, through the fourteenth century, Jewish immigrants, fleeing from the continuing persecutions in Europe, arrived to settle in the city. Although there is evidence that they brought with them early kabbalistic manuscripts, the religious importance of Safed in this period was still negligible. Jerusalem remained the Holy City and its sages remained the most respected spiritual authorities in the Jewish world. Life in Safed revolved around the rhythms of the caravan trade along the routes down the Jordan valley and from the Mediterranean to Damascus; tax collection from the surrounding villages at harvest time; seasonal pilgrimages to the tombs of the sages; and the bustle of weekly market days.

Yet after 1492, with the horror and uncertainty of the Spanish Expulsion and the increasing flow of Jewish immigrants toward the Ottoman Empire, Safed was one of the several towns in the Holy Land that received a significant number of refugees. Jerusalem had religious prestige, but, from an economic perspective, had little to offer. Safed represented a more promising frontier. Contemporary accounts record the presence of three distinct congregations in Safed at this period—of local Jews, of immigrants from North Africa, and Jews from Spain. Economic activity in the region of Galilee was already steadily increasing when outside events changed the course of the region's history. With the gradual expansion of the Ottomans toward Persia in 1514, the Mamluks of Egypt brought their armies northward to discourage Ottoman movements into Syria. But in a clash of the antiquated Mamluk cavalry with the highly disciplined Ottoman forces—whose firepower was strengthened by the use of cannon—the vaunted Mamluk power collapsed. Ottoman forces pursued the retreating Mamluks southward toward Egypt, leaving behind Ottoman governors and military garrisons to administer the newly acquired territories. Once again the course of Jewish history in general— and Jewish mysticism in particular—would be profoundly influenced by unfolding world events. For by the beginning of 1517, the Age of the Mamluks was over and the Holy Land had begun a new historical incarnation. All of Syria, Palestine, and Egypt had come under the rule of the conquering Ottoman sultan, Selim I.

For most of the inhabitants of these conquered territories, the victory of the Ottomans had brought a merciful termination to the increasingly oppressive Mamluk feudal regime. The self-serving tyranny of the Crusader lords had merely been replaced by a Muslim military aristocracy who had stifled significant economic development in the region, content to support its lavish courtly lifestyle through the continuing, violent exploitation of the peasantry. As the Ottoman armies passed through the country, there seems to have been considerable popular support for a change of regime, even if the future was unclear. The Jews, in particular, seem to have been enthusiastic supporters of the Ottoman conquerors as the Mamluk lords were defeated in battle or fled their strongholds without a fight. But the open enthusiasm of the Jews for the defeat of the Mamluks proved to be somewhat premature. As soon as the main Ottoman forces left the area, the old Mamluk lords emerged from hiding to reclaim what they believed was rightfully theirs. Gathering all their surviving forces and promising the local Muslims that they would be rewarded for their loyalty, they mounted a counter-attack well behind the Ottoman lines.

The bloodiest outbreak occurred in Safed in January 1517, when a mob of local Muslims, inflamed by their former overlords and by rumors of the defeat of the Ottomans in Cairo, led an open rebellion with great bloodshed in an attempt by the now-dispossessed local nobles to reassume control. A crowd of Muslims, inflamed by their former overlords, murdered the Ottoman governor and plundered the Jewish Quarter, killing or wounding many in the community. In any event, this violent outbreak proved to be the last gasp of a dying regime. The Ottomans were well aware of the economic and strategic potential of Safed, and they proved determined not only to restore order but to make it one of the cornerstones in their rule in Palestine. To that end, they encouraged intensified Jewish settlement in the city, and within just a few years, urban life and trade began to flourish on unprecedented levels and the population soared. Thus even before the recorded arrival of a single kabbalistic

scholar, with the establishment of a new regime on new principles of the Ottoman Empire, the Golden Age of Safed had
begun.

AN ECONOMIC MIRACLE

Trade and profit, more than divine inspiration and mystical visions, would fuel Safed's renaissance. The down-to-earth reality of commerce, negotiation, and camel trains loaded with
merchandise bought and sold to the highest bidder was what set
this place and time apart. In less than five years after the Ottoman conquest, Safed had already become one of the most active economic centers in the region. Moses Basola, an Italian
rabbi who went on pilgrimage to Palestine in 1521, reported
that "the whole city is filled with every good thing and fine provisions such as grain, wine, and oil in great quantities, and at a
low price. Buyers can obtain every commodity in its season,
and were it not for the fact that that large quantities of wine and
produce are exported to Damascus and other places, these
products would cost almost nothing. All kinds of fruits and delicacies are found there, and anything that is not available is
brought from Damascus. The land is filled with merchandise —
woolen textiles, finished clothing, and perfumes — and for the
sale of these three products, there are many shops in the bazaar
owned by Jews." To the urban commerce was added that of the
peddlars who roamed throughout the surrounding villages selling clothing and other items, often bartering them for raw cot-
ton, spun thread, wax, healing herbs, and agricultural produce.
Basola concluded that "the whole country is far more active in
trade even than Italy." Trades, crafts, and heightened economic
activity now added an element of bustle to the basic agricultural
richness of the Upper Galilee. And the situation would change
even more dramatically with the first industrial revolution in
Safed's history.

Cloth was the source of wealth and status in those days of
Renaissance and imperial greatness — not only for those

grandees who draped themselves in Spanish-style finery and appeared in the glittering courts of Europe or strutted through its magnificent public squares. Throughout Europe and the Mediterranean, the bolts of fine woven goods, ranging from oriental silk to the tightly bound bolts of woolen fabric from Flanders and Iberia, represented a form of investment and wealth handed down in dowries and estates from generation to generation. And its manufacture, perfected in the workshops of Aragon and Castile by the Jewish craftsmen, brought wealth to those nations and those entrepreneurs who could bring together the raw materials, the workers, and the equipment to turn out cloth in sufficient quantities.

For half a century since its conquest of Constantinople and ascent on the world stage as a superpower, the courts and armies of the Ottomans had been spending their treasure to import Western cloth and woolens. But now their new Jewish settlers brought the know-how and capital to set up an initial manufacturing center in Salonika. Its phenomenal success in the sale of high-quality woolens in the Balkans convinced some of its leading entrepreneurs that markets in other parts of the rapidly expanding Ottoman Empire could also be profitably served. The bureaucrats and local elite of Damascus, Aleppo, and Sidon were potential customers. And Safed beckoned as a great new manufacturing center. Property could be bought relatively cheaply, and there was plenty of flowing water in the nearby ravines for the construction of fulling mills and dyeing vats. And no less important, the Jewish population of Safed was rapidly growing and there were plenty of wives, children, and local villagers who could be recruited for the various stages of the work. The only drawback was the basic raw material: the fat-tailed, coarse-coated Awassi sheep of the Middle East were the only livestock available in the region. Yet in Safed, innovation was a requirement for survival, and it was soon recognized that Awassi wool could be used to produce an acceptable (if slightly cheaper) blend of fibers when spun together with imported Merino fleece.

Even today, among the thick underbrush in the deep ravines

of Nahal Amud—Wadi Tawakhin, the "Valley of the Mills," in Arabic—near Safed, the archaeological traces of this production process can still be found. And in its intricate mixture of natural and human processes, of technology and shrewd utilization of natural resources, it offered the material wealth on which the edifice of Safedian Kabbalah was built. In fact, the complex process of textile production provided a new yearly cycle to complement the agricultural seasons and the fasts and festivals of the Jewish ritual calendar. In the springtime, even before Passover, purchase agents fanned out through the countryside to purchase newly sheared wool from the local flocks of Awassi while the bales of imported Merino wool came overland on donkey or camel caravan from Sidon. Through the late spring, the mountains of wool were washed in the flowing streams in the valleys, and the workers and the foremen carefully graded and separated the fleece containing long fibers (to be spun into the finer thread) from the shorter fibers (to be used for the production of felt). Once separated and dried, the wool was brushed clean of all sticks, thistles, and pebbles; thoroughly combed to straighten and separate the fibers; and then apportioned among dozens of village families throughout the vicinity for the next stage of the production process.

We have no hard evidence on the precise method of spinning the raw wool into thread in sixteenth-century Safed. The traditional Near Eastern implement was a hand bow in which the fibers were twisted, but it also seems reasonable to assume that with so many Spanish and Portuguese immigrants in Safed, Spanish-style spinning wheels were used. And once the spinners had produced large bobbins of thread, the thread was collected and distributed to the weavers all over town. In courtyards and hearth rooms, wooden hand looms stood ready for the weavers to turn out cloth of varying categories, receiving their pay by the piece, and working in family groups. The final stages of the process—the finishing of the fabrics—was most likely carried out by the skilled craftspeople who had come from the centers of Jewish textile production in the Balkans or Greece. Operating the fulling mills down in the valleys, they passed the bolts of fabric under the large, pounding hammers to flatten and stabilize the woof and the warp. In the case of the highest-class fabrics, dyeing was often also a part of the process. The geographical location of Safed, close to major overland caravan routes from Baghdad and the Persian Gulf, made indigo — the main color used in both Salonika and Safed — less costly than in production centers farther west. Anatolian crimson was also used since it was wildly popular with the Venetians and the markets of northern Europe. By late summer, the cycle of production was over. The finished bolts were dispatched to the port of Sidon just after Rosh ha-Shanah to celebrate the start of a new year with prayers, calculations of profit, and the arrival of ships from the west with their cargo of raw Merino wool.

The growth of this industry was nothing short of explosive. By the middle of the sixteenth century, the former village in the upper Galilee had become a bustling city, producing tens of thousands of bolts of finished cloth every year. "Anyone who saw Safed ten years ago and came back now would be utterly amazed," wrote the Jewish traveler David de Rossi in 1535, "because Jews are constantly arriving, and the textile industry is growing by the day." Who were these people? A close examination of the descriptions of passing travelers and modern scholarly analysis of the figures recorded in Ottoman tax registers has uncovered the secret of Safed's demographic explosion. In 1525, less than ten years after the Ottoman conquest, the Jewish population of Safed numbered 233 families, divided into three congregations. The majority were local Arabic-speaking Galileans, numbering 131 heads-of-household. Next came the Ashkenazim at 48 households. Next were immigrants from north Africa at 33 households. And fewest of all were the settlers from Portugal ("Purtukal" in Turkish) numbering 21 heads-of-household, or only 9 percent.

By the next recorded census in 1555, just thirty years later — and after the Inquisition had been established in Lisbon — the demographic shape of the Safed Jewish community had dramatically changed. The population had almost tripled, and while the native-born heads-of-household had declined to a mere 14 percent of the total, immigrants from various parts of the Iberian peninsula now comprised a full 60 percent of the Jewish population. The congregations of Jews originally from Castile alone represented 25 percent and those from Portugal 20 percent of the whole. The cultural flavor of the city was now clearly Hispanic in language, dress, and, presumably, turn of mind. One of the spiritual leaders of the main Sephardic congregation, Rabbi Moses di Trani, found that a great deal of his work in Safed involved intervention with the Ottoman authorities to facilitate land purchases and settling legal differences between his own congregants. "God put it in my heart to build up the desolate places thereof," he later wrote. "I have watched over them in most of their building enterprises, that no man should encroach on the property of his neighbor." Business problems, however, were not the most serious challenge that the new settlers faced.

It is easy to forget that many of those who arrived in this new, massive wave of immigration in the late 1520s and 1530s — especially those originally from the Iberian Peninsula — were the children of, or had themselves been, forced converts to Christianity. And among the most recent arrivals, there were those who had lived under threat of the Inquisition for an entire generation longer than those who had fled to Turkey in the earlier waves. There was thus understandable grounds for resentment among those Jews who had sacrificed and suffered for their Judaism. The "New Christians" had actually benefited from their apostasy, succeeding in trade and living the good life as no faithful Jew had been able to do. Only when conditions in Portugal became unbearably repressive — and their lives and property seemed to be in immediate danger — did they make the decision to move eastward, to the Holy Land. Who could say that their arrival in Safed was not motivated by the same kind of economic opportunism that led their parents and grandparents to embrace Christianity? What was to be done about them when they joined the Jewish communities of the East? In terms of Jewish ritual law, they were to be accepted back into the community, but the fate of their souls was in doubt.

In spite of their subsequent economic success in the Ottoman Empire, they were still subject to the fearful biblical curse of *Karet*—the divine punishment for falling prey to idolatry and failing to fulfill the commandments. According to some authorities, it entailed extra punishment of the soul after death. Yet with hopes for the imminent redemption of Israel, a major preoccupation in the spiritual life of Safed, something had to be done to enable the New Christians to atone for their sin of apostasy. And the newly arrived sages of Safed characteristically attacked this problem with the same concentration and scientific precision that had fueled the booming textile trade.

THE BATTLE FOR REDEMPTION

In times and places of prosperity, intellectual and philosophical pursuits tend to flourish, and it was from the scholars who flocked to Safed in the 1520s and 1530s that a solution to the problem of the New Christians arose. There were surely places with a holier reputation than Safed on which to build a new mystical movement: Hebron, with its patriarchal tombs of Abraham, Isaac, and Jacob; Shechem, with its tomb of Joseph; and, of course, the Holy City of Jerusalem. In fact, Jerusalem possessed another distinct attraction for religious scholars. In 1509, the leaders of its Jewish community had declared that any full-time scholars settling in the city would henceforth be exempt from all government taxes—with the community funds bearing the expense—so that they could devote themselves entirely to the study of scripture and Law. This economic inducement brought many prominent scholars to Jerusalem from the various places that they had been displaced in exile. Yet after the booming textile industry had been established in Safed, an even greater opportunity arose. The leaders in Safed extended their own offer of tax exemption. And where Jerusalem was a conservative community, with an anemic economy and a strong

Muslim presence, Safed drew an entirely new type of rabbi-entrepreneur. We have already mentioned the active involvement of the Sephardic rabbi Moses di Trani in facilitating land purchases and settling business disputes. Yet far more influential in shaping the unique character of scholarship in Safed was Rabbi Jacob Berav, an exile from Spain, who combined his Talmudic and kabbalistic studies with an active involvement in trade.

Berav was nearly fifty when he settled in Safed in 1524, and by that time he had gained a reputation as an outstanding religious authority throughout the Jewish world. Born in the small Castilian town of Maqueda, he had studied in the famous yeshiva of Isaac Abuhav in the royal city of Toledo; after the Expulsion of 1492—at age eighteen—he found a new position in North Africa as rabbi of the exile community in Fez. While there, he became involved in international commerce and succeeded in becoming a wealthy and respected merchant, with his long-distance buying and selling putting him in close contact with many other Jewish communities. After a brief sojourn in Egypt, he settled permanently in Safed—no doubt attracted by the tax exemption and the city's growing commerce—and soon established his own yeshiva in the city, modeled after the academy of his teacher and mentor, Rabbi Isaac Abuhav, in Castile.

In the nostalgic memories of Jewish life in Castile before the expulsion, Abuhav's academy was described as a unique place of learning—not a strict seminary where students were required to learn by rote from their teachers. It was, rather, remembered as a lively house of debates and discussion, where scholars from many different backgrounds learned to think for themselves. Berav was anxious to recreate that atmosphere in Safed. While the normal practice had been for each congregation to support its own house of learning, he now invited the best and the brightest from all backgrounds to gather at his yeshiva and debate the fine points of the Law and the future of the People of Israel. Before long he had gathered a glittering assembly of intellects—rather than students—including Moses di Trani and Joseph Caro, newly arrived from Nicopolis. And in the great and noisy study hall of Berav's academy in Safed the convocation from exile of so many scholars and accomplished sages seemed to possess its own mystical significance. And they regarded themselves, perhaps a bit immodestly, as the most learned and authoritative deliberative body anywhere in the Jewish world.

Yet Berav's ambition to lead a supreme court of the Jewish people required a daring act to secure its fulfillment. The full exercise of religious authority to debate the Law and mete out biblically mandated punishments was technically permitted only to those who had been granted *semikhah* or "ordination"—a chain of authority that was traced back to Moses in traditional lore. It was the divine sanction that was passed on to Joshua and the seventy elders who composed the deliberative body called the Great Sanhedrin as long as the Temple of Jerusalem stood. As ordained judges, they were permitted to pass judgment in criminal cases of capital punishment, to determine the calendar, and to apply excommunication. In short, they were an essential component of the independent life of Israel. But in the aftermath of the destruction of the Temple, the chain of semikhah was broken. In the subsequent centuries of exile and dispersion, rabbis had been informally ordained upon graduation from a yeshiva, but they did not possess legal authority that extended beyond the confines of their own communities. But now something more than a congregational rabbi or judge was needed. With many of the returning exiles to Safed bearing the guilt of apostasy and imperiled by the curse of karet, a source of authority was needed to grant them the proper atonement for their sins.

Only in a place like Safed—and in an intellectual center like Berav's academy, where the theoretical bases of Jewish thought spanned the gamut from strict law to mystical speculation—would anyone dare to attempt a daring reversal of history. In the earlier Golden Age of Spanish philosophy, the great twelfth-century sage Moses Maimonides had speculated on the possibility that semikhah might be restored. In an almost abstract hypothesis, he suggested in 1168 that if all the sages in the Land of Israel made a decision to restore the chain of ordination, and acknowledged that one of them was the indisputable leader, the chain of semikhah could begin again.

The massive influx of sages back into the Land of Israel in the early sixteenth century—and the emergence of a towering leader like Berav—seemed to fulfill the necessary conditions. And for those many mystically inclined sages in Safed, the restoration of ordination was an essential part of the millennial drama about to unfold: victory over the forces of evil, the purification of the People of Israel from foreign contamination, and the reestablishment of a center of divinely appointed authority. Isaiah 1:24–26 had described the scenario: "Therefore the Lord says, the Lord of hosts, the Mighty One of Israel: Ah, I will vent my wrath on my enemies, and avenge myself on my foes. I will turn my hand against you and will smelt away your dross as with lye and remove all your alloy. And I will restore your judges as at the first, and your counselors as at the beginning. Afterward you shall be called the city of righteousness, the faithful city." Isaiah had clearly intended Jerusalem to be that city, but perhaps Safed was the true place for the fulfillment of that prophecy. So in 1538, Berav and his followers took the fateful action. Without prior consultation with any other community, twenty-five senior scholars in the Safed Academy gathered together and formally declared Berav to be their duly ordained leader. And in this solemn act of semikhah—the first since the days of the earliest rabbis—the sages of Safed declared independence for themselves.

With the record of the proceedings carefully inscribed on parchment, a messenger was sent southward from Safed to Jerusalem to bring the news of the action to the leaders there. Yet the rabbis in Jerusalem reacted in horror and anger, regarding the Safed sages' action as outright blasphemy. They denied that semikhah could be restored without clear divine intervention, and they accused the Safedians of being arrogantly disrespectful of the ancient holiness of Jerusalem. And in a subsequent flurry of angry letters dashed off to various Jewish communities, the Jerusalem leadership gained the support of

David Ibn Zimra, the *nagid*, or spiritual leader, of Egyptian Jewry. They would not stand idly by as the upstarts in Safed unilaterally proclaimed the beginning of a new stage in the sacred history of Israel.

Part of the passion was surely personal: Berav was clearly a dominant and sometimes domineering personality. He was not merely a cleric, and perhaps it was his personal wealth and the burgeoning economy in Safed that made his plan seem so dangerous to the older and less prosperous communities. In other times and in other places, the pursuit of commerce required too much time and attention to permit serious scholarship, so the spiritual authority was left to the specialists. But in sixteenth-century Safed, with the establishment of the "putting out" system for textile production, only the initial organization and general supervision of the work was required of the entrepreneur. In the rising profits of imported wool, weaving, dyeing, and the sale of finished bolts of cloth to the major cities of the region, the new class of spiritual entrepreneurs arose. Berav himself was but one of many. And the combination of Safed's economic power with its sages' spiritual ambition fueled the intense opposition. It also paved the way for Rabbi Berav's sudden downfall.

"Is it because of the great quantity of clothes that are manufactured in Safed," asked Jerusalem leader Rabbi Levi Ibn Habib, "that they presume to be the leaders of the Jewish people?" Even business competitors and rivals of Rabbi Berav found the semikhah controversy a convenient pretext to denounce him to the local Ottoman officials, who were ever vigilant for signs of political unrest. Thus by the end of 1538, with the controversy at its height, Berav was ordered to leave the country for the good of the public order. Yet before leaving for Damascus—knowing that once outside of the Land of Israel in exile he would not be able to exercise the power of semikhah—Berav ordained four of his most trusted colleagues—among them, Joseph Caro and Moses di Trani. They, in turn, would have the power to ordain new judges themselves.

In the years that followed, as Berav settled in Damascus and then returned to Egypt, the idea of the renewed semikhah was gradually abandoned by all but his most faithful followers. In Safed, Joseph Caro inherited Berav's spiritual mantle, presiding over the local court and heading the great academy. Undaunted by the criticism of the other communities, he continued the practice of ordination. And with the goal of reintegrating the Jewish people after the horrors of exile, he condensed his great treatise on Jewish Law into a usable reference work, the *Shulkhan Arukh*, or "The Prepared Table," which remains an authoritative statement on normative Jewish observance even today. Caro's other works helped to standardize such varied activities as dietary laws, collection of interest on loans, purity, mourning, marriage, divorce, and civil and criminal law. The sages of Safed were busy creating a world of their own ideals. And they were completely convinced that in their words, thoughts, and actions the redemption of the world had begun.

INTO THE GROVE OF
THE POMEGRANATES

Moses Cordovero was only sixteen years old when the great ordination controversy swirled around the famous rabbinical academy of Rav Berav in Safed. Yet within just a few years the young Cordovero would found a powerful, new kabbalistic movement that would succeed in establishing Safed as the spiritual capital of Israel. His physical appearance is unknown and his personal origins are uncertain; subtle clues are all we have to go on in reconstructing his personal history. A few suggestive facts offer at least the outlines of a biography. He was born in Safed, in 1522, and his surname indicates a possible family origin in Córdoba. And his later appointment as head of the academy connected with Safed's Portuguese community hints at a direct connection to that ethnic group—perhaps through parents, aunts, uncles, or grandparents who migrated to Portugal in the wake of the expulsion from Spain. And although there is no trace of any New Christians in his family background, his later dealings with the growing Portuguese congregation surely placed him in close contact with the hundreds of New Christians who were settling in Safed, especially after the imposition of the Inquisition there in 1536.

In his teens, Cordovero entered the yeshiva of Joseph Caro and was soon acknowledged as one of Caro's most brilliant students, yet he was not destined to be a judge or legal scholar. Mysticism always exerted a profound attraction, and in 1542, at age twenty, he reportedly received an otherwordly visitor—a magid, or celestial messenger, like the voice which had spoken to Joseph Caro—who solemnly announced to Cordovero that it was his destiny to "heal the altar of the Lord which is broken down." In this age of world-transforming changes and messianic expectation, it was not enough to study the laws of the Torah and Talmud and to regulate the life of the here and now. Beneath their surface lay the profound secrets of the unfolding age of redemption. And while many of the sages of Safed were fully occupied with matters of business and ritual practice, Cordovero was drawn to the teachings of the charismatic kabbalist from Salonika, Solomon Alkabetz. Now in his forties, he led a small mystical circle at the site of the ancient tomb of Rabbi Simeon Bar-Yohai—the revered hero of the Zohar—near the mountaintop village of Meron.

It is difficult to know precisely where the study of the Kabbalah fit in at this period of Safed's history, for the main emphasis in Joseph Caro's academy and in the academy of Rabbi Moses di Trani was interpretation of ritual law. And in a rapidly growing community, composed of congregations from so many places, with so many different traditions and customs, agreement on the basic legal and judicial procedures was difficult enough. Yet each group had also brought with it their own mystical traditions—from Germany, Italy, Turkey, North Africa—and none more intensely than the refugee families from Portugal and Spain. For almost a generation, the mystical excitement had been spreading, and the new interest in the Zohar and the arrangement of the sefirot seemed to many people to be itself a clear sign of the rapidly approaching end of times. Cordovero delved deeply into the study of the ancient mystical texts — under the guidance of Solomon Alkabetz, whose sister he eventually married. And he gradually came to recognize that in times of great historical crisis in the long saga of Israel, the profound secrets that had once been closely guarded by mystical sages gradually were made known to the wider People of Israel. So it was in the time of Simeon Bar-Yohai, when the Roman repression had all but snuffed out the open learning of the Torah, that Rabbi Simeon received a divine dispensation to commit the mystical secrets to writing. And so it was in the time of Rabbi Moses de Leon in Castile, when he and his colleagues brought the ancient documents together in a single work.

And so it must be even now as the Jewish people hovered between expulsion and redemption, with so many of them lost to forced or voluntary conversion, that the secrets of the Zohar had to be collected and verified and put in a new and more accessible form. Since the failure of the Safed sages' attempt at universal ordination, the former New Christians and even those with far milder failings were desperately seeking more mystical ways of atonement in the perfect confidence that they were living in the millennial age. And Cordovero had learned from his teacher Joseph Caro the necessity of codifying knowledge from different sources, places, and versions that had been carried among the sacred texts of the various communities now converging on Safed. He set himself to this task of mystical refinement and renewal. And after seven years of scholarship and reflection, in 1549, he produced his first large systematic work, *Pardes Rimmonim,* the "Grove of Pomegranates." Like the Shulkhan Arukh, this massive work represented a conscious attempt to recodify and standardize the various aspects of Jewish culture, inviting the uninitiated into a strange mystical garden where the ripe fruit was both sweet and held many precious spiritual seeds. Just as Caro's Shulkhan Arukh codified and simplified the vast body of Jewish ritual law and made it accessible to the layperson, Cordovero's Pardes Rimmonim served for centuries as a basic compenium of kabbalistic lore. Yet an important, perhaps even crucial, element of this stage of kabbalistic development that is often overlooked by modern scholars of this major work is the specific historical background of Cordovero's work. For his mystical synthesis of the flow of power from the transcendent God, through the network of the sefirot, metaphorically resembled the flow of capital, skill, and finished products that was now enriching the city of Safed.

Cordovero's writings comprise not so much an innovative mystical doctrine as an eloquent and accessible summary of the basic concepts of the Kabbalah. In his deep admiration for the saintliness of Rabbi Simeon Bar-Yohai, and his belief that the vast compendium of the Zohar was all written by Bar-Yohai and his followers, he was forced to come up with ingenious ways to reconcile the glaring differences in the widely differing texts. Yet in dealing with this dizzying, often confusing, wealth of the mystical raw materials, Cordovero systematically described the chain of divine emanation as almost an industrial production process that would be at least subliminally familiar to the people of sixteenth-century Safed. From the boundlessness of God the Ineffable and Transcendent (expressed by the term *Ein Sof,* or "Endlessness," in the traditional Kabbalah), a concentrated act of divine will (embodied in the first sefirah of Keter or "Crown") began a process of defined and focussed creation. Only that part of the energy that was needed for the final product was concentrated and emanated outward. And in a series of further stages—corresponding to each of the next nine sefirot—the divine light was further limited and shaped.

Passing from Keter to Hokhmah, the initial will was crystallized into a physical plan for the universe, and then through Binah, where it was further restricted to the creation of physical forms. Step by step, the energy cascaded down through the seven lower sefirot, at each stage losing some of its power but gaining a greater particularity. The modern example of step-down transformers that convert the output of a nuclear reactor to the high voltage of regional substations to neighborhood transformers and then to household current is an easy metaphor to describe this heavenly process. Yet it conveys only the progressive lessening of intensity—not the progressive emergence of detail and character that is so essential to Cordovero's scheme.

A far more appropriate image, in fact, would be the flow of raw materials gathered and processed by craftsmen. Obtaining only those resources necessary for the final product, they pass through each stage of production while the raw material grows progressively smaller in quantity, even as it takes on more sophisticated forms. The raw wool that came to Safed in heavy bales from the Balkans is only one example of the initial infusion of natural bounty. The merchant entrepreneur was the directing will that selected the amount (with an eye toward the quality and quantity of the final product), while the washers, carders, weavers, dyers, and fullers represented the "vessels" through which the raw material would pass. The relationship between the various craftsmen and the balance between the various stages of production determined the quality of the final product and how much of it would be produced.

Only by paying attention to these basic structures of the heavens could the People of Israel—and indeed all of humanity—ever hope to control the flow of divine blessings in the many forms they came to earth. Through directed prayer, mystical contemplation, or by living one's life in accordance with the orderly rhythm of divine emanations, Cordovero later observed, a man's "words have ramifications on high and the sefirot arrange themselves in accordance with the matter he is pursuing." In sixteenth-century Safed, the structures of heaven and the industriousness of humanity suddenly merged.

This abstract scheme of heavenly production and circulation may have struck a responsive chord among Safed's leading citizens and sages. Yet Cordovero would also include some deeply personal spiritual elements in his brand of Kabbalah that made it both an abstract philosophical system and a vivid revivalist faith. The attraction of the Kabbalah was now being shared by ever-wider portions of the population among the urban Jewish populations of Salonika, Nicopolis, Adrianople, and Safed. Yet Cordovero had noted that as the time of the redemption grew nearer, the secrets of creation would become known to the entire People of Israel, who would understand that both their own individual salvation and the salvation of Israel were dependent on ritual reenactments of the arrangement of the heavenly sefirot. Throughout the Middle Ages, the peasants of Galilee — Jewish, Christian, and Muslim — visited and revered the tombs and caves of ancient saints and heroes, hoping for contact with the forces of heavenly power as they had been understood for hundreds of years. One of the most important of these pilgrimage sites was Meron, site of the tombs of the famous first-century rabbis Hillel and Shammai, where local Galilean farmers gathered every year in late springtime to pray for a good harvest and a plentiful supply of rain.

In the late 1400s, around the time of the Spanish Expulsion, the nearby tombs of Simeon Bar-Yohai and his son Eleazar became the central focus of the yearly pilgrimage, no doubt due to the significance of the Zohar to the growing number of immigrants. The site soon also became a center of mystical devotion, under the leadership of Cordovero's mentor and brother-in law, Solomon Alkabetz. Remaining to a certain extent apart from the mainstream of Safed's intellectual life, Alkabetz had long been fascinated with the power of heavenly apparitions and the unique mystical revelation they could give. The Sabbath Bride was only one of the figures he imagined roaming the Galilean forests and hillsides. Surely the soul of Bar-Yohai was available to all who would appeal for insight from the putative author of the Zohar. Alkabetz challenged the traditional boundaries between urban existence and the rural districts, and under his influence a number of the younger generation of Safed kabbalists — Moses Cordovero, of course, prominent among them — began to go out and roam the fields beyond the cramped walls of Safed's study halls. And in wandering over a landscape of ancient sights and potent spirits, they changed the ancient pilgrimage rituals into a new kind of philosophic quest.

Instead of going to sites to pray for water for the coming growing season, they sought fresh insights into the deepest kabbalistic mysteries — of reincarnation, of divine emanations, and the current disposition of the sefirot. Now the mystic had to act out the celestial drama on many levels, not only in study and prayer. The use of penitential rituals as an aid in mystical achievement had been known at least as early as the Hasidim of the Rhineland, with their midwinter immersions in freezing water and scourging of the flesh. Yet the practice of *gerushin,* or "wanderings," that arose among the Safed kabbalists was not intended as a punishment but as a symbolic acknowledgment of the pain of exile. They were meant to reproduce the wanderings of the sefirah Malchut, otherwise identified with the exiled Shekhinah—searching for her reunion with the sefirah Tiferet, her heavenly mate. The practice was fruitful rather than painful, bringing down unprecedented insights from above.

"On Friday, the tenth of Shevat in the year 1548," wrote Cordovero of one such mystical exploration he undertook in late winter with his mentor Solomon Alkabetz, "we went into the exile of the King and Queen as far as the ruins of the Beit Midrash in Nabartin, and there I hit on the following novel kabbalistic idea." The wanderings soon became a regular part of kabbalistic practice, for five days later Cordovero reported that "on the fifteenth day of Shevat, my master and myself were alone, and the words of the Torah were shining in us and the words were spoken of themselves. We went as far as the tomb of Shimon of Yokrat." There, amidst the ruins and the thistles, they received supernatural enlightenment on a particular biblical verse. By summertime, Alkabetz had added additional ascetic elements. Cordovero noted that on another trip "we went as far as Kefar Biriyah, where we entered the synagogue and devoted ourselves to matters appropriate to the gerushin. And my master decided upon the innovation that in the summer months especially we should on occasion walk barefooted in the mystery of the Shekhinah."

Years later Cordovero would recall "what I and others have experienced in connection with the gerushin, when we wandered in the fields with the kabbalist Solomon Alkabetz, discussing verses from the Bible suddenly, without previous reflection. On these occasions new ideas would come to us in a manner that cannot be believed unless one has seen or experienced it many times." In certain respects, these practices resembled the visions of the ancient Hekhalot mystics as they too exchanged the long benches of the study halls for metaphysical realms. But instead of traveling alone, upward into the heavens, the mystics of sixteenth-century Safed visited the very sites that had been the centerpieces of earlier pilgrimage festivals, forging a link between country and city, between past and present, between the individual and the community.

In the practice of the gerushin, each person did not merely reenact the exile of the Shekhinah in order to bring down blessings on himself. It was also an instructive and symbolic behavior. Despite the possibilities for conspicuous consumption and display in a thriving, profitable center like Safed, Cordovero sternly instructed his growing numbers of kabbalistic followers that the true mystic "should always behave like a poor person, standing before his Maker like a pauper, begging and pleading. Even one who is wealthy should accustom himself to this attitude, considering that none of his possessions belongs to him and that he is forsaken and requires the constant mercies of his Creator, having nothing but the bread he eats." Sixteenth-century Safed was no ordinary community of weavers and traders; it represented another important link in the centuries-old mystical chain of tradition onto which a unique new layer of devotion, speculation, and ritual was reverently placed.

"A PLEASANT LIGHT"

By the 1560s, Safed was a revival camp masquerading as a bustling market city, with dozens of weaving and dyeing establishments and perhaps as many as a dozen mystical brotherhoods. This unique mixture of mundane and spiritual was the culmination of the far-reaching changes the city had experienced since the Ottoman conquest a half-century before. For with the decline in the prestige of the Jerusalem community under reinforced Ottoman presence, Safed, enjoying its relative

autonomy in the mountains of Upper Galilee, was now acknowledged by growing numbers of pilgrims and scholars
throughout the Diaspora as the emerging center of world
Jewry. Rarely before had any city so quickly achieved such
distinction in matters of the spirit and amassed such huge profits from its shrewd commercial dealings. And both the riches of
the marketplaces and the public piety of the city's population
aroused the admiration of casual visitors. Rabbi Cordovero was
only the most famous of Safed's numerous mystical leaders,
around whom eager students, merchants, and families gathered
for instruction and enlightenment. Each of the leaders tried to
outdo the others in directing his followers to engage in medita-
tions on the sefirot and meticulous observance of the laws of the
Torah, hoping thereby to increase the flow of divine blessings on
the People of Israel. In synagogues and study houses, public
prayers and fasts were common. Women and children — rarely
involved in this era in public rituals — were encouraged to attend
community-wide classes in kabbalistic knowledge and prayer
techniques.

Every day after sunset when the weaving looms and fulling
mills fell silent, sages, students, and townsmen would gather for
prayer vigils, some lasting almost until dawn. Through the night
hours (which was generally agreed to be the best time for communication with the heavenly powers), the muffled sounds of
chanting and the flickering light of candles spilled out into the
steep cobblestone streets. Among the town's most colorful figures was the elderly Abraham ha-Levi Berukhim — combination
town crier and caller to repentance — who went from door to
door to awaken the tardy for the midnight prayer vigils. And
every Friday, as Sabbath approached, he circulated through
the busy market, pulling people away from their looms and the
piled bolts of finished cloth to prepare for the reception of the
Sabbath Bride. Though originally one of Cordovero's followers,
Berukhim became the head of his own circle of zealous mis-
sionaries, a group that became known as the "Tent of Peace."
And there seem to have been many other societies and fellowships of which only a few are preserved in the records — among

them the "Society of Penitents," who donned sackcloth and ashes and engaged in painful demonstrations of flagellation in their great exertions for repentance like the medieval Hasidei Ashkenaz. And throughout the city and in the outlying villages, poets, sages, and philosophers produced countless works of kabbalistic expression that served to raise the reputation of Safed throughout the rest of the Jewish world.

Yet there was to be at least a brief clash between the earthly and the heavenly in Safed, for the ongoing prosperity of its weaving trade soon brought a serious challenge to the unique combination of spiritual and commercial life carried on there. By the mid 1560s, the textile industry in Safed was experiencing an unprecedented period of expansion and profit. The four main dye establishments alone paid over 12,000 Turkish pounds in yearly tax payments to the Ottoman officials, which was more than the total tax paid by most towns of the province. This level of revenue and potential profit served as an almost irresistible attraction to entrepreneurs from Salonika, where the textile industry was already facing price pressure and stiff competition from the boatloads of English and Flemish woolens, which were beginning to fill the markets of Italy and Greece. Safed, with its protected Near Eastern markets, offered a safer atmosphere for long-term investment. That was its great advantage and its greatest danger. For in 1565, a legendarily wealthy Salonikan textile magnate named Judah Aberlin arrived in Safed, established his own business, and began to make trouble. On the basis of his wealth and reputation in Salonika, he quickly rose to become one of the leaders of Safed's Ashkenazi community and was appointed to a position of authority on its board of overseers.

Aberlin's first priority was strictly business. Today it would be called trying to level the playing field. For the longtime tax exemption of scholars gave them an unfair advantage—at least in the eyes of an investor who kept a close watch on his own capital. Thus his first proposal to the Safed city fathers was reasonable, at least from the standpoint of fairness. The tax exemption had originally been devised to help indigent scholars earn a living while devoting most of their time to study. Yet in most cases, it had turned into a comfortable tax shelter for large-scale merchants who belonged to the mystical brotherhoods. Aberlin had no taste for mysticism—or, for that matter, for scholars—and he demanded that in light of the growing tax burden on the entire Jewish community, there was no reason to subsidize some of the city's most profitable weaving establishments. He therefore demanded that the leaders of the community enroll *all* the Jews of the city in the tax registers.

And there was another pillar of Safed's uniqueness that Judah Aberlin sought to pull down. The normal mode of community organization in Safed and throughout the Diaspora was the ethnic congregation, with its associated yeshiva and social welfare facilities. In Safed, as elsewhere, Ashkenazim, Sephardim, and Musta'riba—the Arabic-speaking Jews of Palestine—all formed their own close-knit communities, sometimes further divided into more specific places of origin. Thus the Ottoman tax rolls in 1555 had—in addition to listings for Musta'riba and Ashkenazim—separate entries for congregations of Jews from Portugal, North Africa, Córdoba, Castile, Aragon and Catalonia, Hungary, Apulia, Seville, Calabria, and the Italian peninsula. Each of these congregations was responsible for a yearly tax payment, and their burden was made even heavier by the unique institution of the mystical brotherhoods. These groups were not based on a particular homeland or ethnic affinity but attracted individuals from all the communities. And not only were these brotherhoods exempted from tax payments, they regularly sent representatives abroad for charitable contributions, thereby harming the fund-raising activities of the ethnic communities. For a conservative community leader like Aberlin, the situation in Safed was insane. He therefore proposed an administrative housecleaning: for tax purposes all Jewish residents of Safed must be associated with their family's place of origin. And he further insisted that all monies coming from abroad should go to the treasurer of the appropriate community.

Never before had such dictates come from Europe. The communities of the Holy Land—Safed among them—had always maintained a sanctimonious independence. In fact, their modes of organization had been models for the communities of the West. A war of insults, mutual threats of excommunication, and curses now inevitably followed Aberlin's proposals, for it was the economic independence of the mystical brotherhoods that had allowed them such great latitude in crafting new forms of devotion and fellowship. Aberlin initially succeeded in influencing the leaders to impose the head tax equally on all Jewish residents, regardless of intellectual status, insisting that the wealthiest scholars also pay their fair share of a wide range of lesser imposts and dues.

Aberlin may have been waging a war against those he simply saw as business competitors, but the scholars, for their part, saw his actions as a direct attack on Safed's unique status as a center of kabbalistic spirituality. The resulting public attacks on Aberlin's greed, parsimoniousness, taste for power, and sheer disregard for the welfare of Israel quickly discredited him among even the city fathers of Safed, and his attempts to obtain favorable rabbinical rulings on the tax matters from leaders in Damascus in Jerusalem failed miserably. In humiliation and disappointment he eventually returned to Salonika where, it is said, he became involved in an acrimonious lawsuit over the disposition of the family fortune that had been left in trust while he was in the Holy Land. The Kabbalah remained the dominating force in Safed, and Caro, Cordovero, and the others were now the notables of the city. They were no longer secret scholars, magicians, or resisters of the standing order, dependent for their material support on wealthy grandees who made their fortunes in secular pursuits.

Yet the apparent triumph of Safed's unique way of life was not as complete as it might have been. Pressures were building both within the community and in the outside world that would soon put an end to the city's golden age. In 1570, Moses Cordovero died suddenly at age forty-eight, leaving his followers to continue spreading the knowledge of the Kabbalah to the People of Israel. Even in death, Cordovero proved to be influential in his transformation of the old mystical brotherhoods, first founded in Salonika, into a new social form. The vibrant Safed brotherhoods broke through the old hierarchies of class and ethnic distinctions. They could be established by mystically inclined individuals anywhere in the Jewish world. More important, membership in these groups offered a chance for every individual to participate in a national revival—by drawing down the divine spirit through ethical behavior, meditation, and directed prayer. And the nature of the hoped-for change was reformist rather than revolutionary. Cordovero had not called for a radical overthrow of the forces of darkness but had rather helped, through the standardization and refinement of kabbalistic tradition, the general understanding of how to manipulate the hidden laws of the world as it is.

In fact, by the end of his life, Moses Cordovero had turned from compiling heavy tomes of esoteric scholarship to writing easily readable mystical handbooks aimed at the Jewish public at large. The purpose of his famous *Tomer Devorah*, the "Palm Tree of Deborah," was to provide a guide for daily life for even the humblest adherent of the Kabbalah. It assured the reader that by acting "at the right time—that is, by knowing which sefirah dominates at a particular time—he can bind himself to it and carry out the adjustment associated with the ruling attribute." And in his unfinished book of kabbalistic instruction, *Or Ne'erav*, "A Pleasant Light," Cordovero insisted that the advantages of the study of the Kabbalah were inarguably superior to any other method of study or religious devotion. "When a man engages in this science," he wrote, "angels and righteous souls from the Garden of Eden will accompany him. It is not the case with other disciplines of the Torah."

The Kabbalah was a way of life that covered every aspect of daily existence. It infused private life with mystical meaning, explaining how even the simplest everyday acts of waking, working, prayer, and sleeping could be directed to battling the forces of evil, and creating a sympathetic balance among the forces of the heavenly world. In one sense, this was a particularly Jewish development, yet in another it reflected the far-reaching social changes going on throughout the West in the sixteenth century. In England, France, Holland, and throughout the other northern lands of the Reformation, new communities of the spirit arose that were not geographically bounded or ruled by hereditary aristocrats and their stodgy, ever-faithful clerics. The "new" men and women of the early modern world — passionate seekers of personal salvation and world redemption — were now the leaders of these communities.

Thus the fame of Safed and its mystical masters gradually spread throughout the Jewish communities of the Near East and Europe, carried along with the merchandise produced by its weavers and spinners and described in the increasingly embroidered stories of the spirits and visions that arose from the midnight mists of the Galilean hills. In time, some of the unique customs of the Safed brotherhoods — particularly the celebration of the Sabbath as a divine marriage and rehearsal for redemption — were adopted as normative Jewish practice throughout the world. A number of Cordovero's colleagues and students popularized these innovations by formulating ever more detailed rules and regulations for daily conduct. Eleazar Azikri composed the *Sefer Haredim,* the "Book of the Pious," which offered a guide to the proper observance of ritual law, arranged by topic, season, and body part. Elijah da Vida's *Reshit Hokhmah,* the "Beginning of Wisdom," described five "gates" of ethical conduct that meshed well with the five books of Cordovero's Pardes Rimmonim, the five main sections of the Shulkhan Arukh, and the five books of the Zohar· and the Torah itself.

At a time of increasing public interest in personal manners, behavior, and achievement — the historical phenomenon now recognized as the emergence of the modern conception of the Individual — the Kabbalah of Safed spread widely, particularly in Italy, where Rabbi Menahem Azariah da Fano of Mantua and Rabbi Mordecai Dato became influential kabbalists. And before long, through the use of that revolutionary new clanking contraption of metal, wood, ink, and paper — the printing press — countless kabbalistic handbooks and pamphlets were printed in Venice and in the cities of Mantua and Cremona to serve the growing public appetite for kabbalistic works. Eager readers hoped to gain the benefit of at least a small part of the powerful magic that brought contentment and prosperity to the people of Safed.

Of course the material prosperity of Safed that enabled this kind of religious experimentation would not last forever. It would continue only as long as the tides of international commerce continued to favor the alignment of raw wool, consumer demand, and relative monetary stability. But for approximately forty years—the span of almost two generations—the material and the spiritual were woven together in a magical pattern that seemed powerfully real. The mystics of Safed unhesitatingly looked toward the heavens for the source of their prosperity and personal fulfillment. And long after Safed's Golden Age had ended, the memory of that brief era of spiritual and material blessing would bestow upon that strange city in the mountains of Upper Galilee an aura of sanctity and abundant spiritual blessings. The legends of the mystical city would remain potent—and seductive—centuries after the dangerous chaos of violence, power, and hatred returned to this enchanted corner of the world.

Chapter 6

LIFTING THE SPARKS

A new generation arose in those days of wonder, textiles, and riches—learning their trades and studying the Kabbalah's mysteries, mixing commerce and metaphysics—just as other young students in sixteenth-century Paris, London, and Amsterdam were doing, in constructing the foundations for a new age. It was a time when the modern world was beginning to take on the recognizable appearance of nations, government bureaucracies, trading companies, and upwardly mobile individuals. By the time of the death of Moses Cordovero in Safed, Spanish conquistadors had swept across the Caribbean and Mexico, constructing sturdy stone fortresses and lumbering galleons to transport the wealth of this New World back to Seville. French, British, and Dutch warships had established outposts along the thickly wooded western coasts of the North Atlantic, and the fiery passion of Protestantism had spread across northern Europe, laying the foundation for a new civilization of urban logic and global economy.

The future loomed large on the horizon, yet the young scholars in Safed—drawn from the mosaic of Jewish congregations that had been created in the tumults and political upheavals of previous centuries—continued to study Cordovero's sublimely static mystical system. They struggled to memorize and visualize the system of balance of the hovering sefirot, shimmering in the heavens like some great radiating clockwork that could be adjusted and manipulated to the best advantage with the proper training and skill. This classical Kabbalah was a science as particular as alchemy, astronomy, or chemistry in its unchanging underlying principles and logic, derived step-by-step from the ancient lore of the divine Chariot, the Book of Creation, Bahir, and Zohar. But for the new generation of scholars who grew up in the years when Safed's prosperity began to falter, such stability was by no means assured. The death of Suleiman the Lawgiver in 1566 had brought an initial wave of political uncertainty—followed as he was by his stout, middle-aged son, Selim "the Sot." For the time being, the threat of encroachment by the great textile magnates had been averted, but there was no telling how the tides of imports and exports would run. Rumblings from "Edom" in Europe gave no easy feeling for the thousands of Jewish communities scattered from southern France to the Russian steppes. The intervention of the heavenly powers was needed as desperately as ever, but the staid mystical codification of Cordovero seemed increasingly flaccid. It would take a radical new voice to transform the Kabbalah into an ideology that matched the explosive potential and sense of individuality that would typify the dawning modern age.

No reliable portraits exist of the young sage who would make this historic mystical breakthrough. Yet in a sense, his invisibility underlines his role as more than a particular guru. Over the centuries, Rabbi Isaac Luria Ashkenazi became known widely from the acronym "ha-Elohi Rabbi Yitzhak," which in Hebrew spells the word *ha-Ari,* "the Lion." And that name, with all its messianic connotations from the symbolism of Judah and its Davidic dynasty, has become something of a magical motto for mystically inclined Jews everywhere. In all the annals of kabbalistic folklore, there is no personality who has left such an indelible impact in such a short career. In the span of less than three years—that seems in retrospect like a lifetime—the young kabbalist burst upon the mystical scene in Safed and convinced a faithful circle of followers that they had not even yet begun to grasp the deepest secrets of the Tree of Life. He offered a way of knowledge that elevated direct spiritual power over erudition; the fact of the matter was that the Ari himself transmitted his teaching through voice, action, and expression. Only a few small fragments of his original written compositions survive.

In a way, Luria's arrival in Safed as an outsider was something of an act of defiance to the kabbalistic establishment. Yet within just a few years of his death, legends sprung up about him, attributing to him the same sort of thaumaturgic power that had been bestowed by folk legend on the great prophets, wonder-workers, and sages of the past. Even today, the Ari remains a living presence for those who maintain faith in the Kabbalah—offering blessings for the storeowner, ease of the pain of childbirth, and resolution of personal problems between husbands and wives. Pilgrims still come to pray at his modest gravesite on the steep, broken ground of Safed's ancient cemetery, hoping to gain even a fleeting contact with the blessings of the upper spheres as they pour forth onto the earth. Yet the Lion's insight was no mere password to the heavens. He offered his followers a profoundly disturbing secret: he helped them understand the nature of *evil* and the means by which it would eventually be overcome.

Seen through the hazy, romantic gaze of later mythmakers, the tales of the Ari's birth and childhood offer only the vaguest indication of the precise historical context in which he was educated and began his career. Yet the basic facts of time, place, and general circumstance fit comfortably enough. According to tradition, the Ari was born in Jerusalem in 1534, the son of a struggling scholar and a wealthy Egyptian merchant's daughter who had joined the tiny kabbalistic circles in Jerusalem.

The reported circumstances of his birth recall the appearance of angelic heralds and heavenly attendants that marked the birth of great biblical figures. No less a heavenly personage than the Prophet Elijah is said to have announced the Ari's birth to his father, Samuel Ashkenazi, a man known for his extraordinary piety and solitary nighttime vigils, praying for the redemption of the Shekhinah from her state of painful exile. Elijah was reported to have announced that the child to be born was "destined to redeem the souls of Israel from the clutches of the kelipot" and reveal the full glory of the Kabbalah all over the world. That destiny could hardly have been expected, for the community in Jerusalem was at that time engaged in an intensifying rivalry with the kabbalists and sages in Safed, who, under the leadership of Rabbi Jacob Berav, were claiming a unique role in the coming redemption of Israel. The story of Elijah's materializing once again to serve as the *sandak,* or godfather, at the Ari's circumcision is surely more of the same later mythmaking. Yet it vividly underlines the mystique of a figure whose greatest power was drawn from a personal relationship with the heavenly forces rather than from the bestowed legitimacy of religious office on earth.

It is clear historical testimony to the poverty and relative weakness of the kabbalistic circles in Jerusalem that when Samuel Ashkenazi died suddenly in 1542, mother and eight-year-old son were left without a steady means of support. A mystic's legacy outside the select group of Safed's kabbalistic textile tycoons was ephemeral. But the birthright of an Egyptian Jewish merchant's daughter offered a secure life lived in the great mansions, khans, and counting houses of Cairo — and a fine scholar's education to a son who was not inclined to try his hand at trade. And thus the story continues that Isaac Luria and his mother left Jerusalem to find new lives for themselves in the household of her brother Mordecai Frances, merchant and tax farmer for the province of Egypt, undoubtedly one of

Cairo's wealthiest Jews. The name Frances bespeaks an origin in Western Europe, and it was among the circulating networks of expelled Jews and New Christians that the commerce of the Mediterranean was carried on. The thousands of yellowed documents retrieved from the genizah of the Ben-Ezra Synagogue in Cairo's Coptic Quarter a century ago offer a close-up portrait of life in that bustling metropolis. It was a place where pepper and silks from the Orient, pearls from the Persian Gulf, vegetable and grain from the Delta, and fine glass and metalwork from Europe met in a swirl of negotiation, calculation, and exchange. From contemporary documents, as we will see, the young Luria became actively involved in commerce, yet in the legend, Luria revealed himself to be a rabbinic prodigy, becoming the greatest sage in Egypt at the age of fifteen. Betrothed to Frances's own daughter, he continued his study, first under the Rabbi Bezalel Ashkenazi and later becoming the protégé of one of Egypt's greatest sages, Rabbi David ben-Abu-Zimra, better known as the Radbaz. These scholars were well versed in the kabbalistic traditions, yet supposedly it was by sheer accident that the young Luria came into contact with his future mystical calling.

According to the story, Luria happened to meet an arriving merchant in a synagogue in Cairo; the man was a New Christian but had come back to the faith. He carried with him a strange manuscript, which he said contained great secrets. Luria was determined to obtain this text and study it completely, and the matter was accomplished in a most businesslike way. Luria's father-in-law and uncle, always anxious to help the young scholar, agreed to exempt the merchant from all customs duties on his merchandise if he would hand over the manuscript. And so it was done, though Frances, his sister, and his newlywed daughter might have come to regret the deal. The strange manuscript proved to be the Zohar, and Luria threw himself into a single-minded study of its mysteries, leaving Cairo and isolating himself in a farmhouse in one of the outlying Nile villages controlled by his uncle — returning to his wife and uncle's home only on Shabbat.

Recent studies of Luria's life, based on contemporary letters and documents, have suggested that his kabbalistic education was not nearly so solitary, nor sudden. There is good reason to believe that he was introduced to the Zohar while still a boy in Jerusalem, and that he furthered his studies in Cairo, not on the lonely banks of the Nile. But these historical facts in no way dim the brilliance of the myth of the Ari. His followers have always deeply believed that he probed the mystical depths of the Zohar to uncover secrets forgotten since the time of Rabbi Simon Bar-Yohai. With his soul soaring into the highest heavens during his nighttime slumber, he visited the celestial academies of the great sages Bar-Yohai, Akiva, and Eleazar. And he returned to earth in the morning with astounding insights about the nature of creation and great revelations about humanity's destiny that the heavenly figures assembled in the divine realm had solemnly entrusted to him.

What was the content of those revelations? How did Luria's mystical insights so profoundly alter the nature of all subsequent kabbalistic technique and philosophy? It had to do with a stunning new—even heretical—understanding of the nature of evil as a deep-seated element of history and reality. Indeed, according to Luria, evil was an integral component of the divine character. Some kabbalistic tradition had understood evil as the result of a flawed, primitive emanation. Others had described it as a manifestation of divine judgment destructively ripped loose from its balanced connection with divine mercy. But Luria rejected these ideas of evil, suffering, and misfortune as merely externals to the essence of God. He had seen around him in the synagogues and bazaars of Egypt how aggressive and destructive intentions can come from the minds and hearts of even the most pious of men. The evil of violent, aggressive empires was all too evident in the history of the People of Israel. But even *among* the People of Israel, in business connections and interpersonal relations, the same evil intention to dominate and subjugate caused misfortune and pain. Somehow God must have devised a way to eradicate its roots in the human soul, in all earthly existence, and in the heavenly spheres. And while earlier kabbalists had envisioned the act of creation as one of conscious, creative emanation, Luria suddenly recognized creation as a process of purification—primarily aimed at destroying the principle of evil from within.

At the heart of this revolutionary theory was a profound paradox: If the Godhead encompassed everything *before* the creation, would not evil be one of its components? As far as we know, no earlier thinker had imagined it possible to even comment on the nature of the Ein Sof before the first emanation, but didn't a transcendent God who encompassed *all* potentialities necessarily encompass the potentiality of evil as well? Earlier kabbalists had often used the symbol of an outer husk or nut shell to denote the most basic qualities of evil—that grasping, dominating, covering urge to envelop and possess all life and light within itself. Yet Luria perceived that this quality existed— at least in potential form—within the Ein Sof. And if left unchecked, it could hardly be expected to remain passive and docile among the countless other divine qualities. Its potential and very existence threatened the eternal unity of God.

Previous Jewish mystics had envisioned the process of creation as a graceful and beneficent outflow of divine energy from the depths of the Godhead—and had devoted themselves to developing techniques of increasing or directing the flow of God's blessing. Whether in the ancient amulets intended to placate the hostile angels who guarded access to the Divine Presence or in mathematically precise prayers to restore sefirotic balance, evil was always regarded as essentially an absence of divine light. Yet Luria saw evil as a structural element of the present creation that could be rooted out only in the painful process of convulsion and crisis. And the biblical story of creation was a profound metaphor for the first fateful steps in a process of cosmic exorcism to destroy the principle of evil once and for all. Already in the biblical interpretations of the mystical book known as *Galya Raza,* or "Secrets Revealed"—popularized among the first mystical brotherhoods in Salonika in the decades after the Spanish Expulsion—evil, not good, had been seen as the catalyst for the very first act of creation.

The mystical reading of Genesis 1:1 that "darkness covered the face of the waters" suggested that it was the grasping of the forces of darkness that prompted God to begin the process of creation and differentiation. But where most kabbalists had envisioned God's creative work as one of emanation, with energy cascading downward through the network of the sefirot, Luria conveyed an image of crystallization. He explained that God's first act was to distil the dispersed and diluted roots of evil, concentrating them in a single spot "like a grain of salt distilled from the vast saltiness of the sea." Once that distillation was accomplished, God "withdrew Himself" from the small space around that spot of concentrated evil, physically distancing Himself from it. That act of withdrawal, known to kabbalists as *tsimtsum*, or "contraction," was regarded by most as an "exile" of God from the presence of evil, but Luria offered a stunning reinterpretation of that act. He saw the tsimtsum as the first step in an inexorable process of purification. For immediately after the tsimtsum, evil took control of the space God had vacated, encasing it with a dark, enveloping shell. However, evil's control of that newly vacated space—where all created worlds would eventually be formed—was to be the first stage in its self-destruction. Luria believed that God's continuing acts of creation were designed to isolate evil from all that was good, positive, and holy—and to force it to destroy itself.

IMAGINING THE GREAT CATASTROPHE

From the ethereal, saintly image that Isaac Luria has maintained in the popular imagination over the centuries, it is hard to believe that he lived his life in a place and a time where Jewish survival required skillful and constant involvement in worldly affairs. The legends of his boyhood and early years after marriage speak only of the Ari's deep involvement in religious study. And a casual or credulous reader might actually believe that, growing to adulthood, Luria lived an entirely isolated existence—as the legend went—studying the Zohar in complete solitude in a lonely farmhouse by the banks of the Nile. Yet among the thousands of medieval documents retrieved from the genizah of the Ben Ezra Synagoue in Cairo at the turn of the last century, there is vivid evidence to demonstrate that Isaac Luria was actively involved throughout his entire adult life in regional and even international trade.

As we have already seen in the bitter debates and conflicts in Safed over tax matters, scholars and sages were often involved in business ventures, and their exemption from community tax payments made their special position a potentially lucrative one. The scholar-entrepreneurs of Safed were deeply involved in the textile industry and were able to devote a relatively small proportion of their time to business through the use of the "putting-out" system. That is, they could devote themselves to their studies while the raw materials were being transformed through the various production stages by the craftspeople of Safed and the surrounding villages. Luria, however, involved himself in another economic pursuits that allowed even more time for study: the purchase of valuable commodities from importers or farmers and their later sale in distant markets when the balance of supply and demand was just right. One of the documents found in the Cairo synagogue records his purchase in 1554, at age twenty, of a considerable quantity of pepper. It had been imported from the Far East, was transshipped by caravan across Egypt, and deposited in the port of Alexandria for transshipment to European markets. The sale was made possible by a complex network of Jewish merchants and agents—in this case largely a paper transaction—deducting from the amount of pepper already stored in an Alexandria warehouse to the credit of Luria's account.

Luria's name also appears on a list of borrowers from a prominent Cairo merchant capitalist, further indicating how deeply involved he was in the give-and-take of speculation and trade. Another document records a shipment of imported silk goods, brought to Egypt by caravan, via Safed. The international commerce in luxuries and spices gathered from the Orient was—despite the continuing attempts of the Portuguese to gain a monopoly of the trade of the Indian Ocean—still a significant economic activity within the Ottoman Empire, and regional routes of trade were growing in importance as well. Egypt had for centuries been the breadbasket of the eastern Mediterranean, with its vast river valley and numberless village peasants, a dependable source of grain and fresh vegetables to the bulging cities of Italy, Greece, and Anatolia. In a document that has been dated to 1562, Luria acquired the services of a purchase agent in the heart of the farm regions of the Nile Delta—Rabbi Moshe Benjamin—for the purchase and transport of large shipments of locally produced wine, cattle hides, and cucumbers to Ancona in Italy. And yet another document records his import of Cretan wine back to Alexandria. It is clear that Luria was also involved in kabbalistic studies during this period. Yet in the midst of his down-to-earth negotiations of purchase prices, potential profits, and repayment schedules, he developed a striking new vision of the role that humanity could play in the repair of the heavenly worlds.

Luria presented himself as more of a mystical master than a teacher. His vivid explanation of the ongoing battle between good and evil—rather than his erudition or his modest literary output—ensured him a place of unparalleled reverence in the history of the Kabbalah. Moses Cordovero and his followers in Safed had combed the traditional sources to develop a mystical understanding of creation as a process of directed production—of the specialized stages in which all material forms were gradually articulated as finished products. Yet Luria, living among the merchants, qadis, and business agents along the Nile in Cairo, envisioned a quite different outcome to God's plan for creation. He denied that the divine goal was the gradual accumulation of prosperity and well-being from a process of orderly production. Luria insisted, instead, that the process was one of continual purification—a directed and focussed attempt by the divine powers to eradicate the principles of greed and domination that produced inequality and suffering. We can only admire such a wide-ranging Renaissance intellect who could at one moment be deeply concerned about the going price of pepper or wine on the dockside at Herakleion and at another moment engage in speculation about the heavenly dramas that unfolded at the creation of world.

Far more abstract than Michelangelo's romantic vision of creation on the ceiling of the Sistine Chapel—and far less mechanistic than Moses Cordovero's carefully drafted diagrams of the sefirot—the Lurianic myth depicted the bizarre image of evil, like a thick husk or nutshell, tightly encasing the *tehiru*, or empty space that God had vacated intentionally. Yet the space inside the husk of evil, where all worlds and beings would be created, was not completely empty. Trapped inside the hard shell of evil were the faint traces of the unfathomable divine brightness that had once been there. And emanating a straight line of searing divine energy through the outer shell and into the space within it, God separated light from darkness, forming it into an initial configuration that Luria called *Aðam Kaðmon*, the "Primordial Adam."

It is impossible to know what precisely Luria meant by this anthropomorphic image, often described in shockingly crude terms of arms, legs, head, eyes, ears, and reproductive organs. Later kabbalists insisted that this initial separation between light and darkness—the master pattern for all that would come afterwards—was, in fact, the creation described with the words "in our own image, after our likeness" in Genesis 1:26. But the Primordial Adam was to be just the beginning of a further process of emanation in which God's light would eventually root out and destroy the powers of evil in the universe.

Unlike his mystical predecessors down through the ages, Luria made no attempt to connect the events of his time directly with political events or public personalities. He saw the power of the heavenly forces working at a far deeper level than kingdoms and empires. Their battleground was a conceptual one, and Luria utilized the surrealistic images of streaming light, human form, and the hard crust of evil to produce a dazzling drama. It was both more haunting and more profound than the staid sequence of emanations of the medieval kabbalists or the primitive vision of the Chariot of earlier mystical seers.

In the vision of Isaac Luria, a further emanation of divine light streamed into the body of the Primordial Adam, quickly filling it completely and bursting forth in rays of dazzling light from its "ears," "mouth," and "nostrils." And it was with this act that the ten sefirot—Keter, Hokhmah, Binah, Hesed, Din, also known as Gevmah, Tiferet, Netzah, Hod, Yesod, and Malchut—were initially created as a composite mass of brilliance, the "world of the Bound" according to Lurianic parlance, hovering like an aura around the upper part of the body of the Primordial Adam.

That was not the end of the process. The unceasing flow of divine light continued to stream outward, this time through the "eyes" of the Primordial Adam, cascading downward to become known as the "world of the Spotted," a realm in which the sefirot were fully differentiated, each manifest in a separate entity. This realm of differentiation was—in the imagination and mind of Luria—the system of the sefirot that had been the centerpiece of all earlier Kabbalah. The earlier mystics believed this network of separate heavenly powers to be the highest world of divine emanation. Yet Luria saw it as a distinctly lower stage in the process of emanation, hovering around the lower extremities of the body of the Primordial Adam, from his navel to his feet. And its creation culminated not in a stable world of balance, to be maintained and prayed for, but in a sudden violent catastrophe. It is important to remember—when we struggle today to form a coherent mental picture of Luria's surrealistic visions of light streaming through the orifices of a colossal, human-like figure—that the Lurianic myth describes a process, not an event.

At each stage of emanation, the forces of evil inevitably enveloped each newly created structure, in its attempt both to retain life-giving contact with the source of all being and to maintain control over the structures that had been formed. Yet the process turned explosive when the divine light began to stream from the eyes of the Primordial Adam into the waiting vessels, formed by a combination of divine emanation and the enclosing shells or *klippot* of evil. And like a torrent of water gushing through interlocked glass containers, the divine light rushed through the upper three vessels — Keter, Hokhmah, and Binah — filling each with its appropriate measure of divine energy. But when the light flowed on with a great rush through the seven lower and weaker vessels, they shattered into jagged shards, tumbling downward to the lowest level of the tehiru, the space given over to the dominion of evil, farthest from the source of the divine light. With that fateful event, the realm of earthly reality was established, with its confusing, chaotic, and complex mixture of darkness and light. And this lowest level of the tehiru, with sparks of divine light trapped by jagged fragments, was the cosmic locale for the centuries-long sufferings of the Jews.

Could this crashing, smashing catastrophe in the course of creation be the result of a divine miscalculation? Was it a sign of a deep and permanent flaw in the cosmos? Or was it a way that the tehiru — the sole locale of evil — could eventually be purified? There were some important events in the upper worlds that paved the way for the eventual repair of the heavenly structures. While the shards of the shattered vessels fell down to the lowest depths of reality, most of the light that had flowed through them rose upward, returning to their source above. And as if to reform and refashion the remains of the seven lower vessels, divine light once again flowed through the third sefirah, Binah, to give birth to what the followers of Luria called the "speckled" world. Here at last was a world of balance, distinct from the upper world of the "bound," where the ten potencies were inseparably coagulated and different from the world of the "spotted," where the seven lower vessels could not physically contain the divine force that flowed through them. The creation of this new world between divine light and ultimate evil was therefore intended to establish a realm unmixed with evil, but while it was in formation, a potentially deadly danger existed below. For the shards of evil that had been shattered became more aggressive in their separation from the nourishing light. No longer directly connected to the Godhead, their only source of sustenance was the few sparks of divine light—288 in number—that had clung to the sides of the broken vessels and were now trapped in the realm of darkness below. But even though they were trapped and enslaved in the midst of darkness, those sparks had enormous potential power. Like slave subjects or persecuted minorities, they provided the vital, exploitable source of energy for evil's continued existence, and its unending quest to encompass everything.

Thus the Breaking of the Vessels could be seen as a metaphor or symbol of the basic weakness of evil. Like the revolts that led to the destruction of the First and Second Temples and the expulsion of the Jews from Spain, it was not simply a terrible tragedy, redolent with suffering and pain. It was the start of a process of gradual separation of the forces of light from their captivity by the forces of darkness. On an earthly level, each of the great historical tragedies experienced by the People of Israel illustrated the dangerous folly of dependence on foreign kings. Ezekiel had preached passionately against Judean entanglement in the imperial struggles of Babylon and Egypt. The apocalyptic mystics of the first and second centuries C.E. had fought with all their might against submission to Rome. The Hasidim and kabbalists of the Middle Ages had waged spiritual war on crusading kings and inquisitors. And now, in an age of seeming prosperity, Luria was convinced that the entangling tentacles of imperial life were again threatening the People of Isreal.

The Jews of the Ottoman Empire enjoyed relative freedom, but they were dependent on the sultan's good will. At the same time, they and the other subjects of the empire were the very foundations of his power and prosperity. For there could be no tyranny—on earth or in the heavenly realms—without a source of energy and creativity to provide nourishment and sustenance for the ruling echelon. From the cosmic perspective perceived by Luria in his mystical visions, the only thing supporting the kingdom of darkness (and all its earthly counterparts) was the exploitable presence of divine sparks trapped within it. And if somehow those sparks could be rescued from the captivity of the husks, the utter banality and weakness of evil would be revealed.

With the lifting of the sparks, the principle of evil that had begun as an integral part of the Godhead would be deprived of its life force and reduced to nothingness. More than that, if the 288 trapped sparks could be liberated, they would rise upward to find their place among the reformulated sefirot. If by their lives and actions the People of Israel could free the sparks, the final separation of light from darkness would be accomplished. And as a result, two transcendent goals would be simultaneously achieved: The unreconstructed forces of evil would be deprived of any power, and the purified foundations for a perfect, eternal universe would be set in place. The Jews as a people were a part of the drama—no longer as individuals praying to the sefirot with certain intonations, but as the hidden sparks among humanity, longing to complete their separation from the powers of doom. This was the heart of Isaac Luria's vision, formulated between 1554 and 1570, as he studied Kabbalah, undertook merchant ventures, and dreamed of the world to come.

THE CIRCLE OF THE LION AND HIS CUBS

In 1569, at age thirty-five, Isaac Luria packed up his family, wrapped up his business dealings in Egypt, and moved to Safed, which was still at the height of its prosperity and spiritual fame. The traditional biographical legends attribute this move to yet another encounter with the Prophet Elijah. Materializing suddenly on earth, the ancient prophet admonished the Ari—after returning from one of his ascents from the banks of the Nile to the yeshiva of Rabbi Simeon Bar-Yohai and his colleagues in heaven—asking, "Why do you stay in this impure land? Go to Safed in the Upper Galilee and there you will merit the right to ascend to an even higher level. Also know that your days are short and you will be buried there." As with most legends, this explanation was clearly formulated after the fact. Yet it is reasonable to assume that there were other, less metaphysical motives that persuaded the rabbi, mystic, and trader to leave his familiar surroundings in Egypt and go to the Holy Land.

Some modern scholars have suggested that contemporary messianic prophecies—declaring that the year 1575 would mark the beginning of redemption—may have influenced such a radical change in the course of Luria's life. The negative biblical associations of the Land of the Nile as a place of slavery—not fit for the proper study of the Torah—may have encouraged Luria, as an up-and-coming scholar, to leave when he had a chance. And even though the economy of Egypt was flourishing and great fortunes could still be made there, the Mamluk governors of Egypt kept close watch over the Jewish community and regularly took sizeable kickbacks from their commerce. Under the contemporary circumstances, there was far greater freedom of action in Galilee. But as events would show, there was another, far more personal element that influenced Isaac Luria's plans. He was convinced that nearly all the sparks trapped by the sherds of darkness had been released and a cosmic transformation was imminent. And he believed that he could play an important role in completing the process of freeing the last of the sparks—by packing his belongings and family and travelling north across Sinai and then up the coastal plain into the mountains of Galilee.

No one could possibly have predicted that the prosperity of Safed was about to crumble, scattering the assembled scholars and their precious mystical texts all over the world. The textile trade still provided employment for most of the city's inhabitants. And the profits and charitable contributions streaming into the city still supported a wide range of communal institutions and religious academies. The various mystical fellowships were flourishing, each with its own membership, costume, and rituals. Moses Cordovero and the now-aged Joseph Caro remained the city's dominant figures and continued to set Safed's reverent, respectable tone. We know nothing about the circumstances of Isaac Luria's arrival and settlement in the city or whether he continued to support himself as a merchant (though there is some possible documentary evidence that he did). The only certain bit of information is that soon after his arrival, he joined the academy of Moses Cordovero, taking his place among Cordovero's eager students, attending lectures on the nature and characteristics of the sefirot.

Like the stable logic of the textile trade or international commerce, the Kabbalah was seen as the foundation on which all other intellectual advances would be built. Some dabbled in astronomy, astrology, and alchemy, for in those days of kabbalistic experimentation, nothing seemed out of the reach of human reason—be it medical, metallurgical, or chemical—with the application of the right elements. Yet the arrival of Isaac Luria in Cordovero's circle of students suddenly shattered the complacency of many of them. He had brought with him a radical new vision in which evil was no longer just the demonic Other Side nipping at the skirt hem of the Shekhinah, carrying her away from the tender embrace of her husband, Tiferet, the Glory of God. He convinced them that the principle of evil was to be found all around them—in the loom houses, in the counting houses, and in the kabbalistic academies.

Rabbi Haim Vital, one of Cordovero's most loyal students, later reported a premonition of the fateful encounter he would have with Isaac Luria. Fifteen years before—in 1554, when he was only a lad of twelve in the streets of Safed—Vital had been warned by a local palm reader that he would eventually have to "choose between the road to heaven and the road to hell." That road would lead from the courses and disciplines of Cordovero, to a brief dabbling in the occult art of alchemy, to the entirely new field of mystical speculation pioneered and promoted by Isaac Luria. For Vital was one of the new generation of Safed mystics, born long after the upheavals of the Spanish Expulsion and the Ottoman conquest of the Holy Land. For them, the prosperity and mystical prominence of Safed were not miracles but the everyday reality that they had grown up with. And here was the irony: while the older generation of scholars and mystics—among them, Joseph Caro, Solomon Alkabetz, Moses Alsheikh, Abraham ben Eliezer ha-Levi Berukhim, and their younger colleague Moses Cordovero—had all weathered the storms of unprecedented social, economic, and political upheaval, they had crafted a mystical ideology in which *stability* was the ultimate goal.

Luria and his contemporaries would come to share a vision in which stability benefited only the powers of greed and domination. He had conceived a far more violent, apocalyptic drama in which the distinctions of darkness and light, high and low, heavenly and earthly would become utterly irrelevant. His mystical ideas were simultaneously populist and utopian, and even though they were shrouded in the most bizarre images of husks, sparks, and heavenly emanations, they were the manifestations of a distinctly modern kind of ideology. For the lifting of the sparks trapped among the shattered sherds of evil—and their return to their rightful places in the heavenly realm—was not merely to be done through the *kavvanot,* or directed, focussed prayers, of faceless, chanting congregations. Luria had fashioned an entirely novel interpretation of the sin of Adam in the Garden of Eden that offered highly specific roles in the grand eschatological drama to each and every Jew.

For the first time in the history of Jewish mysticism, the specific characteristics of the individual—and the progress of his or her soul in the process of reincarnation—was held to be central to the national quest. And it all had to do with Adam and Eve who, according to Luria, were literally the flesh-and-blood father and mother of every human being. In the earlier biblical literature and the traditions of the Zohar, Adam and Eve were the legendary figures whose actions in the Garden of Eden condemned humanity to lives of constant struggle for their direct disobedience of God's command. In the Lurianic system, the Adam of Genesis was not yet a man, but in essence another emanation of divine energy—again, on the pattern of the Primordial Adam—sent down among the shattered sherds to attract the sparks back to their source. Like some cosmic lodestone, the emanation of Adam was meant to draw in sparks of divine light, yet remain uncontaminated by the forces of the klippot, or shattered shells. This Adam contained within him all the "humanity" that would ever be created, all that would ever be needed, for if he succeeded in his mission, the scattered sparks of light would be snatched from the sherds and returned to their proper place. The sefirot would achieve eternal balance, the forces of darkness would be deprived of nourishment, and this "Adam" would live forever in a heavenly garden of plenty and bliss.

Yet something terrible happened, hardly less catastrophic than the first Breaking of the Vessels. With the descent of Adam into the realm of the klippot, he became entangled in the forces of darkness himself. How and why that happened—and what role Eve played in it—is one of the deepest mysteries of the epic. It is described in terms ranging from sexual intercourse with material spirits to the more famous eating of the apple of the "Tree of Knowledge of Good and Evil," through which the forces of evil penetrated him. And with his body now covered with "flesh" rather than "light" (the Hebrew pun is unmistakable in the text of Genesis 3:21), the animating light streaming through his now-fragile body shattered it into 613 scattered organs, ligaments, and limbs. The number 613 was highly significant, for that was precisely the number of commandments and obligations detailed in the Mosaic Law.

This explosion of Adam's metaphysical body parts apparently included a second detonation, for each part was eventually broken up into 613 more pieces, now totalling 375,769 fragments—each of which became individual human souls. Adam's assignment was now made immeasurably harder. For in order to raise up the sparks and to restore the divine powers, the pieces of the First Adam somehow had to be put back together. Humanity's quest—and in particular, the quest of the People of Israel who constituted the shattered body of Adam—was one of Tikkun, or reconstruction. They had first to separate their own souls from entanglement with the forces of darkness, next recognize which "soul root" they belonged to, and then slowly join like with like to reassemble the various body parts and piece together Adam's original form.

According to Luria's system, each man and woman had a particular identity in the cosmos, characterized by the precise place of origin of their soul. Each therefore was given a different mission—not only in meticulously observing all 613 of the Torah's commandments, but also in seeking out soul mates for the work of Tikkun. Luria offered the younger generation of kabbalists in Safed a specific role in redemption, far more complex and personalized than that taught by the Cordoverian school. Moreover, Luria believed that the work of Tikkun had to be accomplished in daily life and work, as well as in special rituals and prayer. Adam and Eve's fate—of having to work and to suffer and to live and die—was not so much God's eternal punishment as it was the only way that harmony in the heavens and earth could be restored.

In every hardship imposed on the banished Adam and his descendants—working by the sweat of their brows, planting crops, building cities, and even weaving textiles—could be discerned aspects of a vast project of separating light from darkness, establishing order, and improving the order of the world. This vast and diffuse enterprise of Tikkun was no longer a mystical vision or expression of ideological resistance to a dominant order. It became an aspect of every facet of life. Redemption became a matter of creating a harmonious order in which the power of violence and cruelty could be broken once and for all. What Isaac Luria offered his fellow students at the academy of Moses Cordovero was the idea that each one of them had a unique and definable place and role in the history of the world. And when Cordovero died in 1570, just a few months after Luria's arrival in Safed, Luria began to be recognized as an even greater master of Kabbalah. For he had not only brought an entirely new concept of redemption, he had the spiritual power to show his followers how they might fulfill their individual destinies.

WANDERING SOULS AND
DEMONIC SPIRITS

It is said of the holy Ari, in one of the many books of praise that began to be written about him after his death, that he had "acquired all kinds of wisdom in the world, the knowledge of the face, the knowledge of palmistry, communication with plants, communication with birds, reading the meaning of flames, and conversation with the attending angels. He could tell from a person's forehead what were his sins and what kind of a soul he possessed and what he came to this world to repair. He could also tell if the soul had undergone two reincarnations or only one, or whether the particular soul was from the tannaim or amoraim, or gaonim, or prophets, and he could also identify the souls of the wicked who had been reincarnated as trees and stones, animals of the field."

As a saintly mystic of unparalleled ability and charisma, he reportedly "knew what had happened to every person and what was likely to happen in the future. And all this in the blink of an eye! He also knew what sins a person had committed from the earliest days of his childhood to the present. And he knew what kind of soul each possessed in order to help them with the fulfillment of the mitzvot. He could also read the thoughts of others and coax out their souls from their bodies so that he could converse with them." But all these were not merely the tricks of a talented shaman; there was a far grander scheme involved in this supernatural virtuosity. In order to help mend the scattered souls of the First Adam—the first step in lifting the sparks and restoring the structure of the heavenly powers—Luria and his followers began an unprecedented concentration on the principle of reincarnation and its accompanying magical evocation of demons, saintly spirits, and wandering ghosts.

As early as the time of the Sefer Bahir in the twelfth century, the principle of reincarnation had been taken for granted in the kabbalistic tradition. It was seen as a fact of nature, part of the constant circulation of divine emanations from the Tree of Life. The sefirah of Yesod, in particular, sometimes pictured as a heavenly phallus, was identified as the source of all souls, which circulated generation after generation until they had been purged of their sins, and the unblemished soul of the Messiah could be born. In the Zohar, the principle of reincarnation was narrowed and given the technical name *gilgul,* or revolution, requiring new incarnations for persons who failed to procreate (and thereby obey the basic biblical injunction to "be fruitful and multiply") in earlier lives. Gradually the idea of reincarnation began to be seen as a generalized means of moral and spiritual improvement. Though never totally accepted by the mainstream rabbinic authorities, it offered reassurance to those pious poor whose daily dose of insults and indignities at the hands of the wealthy wicked seemed to make a mockery of the concept of divine justice in the world. The scriptures were combed for evidence of improvement over several lifetimes, and certain biblical personalities like Abel, Cain, Jethro, and Moses were seen as chapters in the stories of the progress of individual souls. But with Luria's vision of the shattering of the body of Adam, the process of reincarnation took on a larger meaning. Soul sparks from the various parts of his body bore special qualities that could be recognized by those with mystical vision. And once informed of their affinity they could band together and raise up the fallen sparks.

Here was a brand of Kabbalah in which a unique kind of soul psychology replaced the more methodical study of the relationships of the sefirot. And the process became an all-consuming passion, with the earlier meditative exercises — directed heavenward and dedicated to the union of sefirotic couples — now combined with frightening personal descents into hell. Since Luria himself left only a few short compositions, our knowledge of his teachings is derived almost entirely from the later recollections and notes of his followers. But when Luria began to lead his own mystical circle, he fashioned a striking new conception of the standard liturgy. The central prayer of praise to God and meditation on the heavenly powers — the

Amidah—was followed by a harrowing imaginary descent from the greatest heights to the most frightening abyss, as each individual probed the darkness of his own soul to lift up the sparks that existed deep within. And beyond the appointed prayers and regular rituals, each person was required to cleanse his or her soul through painful, penitential practices of fasts and self-mortification that harked back to the customs of the Hasidei Ashkenaz several hundred years before. In such acts, Luria sought to have his followers cleanse their souls of the earthly attachments to pleasure and comfort that stained them like rust or covered them like filth and thus prevented their attachment to related soul sparks.

The paths of reincarnation had become the main avenues to redemption, for Luria was convinced that almost all the sparks had already returned to their heavenly positions and only a few recalcitrant spirits remained to be saved. The souls of the wicked were subject to the whims of the demons, who trapped them in the bodies of owls, snakes, donkeys, and cats. And the seeming frequency of demonic possession was—in the eyes of Luria and his followers—evidence of the attempted escape of a haunted spirit into the body of a person who had recently sinned. It is ample testimony to the unthinking misogyny of this age and this mystical circle that nearly all the demonic possessions recorded in Safed in this period were of women, possessed by the wandering spirits of wicked men. And the process of exorcism seemed to have been standard: after Luria or one of his associates questioned the possessing spirit and determined its identity, they proceeded to force it out from the unfortunate woman's body with the use of acrid, billowing sulphur smoke and the repeated sounding of the shofar. In some cases, the subject did not survive the procedure—a circumstance that was ascribed to the evil spirit itself. If, somehow, the woman was relieved of her demonic symptoms, specially inscribed amulets were placed on her body and clothing to ward off further demonic infestation by the protection of the sefirot.

Yet even more than the control of the demonic forces, the circle of the Ari was most interested in lifting the final few sparks trapped among the sherds of darkness, so convinced were they that redemption was at hand. Scattered throughout the Galilean countryside around Safed were the fallen tombs of the ancient sages that had played such a prominent part in the gerushin or mystical wanderings of Moses Cordovero and Solomon Alkabetz. But now the tombs of the sages were no longer just sources of holiness and mystical inspiration. They became the focus of what can only be called a kabbalistic cult of the dead. As repositories of the earthly remains of many of Adam's most eminent soul roots, they were a valuable resource for the great work of Tikkun. Once Luria had identified the character of the soul of a particular follower, he would direct him to the tomb or monument of ancient soul mates and prescribe elaborate meditative techniques for the bonding of their spirits.

The later writings of his protégé Haim Vital are filled with detailed lists of the location of sacred gravesites and the soul history of the particular sages buried at each place. Luria would prescribe detailed meditative exercises called *yihuðim,* or "unifications," for his followers to perform at the tombs of the kin spirits, and he would regularly participate in this kabbalistic channeling himself. After arriving at the gravesite and performing the suitable yihudim, Luria would stretch out on the surface of the grave with his arms and legs extended, drawing down the soul of the departed to converse with him. To his closest followers it seemed as if Luria had the power to bring the departed soul back into consciousness through the power of prayer and sympathetic acts. And when the departed spirit communicated word of the progress of the great cosmic drama, Luria's face would, according to later accounts of his followers, "light up like the sun, so brilliant, that none of his fellows could even look upon it."

Legend reveals how close they must have felt to the culmination of history in those few brief months of ecstatic metaphysical engineering—separating wicked souls from the righteous and uniting the long-separated sparks of the same Adamic soul root. It did not matter that they had almost completely lost touch with the events in the surrounding world, or even the tangible, social dimension of the battle against evil and tyranny. So close did they feel to redemption that the story is told that "one day the Ari turned to his disciples and declared that they must set out for Jerusalem at once. The disciples were taken aback, but half of them had such perfect faith in the Ari that they stood up ready to depart. But the others grew afraid. The Ari looked at them, brokenhearted, and said: 'I heard a heavenly voice proclaim that if we journey to Jerusalem at once, without the slightest hesitation, the footsteps of the Messiah will soon be heard. But as soon as you raised your objections, I heard the voice say that the chance to bring the Messiah had been lost.' "

An even more serious obstacle was the frail humanity of the Ari who had served as their guru and spiritual guide. Epidemics of cholera and typhus were all too frequent in the close-packed cities and towns of the Ottoman Empire, and in 1572, at age thirty-eight, Isaac Luria fell victim to a disease that even the greatest mystical exercises could not cure. His followers experienced a feeling of panic, fearing that their mentor was about to leave them with the work of Tikkun still incomplete. But according to the later traditions, the Ari calmly gathered his closest protégé, Rabbi Haim Vital, and the rest of his followers around his deathbed and revealed to them the deepest of his mysteries—those that not even the ancient sages had known. And even his deathbed, the Ari's concerns continued to be the fight against the principle of evil in his own business transactions no less than in the realm of the klippot.

"The Ari would spend most of the day engaged in business," recalled a later account of his passing. "And three days before his death, he put all his books in order and said to his disciples: 'If any one cheated me, I forgive them, and if I cheated any one, let him come and I will settle my accounts with him.' " Then gathering his followers together, he promised them that he would return in another incarnation if they needed help to finish the work. Isaac Luria thus died in the summer of 1572, with the Ottoman Empire and the forces of Christendom entirely intact. But he was surely not forgotten. His vivid vision of the

Breaking of the Vessels and his legacy of spiritualism—if not the reality of redemption—would grow into a vast popular movement in Jewish communities throughout the world during the next century.

DREAMS OF RICHES IN AN AGE OF HARD TIMES

The Golden Age of Safed was over, even if the hope still burned brightly among the followers of the Ari that only a few sparks remained in the realm of darkness—and that they could be lifted by just a few inspired individuals. In the summer of 1575, barely three years after the death of their great master, seven of them gathered in Safed with their new leader, Haim Vital, to draft one of the most unusual legal documents known in the history of Judaism. The seven were passionately convinced that by affixing their signatures to the single sheet of parchment, they would inherit the power to redeem and remake the world.

"We, the undersigned," reads the Hebrew text, "have taken it upon ourselves to form a fellowship for the worship of God and the continual study of His Torah, day and night, as taught by our teacher, that rabbi of perfect wisdom, the saintly Haim Vital. We will study with him in the wisdom of truth and will be faithful in spirit. We will promise to maintain complete secrecy about all the things that we learn from him and promise not to ask him to teach us those things that he does not want to reveal. Under no circumstances will we share his teachings with outsiders, nor any of his earlier sayings, or even that which our saintly teacher Rabbi Isaac Luria Ashkenazi taught us while he was alive. Only Rabbi Haim may give us permission to reveal those teachings, since it is only through Rabbi Haim's explanations that we have come to understand what they meant. This agreement is made with a fearsome oath to God administered by our Rabbi Haim and shall be in force for ten years from this date, Monday, the twenty-fifth of Av, in the year 1575, here in the holy city of Safed."

Each of the signatures affixed to the agreement was accompanied by an intricate symbol of intertwined spires and banners whose mystical significance is impossible to understand today. But we can be sure that they had been conceived with intense concentration on the remaining sparks of light, the power of the klippot, the configuration of the sefirot—and the particular soul root and destiny that each of them possessed.

Yet their visionary belief in the workings of the heavenly powers left them blind to the schemes and stratagems of certain earthly powers that would soon destroy the very basis of the wealth of their community. For far beyond the circle of Haim Vital and of the other mystical brotherhoods of Safed—far beyond even the farthest trade connections of the Safed merchants—economic tides were turning. The rising nations of Western Europe were about to shatter the traditional patterns of Mediterranean trade. No longer was Crusade the only option for Western relations with the world of Islam. Since 1525, France had obtained special trading privileges in a treaty with the Ottomans, with the aim of gaining an advantage for their merchants over rivals from Venice and the other Italian ports. And England, long just an underdeveloped source for raw wool for the weavers of Flanders, was also coming into its own.

During the reign of Elizabeth I, the island nation began to take a genuine interest in exploration—sending off the freebooter Francis Drake to harass the Spanish in America and forming the "Levant Company" in 1581. And here was the brilliant secret of English commercial success: the directors and stockholders of the Levant Company had been granted an official monopoly on English trade to the Ottoman Empire and could charge whatever price they chose on merchandise they brought back. And because their potential profit on Middle Eastern spices, metalwork, dyes, pearls, and coffee back in England was so high, they could afford to take a loss on their own exports just to obtain the highly saleable Middle Eastern goods. The English had little to barter except woolen goods, and the sudden "dumping" of large quantities of English textiles at Ottoman ports—at prices far below their fair market value—

quickly sent the price of *all* textiles within the Ottoman Empire into a steep tailspin.

The rulers of the Ottoman Empire, for their part, had little interest in protecting their domestic industries. Textiles, after all, were an almost entirely Jewish concern. And so the profits of Safed's once-booming industry quickly disappeared. Already in 1574, the merchants there noted the sudden, steep drop in textile prices when the time came to market their finished goods in Damascus and Sidon. As the prices continued to fall through the 1580s and 1590s, many of the city's most active textile entrepreneurs closed down their operations and packed up their belongings, hoping to find more profitable conditions elsewhere in the Ottoman Empire. This left thousands of Jewish textile workers in Safed without a steady livelihood, and Jewish communities in the Balkans began to send shipments of subsidized raw wool to Safed to help prop up the industry. But there was no turning back the tides of commerce, and before long most of the skilled tradespeople had left Safed to find work in Salonika, which, though also suffering an economic decline, was a far larger city. Eventually even the sages of Safed departed for greener pastures, leaving behind only a dwindling number of mystical brotherhoods and a population increasingly composed of the aged, the sick, and the poor.

Had Haim Vital been as visionary or as charismatic as his master, he might have been able to maintain the spiritual intensity of his brotherhood, at least for a time. But the competition of other disciples who had not signed the mystical pledge of allegiance — and the steadily declining economy in Safed — persuaded him to follow his destiny to other locales. In 1577, he left for Jerusalem to establish a new yeshiva in the Holy City dedicated to the study of Lurianic Kabbalah. It is important to remember that even though the saintly figure of Isaac Luria has acquired such a prominent place in modern understandings of the Kabbalah's development, the man and his teachings were virtually unknown outside Safed at the time of his death. His immediate legacy was the conviction of his closest disciples that they were the small, select group of exalted soul sparks who would bring on redemption. And even though Vital was unwilling to share Luria's teachings with a broader public, he spent the next eight years in Jerusalem with a single-minded aim. He wanted to ensure that the master's secrets would not be misinterpreted or corrupted, and he set to work compiling and editing a wide variety of texts describing Luria's visions of God's Great Withdrawal, the Breaking of the Vessels, and the work of Tikkun.

Through the years, a number of would-be mystics had approached Vital to gain more information about the Ari's kabbalistic teaching, but still believing that redemption was near and that he would play a part in its advent, Vital had refused to reveal what he knew. In 1586, he returned to an increasingly impoverished Safed—and here the story gets murky. For the evidence seems to suggest that when Vital fell ill and was unable to conduct his teaching and writing, his brother Moshe secretly sold six hundred pages of his collected notes to an eager scholar for five hundred gold ducats—by that time, a very significant sum.

Who was so desperate to gain the secrets of this circle that he would conspire with a desperate brother? The most likely suspect is a wandering, Egyptian-born mystic named Israel Sarug. Sometime between 1597 and 1604, he took the material to the centers of Jewish culture in Italy, where Cordoverian Kabbalah was already well known and respected. Yet now he found a ready audience for Luria's far more esoteric vision of the sparks and the klippot. The atmosphere among the Jewish communities of Italy at the turn of the seventeenth century was darkened by apprehension. The offices of the Counter-Reformation had imposed new restrictions on Jewish life and commerce, creating a depressing contrast with the earlier freedom and relative prosperity of the Renaissance. Yet the tenets of Lurianic Kabbalah—as recorded by Vital and reinterpreted by Sarug—offered an explanation for every misfortune in the drama of reincarnation and the ongoing battle between darkness and light. And with the charm that he evidently possessed, Sarug passed himself off as one of Luria's closest disciples, telling stories about the heyday of Safed and performing psychic readings of the previous incarnations of the many prominent rabbis and scholars he met. Gaining great acceptance for his preaching, Sarug established kabbalistic schools throughout Italy in the first decade of the 1600s—influencing such outstanding Italian kabbalists as Menachem Azariah da Fano and Aaron Berakhya Modena. Travelling onward to Ragusa and Salonika, he ultimately made his way northward to Poland, where distant Jewish communities who were suffering under their own political upheavals and economic changes eagerly grasped at the stories of the wonder-worker of Safed.

And with the way paved for the acceptance of the Ari's teaching, Haim Vital—now recovered from his illness and resettled as a rabbi and teacher in Damascus from 1598 to his death in 1620—began to compile what he considered to be the authoritative versions of Lurianic teachings. They included his most famous work on the main outlines of Lurianic speculations, his mystical prayers, and his doctrine of reincarnation, entitled *Etz ha-Hayyim*, "The Tree of Life." Both the new versions of Lurianic Kabbalah, of Sarug and Vital—and occasional other writings from disciples like Joseph Ibn Tabul—promised redemption to all who would grasp it. The result was the transfer of focus from the historical struggles of the entire People of Israel to the microhistorical—even psychological—study of every individual. And as the figure of the Ari became a popular icon for Jews throughout the Middle East and Europe, memories of the Golden Age of Safed took on a distinctly nostalgic tone. In an age of hard times, the myth of Safed's glory glowed brightly throughout the Jewish world.

The postscript was to be strange beyond all reckoning, yet at the same time a natural outgrowth of the phenomenal spread of Lurianic Kabbalah. By the mid-1660s, the theory of the soul sparks was a common article of faith, but there were few living mystics who could read them accurately. In 1665, a twenty-one-year-old rabbi named Nathan Ashkenazi, living in the Palestinian seacoast town of Gaza, became fascinated with the kabbalistic literature of communication with angelic spirits—

and before long they began to appear to reveal to him the secrets of the heavenly realms. In the course of a self-imposed fast before Purim, he was solemnly informed that the time of redemption was quickly approaching, and he received the miraculous power to discern the nature of the soul of any person who spoke with him.

Word quickly spread through Gaza about the gift of the young soul-reader, which seemed to rival the powers of Isaac Luria himself. Soon people from Gaza and from towns throughout the Land of Israel were flocking to him for psychic readings, hoping to learn the nature of the sins they may have committed in former lives so that they could perform the appropriate atoning prayers. The news of Nathan's powers eventually reached the Jewish community of Cairo, and emissaries were immediately dispatched to Gaza to determine if the excited reports were true. They returned to Cairo with glowing reports of the young rabbi's amazing ability to still troubled spirits. Yet there was one aspect of his revelations that Nathan maintained, for the time being, as a closed secret. He had been granted a sublime vision of the divine Chariot and had learned the identity of Israel's Messiah—a man living in the present generation who would soon make himself known to the world.

Chapter 7
THE FORGOTTEN LEGACY

Who would ever have dreamed that the ancient mystical tradition would culminate in a messianic debacle—pinning the centuries-long hopes of the People of Israel on a man who was held hostage to fits of deep depression and manic illumination? Who would ever have guessed that the brilliant insights of the early kabbalists would become grounds for the irrational worship of this man as the Messiah of Israel? The Kabbalah, and those who study it, even today, has been profoundly affected by an otherwise forgotten tale of madness, hysteria, and messianic hope that took place in the middle of the seventeenth century. Seldom again would the Kabbalah become the basis for a down-to-earth political movement, with tangible political goals. Accusations of magic and heresy would continue—but never again would the Kabbalah be viewed as a serious threat to vested interests, sultans, or kings. The heavenly powers would henceforth be restricted to heaven, with redemption reduced to a dream beyond the reach of the living. Divine energy would henceforth be available only to those who, as individuals or groups, sought ecstatic union with the heavens, as a purely religious exercise. It would be relegated to the spiritual shadows, a hidden presence deep within mainstream Judaism.

The story of this transformation began innocently enough, with a single tortured soul simply seeking relief. He was a thirty-nine-year-old rabbi and mystic named Shabbetai Zvi who arrived in the humid, seaside town of Gaza off the coast of Palestine in the spring of 1665, seeking nothing more than to rid himself of the demons that had darkened his soul since youth. They would prey on him in times of his weakness, draining the life force from him, making it impossible for him to pursue his religious studies and forcing him to despair of life itself. This was a nightmare that had dogged him from his boyhood in the great Turkish port of Izmir. By the early 1600s, the days of independent Jewish production and trade were over and Shabbetai grew up in a world where Ottoman officials and European diplomats and commercial representatives were the most powerful figures in society. Born the youngest son of a local Jewish merchant who had grown wealthy as an agent for the Dutch and the English, Shabbetai proved unsuited for such a life. Supported by the wealth of his father and brothers, he devoted himself to the life of a scholar, studying under the most prominent rabbis in Izmir. Already in his early teens, Shabbetai was recognized as a brilliant Talmudist, learned and skillful in the interpretation of the Law. With a bright future ahead of him, he was a rabbi at age eighteen.

But there was a darker side to Shabbetai's personality that first manifested itself in continuing nightmares and visions of demonic attacks. He turned to solitary penitential rituals to free himself from their continuing threat—and he embarked on a private study of the Kabbalah. And in his personal quest to study the nature of evil he was drawn to the doctrines of the Zohar and especially to those of the *Sefer ha-Kanah*, that strange commentary on the biblical commandments written in Spain at the time of massive, forced conversions of Jews to Christianity. In studying its teaching of the deeper mystical truths that lay beneath—and sometimes in contradiction to the normal ritual laws—Shabbetai became a charismatic leader of the younger generation of scholars in Izmir. He led them in penitential exercises, ritual immersions in the sea, and long walks through the countryside in imitation of the gerushin of the sages of Safed. Yet he occasionally shocked them with his strange pronouncements about his own semidivine status, declaring that his prayers were specifically directed not to God but to the sefirah Tiferet. And he repeatedly hinted that *he* was the figure alluded to in Isaiah 14:14, "I will ascend above the height of the clouds; I will make myself like the Most High."

Gradually the elders of Izmir's Jewish community found Shabbetai's behavior unsettling. Two successive marriages arranged with prominent women in the Izmir community ended in divorce, when the young rabbi-mystic refused to consummate relations with either woman, declaring that the Holy Spirit had revealed to him that the souls of neither was compatible with his. Increasingly incapacitated by alternating states of deep depression and manic euphoria, he became convinced that he might perhaps be the Messiah. His date of birth on the ninth of Av—the traditional date of the destruction of the Temple— seemed to him symbolic of his own role in ending the Exile. And in 1648, at a time when the news of bloody Cossack attacks on the Jews of Poland aroused the entire Jewish world to fear for the future, Shabbetai mounted the *bimah* of his synagogue in Izmir at the weekly Torah reading—shamelessly pronouncing the forbidden syllables of the Ineffable Name of God.

That blasphemous demonstration caused an uproar in the city and his father and brothers tried to rein in Shabbetai's increasingly bizarre behavior—which was now alternating between periods of incessant prayer and penitential exercises and extravagant public displays. Yet their attempts to influence him proved futile, and Shabbetai was eventually banished from the city. Arriving in Salonika, he caused even more violent outrage. Continuing to pronounce the Name of God aloud at synagogue services, he became a strange mystical minstrel, singing before gathered crowds old Spanish love songs whose lyrics he changed to refer to the union of the sefirot Tiferet and Malchut. The climax came when he staged a mock marriage—bridal canopy and all—between himself and a Torah scroll. Branded as a madman and forced out of Salonika, Shabbetai wandered to Istanbul where he joined a circle of kabbalists and sought their help in diagnosing the source of the extreme emotional ups and downs that were in danger of overwhelming his life. He found no relief in their ritual exorcisms and incantations, and after a brief return to his native city of Izmir, Shabbetai proceeded alone to the Holy City of Jerusalem.

Jerusalem had always been a magnet for mystics and madmen, and Shabbetai spent about a year in and around the city, going off in his periods of deep depression to wander among ancient caves and tombs, where he reportedly heard voices. In his periods of illumination, he wandered through the streets of Jerusalem, singing, preaching, and performing extravagant demonstrations of kabbalistic rituals. Now in his late thirties—too old and too eccentric ever to find his place as a teacher in an academy or a rabbi for a congregation—Shabbetai was seen by many as a pathetic buffoon. Yet the leaders of the Jerusalem community knew of his wealthy and respected family back in Izmir. And in 1663, when the Ottoman governor of Jerusalem levied a painful new tax on the Jews of the city, Shabbetai was dispatched to Cairo as an official representative to mobilize funds. In Cairo, he became an entertaining favorite in the court of the head of the Egyptian Jewish community, the Nagid Raphael Joseph Celebi, an aficionado of the kabbalistic tradition himself.

At this time, despite his increasingly bizarre behavior, Shabbetai presented an impressive appearance by the standards of the day. A later description pictured him as tall, with a face that was "very bright, inclining to swarthiness, his countenance beautiful and majestic, a black, round beard framed his face." Dressed in royal robes, "he was very stout and corpulent." Yet his inner turmoil continued. In Cairo he married a woman named Sarah (an immigrant from Europe about whom rumors of prostitution were rampant) in an act that was later termed an imitation of the Prophet Hosea, who was instructed by God to "take to yourself a wife of harlotry" (Hosea 1:2). Yet whatever prophetic or even messianic ambitions he may have had in his periods of illumination, he more than ever sought relief when his deep depressive states arrived. Thus in the spring of 1665, when reports began to filter back to Cairo of the appearance of a charismatic—and highly effective—young healer of souls in Gaza, Shabbetai immediately left Egypt and made his way there.

In those days of widespread belief in the Lurianic theories of reincarnation, Shabbetai had little doubt that his soul spark was somehow entangled in the forces of darkness. Yet only an accurate analysis of the sins he had committed in his former lives—and detailed prescriptions of penitential exercises—might at last break the grip of the klippot. Arriving in Gaza and making his way to the presence of the young prophet Nathan Ashkenazi, Shabbetai found far more than he was looking for. Nathan reportedly fell to the ground overawed by the "very exalted soul" that stood before him. And after spending several weeks together, travelling to the holy sites of Hebron and Jerusalem, Nathan became convinced that Shabbetai's soul was indeed that of the long-awaited Messiah, whose soul was being tortured by its intermittent struggle with the deepest and most dangerous forces in the world of the klippot. This was not a matter of simple exorcism or penitence. It was a cosmic battle that could only be over when Shabbetai defeated those last forces of darkness and thereby brought on the redemption of Israel. And back in Gaza—at the all-night prayer vigil on the eve of Shavuot, a time so many other miraculous manifestations of the spirit had descended over the centuries—Nathan fell into a deep mystical trance. Possessed by a heavenly spirit, he declared that Shabbetai Zvi was the destined king of the house of Israel and the age of redemption, so long and so fervently awaited, would at last begin on May 31, 1665.

It is easy enough to dismiss this midnight revelation as the delusions of a young faith healer and a chronic manic-depressive, but that would be to underestimate the power that had been unleashed by the symbols and rituals of the Kabbalah throughout the Jewish world. By now it had been accepted by many that things were not what they seemed on the surface. The current misfortunes of the Jews as a people—the very fact of their exile—was merely a symptom of the intensifying struggle between the forces of darkness and light. In fact, while the present political and economic situation of the Jews was complex and possibly subject to many interpretations, the Lurianic myth of the shattered vessels, the klippot, and the fallen sparks was utterly unambiguous. Luria had already taught that most of the sparks had returned to their source in the sefirotic realm, and with the freeing of the last few sparks—from the most wicked and tenacious of the klippot—the cosmic battle would be won. As unlikely as it may seem today, Shabbetai masterfully played the part of the Messiah. In his tortured periods of depression and painful withdrawal, he was said to be engaged in that inner battle with the forces of darkness. And when he emerged into one of his public periods of illumination, many could see in his shining face and charismatic aura that he had retrieved yet another of the fallen sparks. And with the number of fallen sparks rapidly dwindling—and the nourishing source of the klippot shrinking—it seemed only a matter of time before those powerful cosmic changes would manifest themselves on earth.

As the news spread throughout the Holy Land about the appearance of Israel's Messiah, the rabbis and leaders of the community in Jerusalem who knew Shabbetai in his earlier period of wandering urged caution, but, at the same time, hedged their bets. Accompanied by Nathan and a growing entourage, Shabbetai appeared at the gates of Jerusalem on horseback and greatly impressed the usually suspicious and hostile Ottoman officials; it was the beginning of what Nathan hoped was an age of far-reaching political change. For his part, Nathan sincerely believed that redemption was within the grasp of the present generation, and as he spread reports of Shabbetai's travels and meetings, he envisioned his personal direction of a vast movement of repentence among Jewish communities throughout the world.

Using his own skills and incantations to diagnose the flaws specific to every soul spark, Nathan hoped that he could enable them to flow together to reconstitute the body of the Primordial Adam and thereby complete the work of cosmic repair or Tikkun. And as word spread to the Jewish communities in Egypt and Syria, men, women, and children began to participate in the focussed acts of penitence, hoping that they might contribute to the coming redemption. During the summer, Nathan dispatched a detailed letter to Raphael Joseph in Cairo, explaining that the cosmic processes were moving quickly and that the prayers prescribed by the Lurianic tradition should be discontinued. All the trapped sparks had ascended and it was now just a matter of faith in the battle of Shabbetai Zvi against the last of the klippot. The growing numbers of Shabbetai's adherents wanted desperately for the reports to be true. They branded any skeptics or opponents as instruments of the demonic forces—part of the realm of the klippot that would soon be destroyed. And they listened with excitement to prophecies of the coming events, visualizing victories that Solomon Molcho had only dreamed of: with Shabbetai Zvi assuming the messianic crown of Israel, deposing the sultan and taking over the Ottoman Empire—and then marching with the Ten Lost Tribes to conquer the world.

In the summer of 1665, Shabbetai traveled northward in what can only be called a royal procession, stopping briefly in Safed where, according to later reports, "ten prophets and ten prophetesses" arose. Then proceeding to the great city of Aleppo, he met privately with the leaders of the Jewish community, and his regal demeanor convinced them that perhaps the Messiah had indeed arrived. And even though Shabbetai made no overt public declarations about his own messianic status and soon moved on to his hometown of Izmir, he left in his wake a whirlwind of excitement that—in other places and times—would have been seen as a political uprising against the established authorities. The streets of the Jewish Quarter were filled with people shouting, singing, and dancing in ecstatic trances, celebrating their sudden liberation by the Messiah from the impositions of their landlords, their employers, from the Arabs and the Turks. Of course nothing had really changed in Aleppo but the emotions of the Jewish population. All business in the city came to a standstill in anticipation of the very different regime that was soon to come.

Arriving back in Izmir, the mass hysteria grew more ominous, for after several months of relative calm, Shabbetai entered one of his periods of manic illumination and had no compunction about making public pronouncements about his messianic status. In December 1665, Shabbetai appeared in regal robes in one of the main synagogues and received a delegation from Aleppo that had come to pay its respects to the Messiah of Israel. Soon thereafter, Shabbetai began to introduce bizarre new customs into the course of the synagogue worship—not only pronouncing the Ineffable Name of God (which had by now become his trademark) but openly violating the dietary laws and other ritual commandments. Believing that the coming of redemption now rendered the traditional Torah a dead letter, he concluded his new messianic liturgy with the benediction, "Blessed art Thou Who hath permitted forbidden things."

Naturally there were some members of Izmir's Jewish community who were unwilling to abandon all that had been considered sacred and proper for the dictates of a would-be Messiah and his growing numbers of local followers. Shabbetai attracted huge, enthusiastic crowds of people who were eager to take part in the emergence of the messianic kingdom. They were later described as the poorest and most common workers, "fishermen, vendors of eggs and poultry, oarsmen in the port, and servants, and more of this sort of nobleman, even the richest of whom had nothing to lose." Yet as the excitement mounted, several members of the local rabbinical council held secret consultations about the unfolding events, an act that was seen as nothing less than open rejection by the crowds—and by

Shabbetai himself. What followed was an open, violent rebellion, with Shabbetai leading his followers, axes in hand, to break down the doors of the main synagogue in the midst of Sabbath prayers. Mounting the bimah himself he conducted a typically unorthodox service, leading his followers in mystical hymns and declaring that the normal prayers were no longer necessary. Then after appointing one of his brothers "king of Turkey" and another "emperor of Rome," he summoned to the Torah "men and even women to whom he distributed kingdoms and he forced all of them to pronounce the Ineffable Name." For several more months a mystical reign of terror gripped Izmir as Shabbetai ruled there virtually unchallenged, declaring that the messianic age would truly begin in just a few months — on June 18, 1666.

By the winter of 1665–66, reports of the upheaval among the Jewish communities of Egypt, Palestine, Syria, and Turkey had reached Europe, through the dispatches of English and Dutch commercial representatives residing in Izmir. And since messianic excitement among Jewish communities was spreading as far away as Poland, Yemen, and Kurdistan—with rumors of Jews selling their property and leasing ships and wagons for their imminent return to the Land of Israel—it was little wonder that the Ottomans became wary. Court officials now prepared to liquidate the obvious threat. The political aspects of Shabbetai's program were now quite evident in his instruction that the dutiful, patriotic prayers in the name Sultan Mehmet IV be eliminated from all synagogue services and the name of Shabbetai Zvi be inserted in its place. Shabbetai and his entourage soon sailed from Izmir bound for Istanbul, the seat of Ottoman power, intending to finalize his rule. But the Ottoman government was ready. On February 6, 1666, Ottoman troops boarded Shabbetai's ship in the Sea of Marmara and hustled him off for a hearing in the presence of the Grand Vizier, Ahmed Köprülü. The hearing was brief and inconclusive, since Shabbetai's latest manic stage had passed. The meek, portly rabbi answered his interrogators' questions politely, and apparently did not seem to pose much of a threat to the imperial order. But because the sultan was about to embark on a campaign in the Aegean, and wanted to avoid unrest in the capital, the would-be Messiah was transported by a heavily armed guard and imprisoned in the great fortress at Gallipoli.

THE GREAT MESSIANIC DEBACLE

Through the summer of 1666—a year whose number had been regarded with ominous apocalyptic significance by some radical Christian movements—rabbis and poets throughout the Jewish world became powerful propagandists for the Shabbetai the Messiah, writing kabbalistic texts that explained his pronouncements and composing messianic poetry. Entire Jewish communities became manic-depressive, alternating periods of fasts and penitential rituals with explosions of prophetic ecstasy. The imprisonment of Shabbetai in the fortress of Gallipoli proved to be a blessing in disguise. Through the quiet bribes of some of his wealthy supporters he received lavish provisions and living conditions and was allowed to receive delegations of visitors. In fact, the closely guarded Ottoman fortress became the headquarters of a vast messianic propaganda machine. Yet the emerging cult of personality of Shabbetai Zvi— in which the details of his life and actions were given a theological interpretation—created precisely the kind of craving for earthly power that the kabbalistic tradition had, from its very inception, attempted to combat.

And so it came to pass that in the midst of Shabbetai's busy court schedule at Gallipoli, a Polish emissary with his own messianic pretensions, Nehemiah ha-Kohen from Lvov, got into a bitter argument with Shabbetai and his retainers. Basing himself on traditional kabbalistic texts about the appearance of the Messiah, he came to the conclusion that Shabbetai's claims were false. In fury, he denounced the entire movement to the Ottoman officials as a mere subterfuge for sedition. And for their part, the Ottomans—already increasingly uneasy with the parade of visitors and delegations streaming in and out of Gallipoli—transferred Shabbetai's "court" to the royal compound in Adrianople in mid-September, just a few weeks before the beginning of the Jewish New Year. And there in the royal divan—with Sultan Mehmet IV, recently returned from Crete, watching discreetly from behind a partition—a bizarre parody of Pontius Pilate's interrogation of Jesus was enacted in Turkish costume.

Examined by the highest officials of the empire, Shabbetai was confronted with abundant evidence of his royal pretensions and his outspoken statements about toppling the sultan and taking over the Ottoman Empire. But now, his delicate psychological state betrayed him. Apparently in a depressive state, he remained impassive and did not defend his messianic destiny but rather put up a weak and unconvincing defense of his own innocence. At the conclusion of the interrogation, he was given a simple choice: convert to Islam immediately or be put to death. Yet there was to be no cross or passion in the life of *this* Messiah. The court officials convinced him to save his life by converting to Islam and bringing his many followers into the Muslim fold. And that was, indeed, what happened. Shabbetai duly converted to Islam. Taking the name Aziz Mehmet Effendi, he was given a handsome pension. Granted the honorary title kapiçi bashi, "Gatekeeper for the Palace," he was now expected to spend the rest of his life in relative luxury.

This stunning turn of events shook the very foundations of the Jewish world that had slowly come to believe that the era of redemption had finally arrived. For many—even most—the circumstances of Shabbetai's sudden conversion caused a painful, humiliating soul-searching. How could they ever have believed that the eccentric Shabbetai was really the messianic figure, described in such lofty terms in the Bible and rabbinic literature? How could they have been gullible enough to believe that this man's emotional ups and downs were the signs of a cosmic battle? And how could they ever have assumed that in a world still so flawed with selfishness, greed, arrogance, and ambition that the power of the klippot was really at an end? In

Jewish communities from Western Europe to North Africa to southern Arabia, any congregational records of correspondence with, or praise of, the would-be Messiah were burned. Former ardent supporters now assumed an uncomfortable, embarrassed silence. Never again, for the vast majority of Jews, would messianic expectations be anything more than a distant longing, an impossible ideal of a perfect world.

Yet there were, here and there, some hearts and minds that had been touched so deeply by the experience of a living Messiah and the possibilities of radical change he represented that they could simply not give up their hope. Nathan of Gaza—Shabbetai's first and most ardent prophet—was foremost among them, refusing to believe that Shabbetai's willing acceptance of Islam was not just an even deeper descent of the Messiah into the realm of darkness to do battle with the last and most demonic of the klippot. In November 1666, he left Palestine and headed to Izmir where there were still many Shabbatean supporters and, staying there over the winter, he was able to formulate a theological rationale for the movement to continue.

Shabbetai's mission, he now proclaimed, was to uplift the sparks concealed at the very heart of Islam—as a first step to toppling that religion and civilization before moving to conquer Christendom. The Bible was filled with stories of biblical heroes entering realms of darkness to strike a blow for the People of Israel—Joseph in the Pharaoh's court, Samson in the Philistine temple, and Daniel in the lions' den were only a few. But Shabbetai's mission of disguise and deception was exceedingly dangerous, for redemption hung in the balance. And because he needed help from his most faithful believers, it was now the duty of the "elect ones"—Nathan insisted—to convert to Islam and descend into the deepest realm of the klippot to help Shabbetai bring about the final liberation of the most recalcitrant sparks.

Nathan himself never converted to Islam, yet he remained the chief theologian and spiritual advisor of Shabbetai's apostate followers, who came to be known derisively by the Muslims as

Dönmeh, or "turncoats." And for a while, Shabbetai and his followers lived the life of new Marranos, practicing Islam in public while observing in private a radical, mystical variation of the faith of Israel. Growing older, Shabbetai continued to be buffeted by the highs and lows of his manic-depression with even his most cryptic sayings accepted by his inner circle as profound mysteries. Becoming more of a nuisance than a threat to the Ottoman authorities, he was eventually sent off to exile in a desolate Albanian coastal fortress called Dulcigo or Ulkün. And even this last humiliation was seen by the Dönmeh as conclusive proof of Shabbetai's messianic identity, for they pointed to Proverbs 30:31 where the description of a "king" is connected with an obscure Hebrew word, *alkum.*

Prophecy apart, Shabbetai's removal to a distant, unapproachable location made his followers even more marginal and few in number, and he died alone and isolated in Albania on Yom Kippur 1676—ten full years after redemption was expected to come. Nathan, still desperately trying to keep the faith alive, declared that Shabbetai's apparent death was only a temporary occultation, a divinely directed translation to heaven, from whence he would return to earth when the time was right. But Nathan never lived to see the second coming. He died in Skopje, in Macedonia, in 1680, leaving the few faithful to fend for themselves. Only in Italy, the Balkans, and distant Lithuania did scattered yet close-knit communities of Shabbateans endure as a strange cult of mystical messianists who remained stubbornly outside the People of Israel.

In the Jewish communities of northern Europe, enthusiasm also continued in some circles long after Shabbetai's apostasy and death. In Prague, Rabbi Mordecai Eisenstadt rallied the faithful throughout Bohemia and southern Germany, explaining that Shabbetai had merely been the Messiah of Joseph—the figure fated to defeat the forces of evil and die in the battle before the advent of the Davidic Messiah. That would mean that the Davidic Messiah was soon to come. Elsewhere, in places as far flung as Morocco and Lithuania, dozens of self-appointed prophets also preached that Shabbetai would surely return.

Among the most colorful of these apostles was a silversmith from Vilna in Lithuania, named Joshua Heschel ben Joseph. During the fateful year 1666, he experienced intense mystical visions of the divine Chariot, which he became convinced were the symbolic contents of the "Torah of the Messianic Age" that Shabbetai had often spoken of. In fact, after the death of Shabbetai, Joshua Heschel became the center of his own movement in Poland and Lithuania, convincing his followers that *he* was the Messiah of Joseph awaiting the return of Shabbetai Zvi. His voluminous writings were eventually gathered in a mystical work, *Sefer ha-Zoref*, the "Book of the Silversmith," that offered commentaries on the prayers and complex numerological calculations about the date when redemption would finally arrive.

Thus by the end of the seventeenth century, small and secret cells of Sabbateans had formed throughout much of Eastern Europe, including one group who called themselves "Hasidim"—presumably after the medieval pietists—who planned to emigrate to the Land of Israel to await the return of Shabbetai Zvi there. The group arrived in Jerusalem in 1700 but met intense local resentment, and its members gradually drifted apart. Another small group formed in the Polish town of Brody, dreaming of the Messiah and speculating on the number of sparks that remained among the klippot. Thus by the beginning of the eighteenth century, all that remained of the once vast movement of Lurianic apocalypticism were the jagged sherds of small, scattered antinomian sects. And from the 1740s, the passion and faith in the kabbalistic tradition as a mass movement passed to the leaders of a great revival in the Ukraine, Poland, and Lithuania, whose theology and social organization is with us still.

TALES OF THE HASIDIM

Even today, they speak of Israel ben Eliezer (better known as *the Baal Shem Tov*, or "Master of the Holy Name") with a reverence bordering on worship. For it was he who transformed the

shattered hopes of the messianic movement, the surrealistic images of Lurianic kabbalah, and the centuries-old magic of the
Jewish mystical tradition into the vibrant *modern* movement of
the Hasidim. It may be hard to speak of an eighteenth-century
rabbi and mystic as founding a modern movement. Yet the Hasidic experience—so deeply connected with the culture, landscape, costume, and social mores of the Jews of Eastern
Europe—represented a sharp break with the more ancient
struggle of the People of Israel. For more than two thousand
years, the mystical lore of the Kabbalah and its predecessors
had been directly aimed at the great empires of antiquity and
their successors. The principle of evil had gradually been crystallized and abstracted, but it had always been viewed as the demonic impetus for the continued existence of emperors, caliphs,
and kings. The experience of Shabbetai Zvi had demonstrated
the apparent futility of putting mystical dreams into action, and
his followers had retreated into a theological fantasy world—
tiny splinter groups of a shattered movement for worldwide
change.

Off in the shtetls of Eastern Europe—in those wooden clusters of houses, synagogues, stables, dairies, and workshops scattered across the fertile agricultural plains of the Ukraine and
southern Lithuania—all politics, and for that matter, all religion was local. Little wonder then that local shamans and faith
healers among the Jewish community would gradually absorb
the terminology and technique of the Lurianic kabbalists and
transform them dramatically. At the time, there were many
baalei shem and traveling faith healers and magicians who
roamed the plains and forests of Eastern Europe, hoping to
give—or sell—solace to the vast Jewish population scattered in
small villages over hundreds of thousands of square miles.

The era was one that desperately needed such solace, for despite the auspicious beginnings of the Jewish communities of
Eastern Europe (officially invited settlers, merchants, and
craftsmen, as elsewhere), they had, by the mid-seventeenth
century, already begun their long slide toward ostracism, persecution, and ultimately genocide. The explosion of violent anti-

Jewish pogroms known as the Chmielnicki Massacres of 1648–49 shattered any feeling of security that might have been left. So the people turned to magic and the mystical brotherhoods founded throughout Poland and Lithuania after the apostasy of Shabbetai Zvi. And in a mix of magical ecstasy and kabbalistic symbols, Israel ben Eliezer, the Baal Shem Tov—or Besht, in the familiar Hebrew acronym—would turn from the toppling of great world empires to resurrect his own community.

It all began with a vision, by now the standard feature of virtually every mystical biography. Born to poor parents in the rural shtetl of Okop in Podolia around 1700, the Besht received only a rudimentary education. As a young man, he worked at a succession of jobs, first as an elementary school teacher at the Talmud-Torah in the regional town of Yazlovets, then as a day laborer in the clay pits near Tluste, and finally as a wandering faith healer and caster of sacred spells. Legend relates that on Rosh Hashanah 1746, Israel "brought about an ascent using the Holy Names . . . and saw wondrous things which I had never seen since the day I attained knowledge." After journeying upward through the heavens and encountering the souls of the departed, "I rose from level to level until I entered the Chamber of the Messiah." And it was there that he learned his fateful destiny to preach and ultimately save the poor and unlettered Jewish masses of Eastern Europe and, eventually, the world. "Through this," the supernal figure of the Messiah told him, "will you know—when your teachings will become known and will be revealed to the world, and your wellsprings shall burst forth, [bringing] to the outside that which I have taught you. And you have comprehended, so that they, too, will be able to make unifications and ascents [of the soul] just like you. Then all of the evil klippot will cease to be, and it will be the era of goodwill and salvation."

From that moment and with that conviction, Israel ben Eliezer embarked on his mission with a love of life and a talent for miracles that soon spread his fame far and wide. He traveled tirelessly among the regions Jewish communities that stretched from the eastern regions of Germany to the rich farm country of Lithuania, to the windswept plains of the Ukraine. As the fame and skill of the Besht became known and respected, townspeople and villagers from the regions around his first residences at Tluste and Medziboh flocked to see him to gain cures and favors. They could also join in the ecstatic rites of *devekut* he preached, in which they could regain union with the divine forces in heaven as well as in their innermost selves. As a movement of rural revival, the rise of the Baal Shem Tov had much in common with earlier peasant prophets and would-be messianic figures. But never before in all of Jewish history was the population dispersed so thickly, under such similar conditions, over so traversable an area as the plains and river valleys stretching from the Crimea in the south to the Baltic coast of Lithuania nearly eight hundred miles to the north.

The contrast with earlier mystical leaders could hardly have been more dramatic. Where Judah the Hasid engaged in painful, unceasing penitential acts and Isaac Luria lost himself in his horrifyingly surreal visions of the realms of darkness, the Besht is recalled as a congenial—even jolly—figure, who loved his pipe and his wine. In his acts, stories, and rituals, he softened the dangerous sting of the Sabbatean heresy by preaching that although we are indeed all condemned to live in the world of the klippot and forces of darkness, all around us are other trapped sparks of divine light. This was a movement that, while bearing the legacy of the kabbalistic tradition, was amenable to the life of the common Jewish population as it did not require great erudition or painful ascetic rituals. It was rather an intensity of devotion in which kavvanah was no longer highly technical meditation on supernal structures but a generalized concentration on "uplifting the sparks" in prayer and in every phase of life.

Dancing, music, joy, enthusiasm, and holy ecstasy marked the Hasidic experience apart from the normative structures and institutions of Eastern European Jewish life, where the rigid hierarchy of social position of the dominant culture had pinned them at the bottom of the heap. And if the vast project of reconstructing the Primordial Adam and bringing on immediate redemption was beyond the Besht's immediate program, he would become the physical channel between the heavenly and the earthly. He became the prototype of the Hasidic Tzaddik, or rebbe—a spirit-inspired leader linking the supernal worlds of the sefirot and divine power with the everyday reality of his followers.

For the first twenty-five years of the movement, the personality of the Baal Shem Tov held the faithful together. Yet with his death in 1760, the leadership passed—after a struggle—to Dov Baer of Mezhirech. From that Ukrainian center, emissaries of the new faith began to propagate legends and praise of the Besht as the core of their teaching, and the movement of revival began to reach the urban populations of Eastern Europe as well. Yet as time went on, the principle of "Tzaddikism" led to the establishment of rival groups centered at different towns throughout Eastern Europe, each convinced that its rebbe was the uniquely inspired Tzaddik who represented the true channel to God. The various Hasidic "courts" developed distinctive traditions—and distinctive theologies. These ranged from the mystical messianism of Nahman of Bratslav (the great-grandson of the Besht) to the scholarly Habad movement begun by Shneur Zalman of Lyady that stressed Torah study and reflection on the Lurianic theories of the sefirot. Little by little the courts of the various rebbes became hardened into lines of dynastic succession rather than infusions of the spirit, almost a parody of the Eastern European feudalism whose stifling culture and social hierarchy the movement first arose to contest.

Yet the Hasidic movement endured against all odds into the twentieth century—and will surely continue into the twenty-first. Surviving the fierce campaigns mounted against them in the 1770s by the urban-based rabbis, the tight-knit communities of Hasidim weathered the famines and destruction of the Napoleonic wars, the pogroms of the late nineteenth century, the privations of World War I, and near extinction during the Holocaust. And transplanted to the major cities of Europe and America, the Hasidic courts continued together in their absolute faith in the holiness of their own Tzaddik. The earlier mystical developments were gradually forgotten, yet the legacy of Shabbetai Zvi, Isaac Luria, the kabbalists of Spain, the earlier Hasidim of medieval Germany, and the Merkabah mystics of the Roman period all contributed to the texture of their customs and beliefs. Hasidism, even today, remains a unique movement of kabbalistic tradition even though the only elements that are distinctive to outside observers are the characteristic black satin robes, flat fur streimels, and calf-length white hosiery. Yet along with their festive garb, adopted as a radical response to the styles of the eighteenth-century Polish nobility, today's Hasidic sages, seers, and would-be Messiahs also preserve the unique mystical ideas of Provence, Castile, and Safed—which are themselves legacies of the mystical ideologies of the ancient Near East.

Epilogue

THE KABBALAH REBORN

S o what is the Kabbalah's continuing legacy in an age when modern nation-states have taken the place of capricious monarchs, where science and technology dominate our understanding of the mechanics of the cosmos, and where religion, even mystical religion, has been reduced to a matter of individual spirituality? Over the last two hundred years, the channels of transmission of kabbalistic lore outside the Hasidic movement and the strictly controlled world of rabbinic study have been severely limited. Yet a "new" Kabbalah of self-help classes, inspirational books, and New Age rituals of personal fulfillment has arisen throughout the Western world. To a certain extent, the new widespread interest in the Kabbalah springs from the European occult tradition in which the tradition of Jewish mysticism has always been prized by religious experimenters and freethinkers as an echo of the *prisca theologica* — the most ancient and venerable religious tradition in the world.

We have already mentioned the interest in the Kabbalah during the Renaissance among Italian Christian scholars, particularly Giovanni Pico della Mirandola (1463–1494), head of the Medicis' Platonic Academy in Florence. Spurred by a quest for ancient wisdom that was animated by the same intellectual curiosity that gave rise to the first archaeological explorations, the Christian kabbalists avidly collected and translated Jewish mystical texts. And in their interpretation of the system of the sefirot and the body of the Primordial Adam, they believed that they had found the true primordial faith—with which Christianity, with its vision of the Trinity and the body of Christ, was completely compatible. More than that, the Christian kabbalists believed that the Kabbalah's precise metaphysical structures and mechanics offered humanity a revolutionary new theological science that could have practical effects. In many of the major cultural and economic centers of Europe, Christian kabbalists consulted with rabbis, pored over mystical texts, and composed their own introductions to kabbalistic lore. Famous works like the German scholar Johannes Reuchlin's *De Arte Cabilistica,* "On the Science of the Kabbalah" (1517), and the encyclopedic handbook *De Occulta Philosophia,* "On Occult Philosophy" (1531), compiled by the Christian alchemist and astrologer Cornelius Agrippa of Nettesheim, created the image of Jewish mysticism as a powerful, secret magic available to all. Though the Christian kabbalists had the highest respect and deepest fascination for the lore of the Kabbalah, their work would forever link Jewish mysticism with the arts of black magic and practical sorcery. It was an association that would result in intensified suspicion and persecution of Jews throughout Europe at times of later anti-Semitic outbreaks.

In time, the Christian Kabbalah gradually lost its initial close contact with Jewish scholars and Jewish sources and became an independent religious ideology of protest and resistance to the established churches of the Protestant and Roman Catholic world. In the seventeenth century, the publication of the *Kabbala Denudata,* "The Kabbalah Uncovered" (1677–1684), by the

German scholar Christian Knorr von Rosenroth, exerted a profound impact on circles of freethinkers and intellectuals throughout Western Europe—particularly on the group in England known as the Cambridge Platonists. And it is in his greatest work, the *Principia—Philosophiae naturalis principia mathematica,* "Mathematical Principles of Natural Philosophy" (1687)—that Sir Isaac Newton of Cambridge established in Western science a concept that had been commonplace in kabbalistic circles for centuries: that the surface appearance and behavior of natural events are mere symptoms and symbols of great natural laws and mechanisms attributable to the divine Architect of the universe.

While Newtonian physics bore within it the legacy of a highly scholarly brand of the Kabbalah, other variants merged into other mystical and magical traditions. And in an eclectic melange of symbols, rituals, and incantations, they formed the secret ideology of a wide variety of European freethinkers, spiritualists, and deists in the mystical societies and brotherhoods—like the Freemasons and the Rosicrucians of the eighteenth century. And in their preoccupation with the occult, with reincarnation, and communications with heavenly realms of light and darkness, they preserved the treasury of lore and symbols that gave rise to the Theosophy movement—of seances and otherworldly communications—that serves as one of the most important metaphysical foundations for the New Age movement of today.

That is not to say that there are no Jewish roots in the current popular revival of interest in the kabbalistic tradition. For most of the People of Israel, the rituals and literature of the Kabbalah left a deep and profound impression. Besides the hymns and poems that were accepted into the liturgy of the Sabbath and the festivals of the Jewish calendar, a more pervasive, subliminal folklore remained. From the images of wandering spirits described in the kabbalistic theories of reincarnation and of continuing struggle with demons came the frightening Yiddish tales of the sudden possession of innocent people by the terrifying evil spirits called *dybbuks.* The popular legends of the construction by Rabbi Judah Loew of Prague of a *golem,* or Frankenstein-like monster, through kabbalistic incantations and instructions, have remained a vivid element of European Jewish folklore. And other nightmarish figures of baby-stranglers, seductive demonesses, and capricious destroyers gave rise to a wide range of sayings, amulets, and bizarre superstitions among Jewish communities from Morocco, to Palestine, to Poland, to Yemen, to the immigrant tenements of Western Europe and the United States. This underlying fear of misfortune—of the "evil eye" drawn to success or good fortune—is, of course, a part of the timeless mystical and magical heritage of Judaism.

Yet the Kabbalah did not endure within Judaism solely as a folk religion. Here and there throughout the Jewish world, a few independent kabbalistic circles continued—even in the wake of the Sabbetean debacle—retreating into the depth of meditation and study, and closely guarding their secrets to all but a few select students. The most famous of these centers was the Bet El Yeshiva founded in Jerusalem in 1737, and made famous by its leader, the Yemenite rabbi Shalom Mizrahi Sharabi. In his intense concentration on the deeper meaning of the Lurianic theories, he and his students entirely withdrew from the affairs of the outside world to effect the task of lifting the sparks and the Tikkun of the world through inner meditation and prayer. This withdrawal from political activism or even participation in the leadership of the community had often been the characteristic response to great failures of apocalyptic or messianic expectations. Drawing inward, the lore was preserved and the faith maintained until God's larger plan for the final unfolding of history was made clear. Thus through the eighteenth and nineteenth centuries, closed—almost monastic— kabbalistic centers arose throughout Eastern Europe, remaining distinct from the courts of the Hasidic rebbes, and maintaining their own, deeply scholarly interest in the classics of kabbalistic literature. In many cases, they were responsible for the collection and editing of ancient manuscripts of the great kabbalistic classics, many of which were not published in book form—and general made available for study—until the nine-teenth century. Through both these channels of spiritual trans-mission, the popular and the scholarly, the Kabbalah continued to spread its basic teaching that an endless state of suffering was not the ultimate destiny of the Jews in exile. Though the time was not yet ripe for action, by understanding the workings of the heavenly powers, students of the Kabbalah could imag-ine an actual end to that suffering—and perhaps even help bring it about.

There were, of course, some bizarre postscripts—like the strange tale of the Frankists who took the Sabbatean idea of de-scending into the realm of evil into the realm of outright heresy. This movement flourished in the 1760s and 1770s, led by a one-time cloth and jewel trader named Jacob ben Judah Leib. He was better known as Jacob "Frank" for the opulent oriental garb he favored (since the Ashkenazi communities of Eastern Europe through which he traveled were used to calling the sephardic Jews of the Middle East "Franks"). Jacob Frank de-clared that all religions were just outward garments for the truly righteous, who were entitled to regard them as costumes, to be put on and taken off at will. At the core of the Frankist belief lay a strange simplification of kabbalistic doctrine: in which God the Father was a distant and unapproachable entity, roughly equivalent to the Ein Sof; the "King of Kings," the beneficent object of all worship, roughly equivalent to the sefirah Tiferet; and the "maiden," or "Virgin," roughly equivalent to the sefirah Malchut or Skekhinah, who was closely connected to the "King of Kings." Seeing himself as the last incarnation of the soul of the "King of Kings"—of which, he claimed, Jesus was an ear-lier occupant—Frank appointed twelve disciples and twelve "sisters," who served as his concubines in the mystical rites of union between Virgin and King.

In their disdain for the distinctly unmystical rituals and legal practices of the established rabbis, Frank and his followers served the Polish church as willing witnesses for the prosecu-tion against the Jewish communities of Poland in a series of unpleasant disputations, which led to the public burning of the

Talmud and waves of by-now routine pogroms. But by the time of Frank's death in 1791, the hunger for mysticism was declining. The first signs of Emancipation had offered to a wide spectrum of the Jewish population of Western Europe increasingly free access to the wider society. And with the gradual opening up of Western European intellectual life to Jewish participation, the Enlightenment cult of Reason and the astronomers' Music of the Spheres came to replace the reliance of many on sefirot, klippot, and hidden sparks as tools with which to understand the deeper workings of the universe.

Along with modern concepts of reason and science came a concerted attack on the Kabbalah itself. In the bitter disputes and recriminations that followed the humiliating collapse of the Sabbatean movement, outspoken leaders of mainstream Judaism—like Rabbi Jacob Emden in Germany—challenged the supposed antiquity of the Zohar and declared that the kabbalistic tradition had brought great misfortune, not redemption, to the People of Israel. In the battle between the rabbinical establishment and the Hasidic movement of Eastern Europe, the Kabbalah was further discredited by the leadership of European Jewry. Yet with the establishment of university-based studies of Jewish texts and history in European institutions of higher learning in the nineteenth century, the criticism of the Kabbalah became even more bitter and dismissive even if—as the modern scholar Moshe Idel has pointed out—there were several noted Jewish scholars like Adolphe Franck in France and Nahman Krochmal in Poland who considered the Kabbalah to be the last remnant of an ancient, mystical faith.

The loudest and most forceful voices were the least sympathetic to the kabbalistic tradition. Foremost among them was Heinrich Graetz, the pioneering modern historian of the People of Israel. His ponderous, twelve-volume *Geschichte der Juden*, "History of the Jews" (1851–1876), portrayed the history of the Jewish people as an epic of national will and destiny, played out across the centuries in strangely modern, nationalistic terms. For Graetz, the Kabbalah was nothing more than a backward superstition, an anti-rational reaction. Dismissing the value of the tradition, he argued that it held back the Jewish people in a medieval state of mind concerned with spirits, phantoms, and demons—when they would be far better off to abandon such primitive beliefs and become progressive citizens of the industrializing world. Graetz's estimation of the Kabbalah was far from unique; it was shared by other noted Jewish historians such as Moritz Steinschneider and Leopold Zunz.

Yet in a generation of young German Jews who came of age during the horrors and insanities of World War I, the old schoolboy faith in the rise of civilization—Jewish or European—simply did not have the same convincing force as it had possessed in the time of Bismarck. For those who sought a deeper spirituality in their Jewish tradition, it was almost too late to save the Kabbalah's rich mystical lore. As the Jewish communities of Eastern Europe began to disintegrate from large-scale immigration, communist reorganization, and ultimately the genocide and plunder of the Holocaust, the collections of centuries of kabbalistic writings (most still in manuscript) were in danger of complete destruction. And if there is a single hero in the modern Kabbalah story, it would not be a mystic rabbi, chanting incantations in a darkened cemetery or prayer room, but an acerbic German intellectual named Gershom Gerhard Scholem. In his capacity as librarian and, later, professor of Jewish mysticism at the Hebrew University of Jerusalem (1923–1965), he tirelessly combed through musty archives in Jerusalem, Berlin, London, New York, and among the ancient rabbinic centers of Poland and Lithuania.

During the 1920s and 1930s, as the war clouds darkened, he reaped the last great harvest of kabbalistic knowledge. For time was short before the forces of Nazism nearly succeeded in wiping out the physical traces and even the surviving memories of a culture that had existed for hundreds of years. And as that world crumbled, Scholem rescued the greatest monuments of the Kabbalah—on parchment, in pamphlets, in handwritten letters, and yellowed books. His single greatest achievement, his book *Major Trends in Jewish Mysticism*, published in 1941, divided the history of the Kabbalah into clearly defined periods and ended with the summary on the importance of mystical thinking in the modern world.

Scholem's passion—beyond the boxed chocolates that he gobbled with an addict's fervor—was the discovery of obscure manuscripts that contained the legends and the symbols of heavenly realms and heavenly prayers that had lapsed into obscurity, whose authors were forgotten, or whose historical context was completely misunderstood. Like a mystical archaeologist, fitting together sherds to form complete shapes and setting them in proper chronological order, he only gradually overcame the decades of reticence that had considered the Kabbalah a magical sideshow and the superstitious underbelly to the noble, civilized face of Judaism. Scholem was convinced that the Kabbalah represented a creative strain in the Jewish experience, one that interpreted the traditional motifs in innovative mythologies and was a force for creativity and adaptation through some of the most difficult episodes of Jewish history.

Yet in his own heart—according to his own admission—Scholem was not a true mystic. He half-jokingly remarked that he approached his study of the Kabbalah with the soul of a certified public accountant, carefully cataloguing and registering other people's mystical treasures but never even tempted to claim any of those treasures for himself. Despite the upheavals taking place in the world around him—Holocaust, world war, and the rise of the state of Israel—he never attempted to realign the sefirot through meditation or to summon Samael and destroy him, so as to hasten the time of redemption. Nor have his many students—chief among them Scholem's protégé, Moshe Idel of the Hebrew University—gone beyond the work of maintaining the spiritual ledger, adding the assets of new clients, and noting and arranging the sequence of ideas but never really believing that the world could be changed.

That was left to others, particularly in the decades that followed the Holocaust, when the sheer horror of the destruction of most of European Jewry caused a renewed interest in the ultimate questions of good and evil addressed by the Kabbalah. Through the centuries, the kabbalistic tradition had always expressed the utopian dreams of the oppressed and down-trodden, concerned to show that the present disposition of powers—in which evil seemed to reign unchallenged and good-ness seemed subject to violence and exploitation—was not the true heavenly state of affairs. Kabbalistic explanations formu-lated in the shocked silence after the Holocaust maintained that perspective, seeing inscrutable heavenly actions behind the hor-rors of concentration camps and mass extermination, working their way inexorably and inevitably for the surviving remnant of the People of Israel, leading them toward messianic times.

In the newly established State of Israel, those questions of good and evil began to be framed in an entirely new context—of an independent state rather than a scattered Diaspora people. And some of the concepts of light and darkness began to take on dramatically new meanings in that setting of government, armies, and continuing war. During the early twentieth cen-tury, some innovative mystical thinkers—chief among them Abraham Isaac Kook (1865–1935), the first Chief Ashkenazi rabbi of Palestine—had suggested how the rebuilding of the Land of Israel by Jews returning from a scattered, Diaspora ex-istence could be seen as a powerful metaphor for the revival of the long-exiled Shekhinah—and through it, the reconstruction of the world. This had been the goal of the sixteenth-century kabbalists of the Ottoman Empire in their mass migration to Safed, but they had never conceived of a sovereign state in the Galilee. But now with the establishment of the independent State of Israel in the midst of a long-running war with its Arab neighbors, vivid kabbalistic images took on a new meaning. The mystical belief in the unending battle between light and dark-ness and good and evil—waged simultaneously in heaven and earth—offered a striking metaphysical subtext to a modern con-flict waged by tanks and fighter planes.

More than that, the land over which Arabs and Jews battled was itself seen as an embodiment of the Shekhinah, the tenth and last of the life-giving sefirot. The Castilian kabbalists in the Middle Ages had imagined the Shekhinah (conceived of as the People of Israel) to be caught in the clutches of the forces of evil. In the sixteenth century, the Shekhinah was personified as the Mishnah, or the Holy Mother of Israel in distress. But in our own times, that personification has become vividly territorial: the occupation of any part of the sacred Land of Israel by Palestinian or other Arab forces is now seen by some kabbalists as a challenge to the free flow of divine energy to the People of Israel—and a threat to the sacred balance of the world.

In the aftermath of the 1967 War, the kabbalistic territorial view became a mystical rationale for territorial maximalism. At least in some radical circles, particularly among followers of the modern mystical leader Rabbi Zvi Yehudah Kook—son of Rabbi Abraham Isaac Kook—the settlement of the entire Land of Israel west of the Jordan became a tactic to maintain control over the entirety of the Holy Land. Their practical and mystical goal was to prevent its falling into the grasp of the forces they saw as earthly representatives of the Other Side. And here it is possible to see how entirely traditional kabbalistic images and mythologies—that had been developing for centuries—burst suddenly into the world's current affairs. For in the eyes of the territorial mystics, any Israeli leader who would willingly give up any part of the Land of Israel/Shekhinah to the demonic forces had become, if not a dangerous demon, then at least an unwitting helper of Samael. Light and darkness could never compromise, shake hands, or sign peace treaties. And this branch of kabbalistic thinking, now deeply influential in the ideology of the modern Israeli religious settlement movement—with a voice in the on-and-off Arab–Israeli peace process—has enormous implications for the world.

In Europe and America—far from the battlefields and killing grounds of the Middle East—the Kabbalah has taken on a far milder demeanor. It has become, for the most part, a Jewish variation on a New Age theme. The deadening conformity and materialism of post-war urban life in the West had led to a painful decline in spirituality. And for many, religion had become little more than a comfortable piety of privilege and position, of expensive places of worship and conservative political stands. Thus it was almost inevitable, in an age of alternative medicine, alternative lifestyles, and alternative identities, that the bits and pieces of the Kabbalah that had survived through the centuries would appeal to at least some segments of the Jewish public again. But this was neither the Kabbalah of national ethical renewal nor of territorial Holy War. It was the Kabbalah of slick workbooks and glib aphorisms, presented in attractive packaging to all who were willing to pay for the lessons and purchase the required books and tapes. It was a Kabbalah that contained some of the most important concepts, of Ein Sof, of sefirot, of lost sparks, and of the union between male and female principles within the heavenly realm. But it was directed not toward the People of Israel but to harried professionals and upwardly mobile individuals, whether Jewish or Gentile.

These are but the latest developments in a continuing process. For from the beginning of the tradition with Ezekiel's searing heavenly vision, the tradition known as the Kabbalah has offered a way to pierce through the conventional wisdom that more often than not was the conventional wisdom of priests, potentates, and kings. As we have seen, the first great visions of heavenly powers and divine forces fueled the quest for freedom of the People of Israel against their Greek and Roman overlords. And later, when the rabbinical sages had recognized the futility of physical resistance, the Merkabah mystics and early Baalei Shem challenged the power of the patriarchs, gaons, and great academies as the only channels of access to the power of God. On and on the controversies swirled through the Middle Ages, through the Golden Age of Spain and the bitter years of exile and wandering. But in every era and epoch the crystallizing doctrines of the Kabbalah provided a heavenly alternative to the self-serving ideologies of the powers that be.

In the world of the twenty-first century, the Kabbalah cannot take the place of science. Hydraulic lifts, antibiotics, and silicon chips can accomplish far more in practical terms than even the most potent Kabbalistic prayers, spells, or charms. Likewise, the reliance by students of Jewish mystical tradition on charismatic leaders, would-be Messiahs, and gurus is a dangerous, if already well-worn, path to tread. In our time, when men's and women's souls—stripped naked of spirituality in the fires of secularization—are often so defenseless against the beautiful mystical metaphor or glib biblical turn of phrase, the Kabbalah's vivid images can offer a feeling of order and sense in an otherwise chaotic world. Yet that is not to say that the Kabbalah has no value beyond its immediate historical context, beyond the pleasing counter images and ideologies it offers against the tyrants and oppressors of every period.

The Kabbalah's greatest power is its vision of an intimate connection between an earthly and heavenly order, and the possibility that humanity may have a crucial role to play in bringing it about. The ideals of heavenly balance loom just out of reach on the horizon, and that was the core of Ezekiel's vision of the Chariot twenty-five hundred years ago. In its wide varieties of forms and expressions, still evolving as we enter a new millennium, the Kabbalah has a great deal to teach about the carefully patterned forces of creation and the role of evil in the very structure of the universe. At the meeting point of politics, theology, economics, and philosophy, the Kabbalah can teach us to see creation as a place of constant struggle between domination and resistance, between slavery and freedom. And with that insight comes involvement. At the hidden heart of the Jewish mystical tradition lies our shared responsibility of looking beyond surface appearances, and—in whatever way we are capable—helping restore balance to the world.

BIBLIOGRAPHICAL NOTES

PROLOGUE: SECRETS OF CREATION

The difficulty of finding a good introduction to the Kabbalah is obvious to anyone who has approached the subject. The challenge is locating basic works that are not completely accepting of kabbalistic doctrine and, at the same time, not coldly scholarly. I have tried to include here a wide selection of books and articles — in English wherever possible — that can serve as the basis for further reading about concepts, personalities, and issues raised in this book. Yet I have also come to realize that much more than a passing acquaintance with the Kabbalah's symbols and concepts is necessary if one is even to begin to appreciate its profound spiritual depths. For the Kabbalah is not a neat system whose symbols have unambiguous meanings. Each time its central mystical concepts are expressed in sermons or written texts, they are cloaked in different earthly guises. And it is only with the recognition of the larger meaning of the *clusters* of symbols that have, over the centuries, come to represent each of the sefirot and processes of creation that the deeper study of the Kabbalah can even begin.

That is not to say that there are not dozens of enlightening introductions. Among the most recent and important are Matt, *The Essential Kab-*

balah; Cooper, *God Is a Verb;* Epstein, *Kabbalah;* and Bokser, *Jewish Mystical Tradition.* Dozens more are available; one's selection of an introduction is largely a matter of finding an author whose style and choice of symbolism somehow evoke meaningful associations in the reader's mind.

Among the scholarly works on the Kabbalah and its history, the most important are in Hebrew, though there have been an increasing number of significant publications in English in recent years. The voluminous writings of Gershom Scholem (1897–1982) are still the first and basic source. I will refer to them repeatedly in the bibliographical notes. Among his English books, his compendium *Kabbalah,* compiled from his contributions to the *Encyclopedia Judaica,* is still by far the best general introduction to the concepts, histories, and personalities of the Kabbalah. Readers interested in exploring specific subjects should first consult Scholem's many authoritative articles in this work. In addition, his path-breaking book *Major Trends in Jewish Mysticism* is the foundation for every subsequent attempt at tracing the history of the Kabbalah—including this one. Of his other writings that have been translated into English, special mention must be made of *On the Mystical Shape of the Godhead; On the Kabbalah and Its Symbolism;* and *The Messianic Idea in Judaism.* All of them are collections of lectures and articles that embody Scholem's eclectic and far-reaching mastery of the secular study of the Kabbalah.

In recent years, a vast literature has arisen to assess the character and extent of Scholem's intellectual impact. Among the most noteworthy are Alter, *Necessary Angels;* Biale, *Gershom Scholem;* Bloom, *Gershom Scholem;* and Dan, *Gershom Scholem and the Mystical Dimension of Jewish History.* In addition, a volume of essays has been published assessing Scholem's major work from the vantage point of a half-century of reflection. See Schäfer and Dan, *Gershom Scholem's Major Trends.*

Professor Moshe Idel of the Hebrew University is among the most active protégés of Scholem today and has become one of the chief critics and refiners of Scholem's early ideas. Idel has himself produced an astonishingly vast body of work on nearly every phase of the Kabbalah, its theology, and history. While most of his specialist articles are in Hebrew, a good introduction to the range of his scholarship, with extensive bibliography, can be found in his *Kabbalah: New Perspectives.* Among the other students of Scholem who have become major forces in the modern scholarly study of the Kabbalah are Isaiah Tishby, Joseph Dan, and Yehudah Liebes. Their works will be mentioned throughout these bibliographical notes. For an enlightening general survey of current developments in the study of the Kabbalah, see Liebes, "New Directions."

Among the new generation of American scholars who have concentrated on the ideology and history of the Kabbalah, special mention should be made of the works of Eliot Wolfson's *Through a Speculum That Shines,*

Along the Path, and *Circle in the Square*, and Lawrence Fine's *Safed Spirituality*. With regard to the general intellectual, scientific, and spiritual history of European Jews during the Renaissance, particularly in Italy, the studies of David Ruderman (among them, *Kabbalah, Magic, and Science* and *Valley of Vision*) are essential reading.

On the modern comparisons between the basic concepts of Kabbalah and astrophysics, see Matt, *God and the Big Bang*, and Friedman, *The Disappearance of God*. For personal descriptions of modern kabbalistic masters and scholars, see the classic work by Weiner, *9 1/2 Mystics*, and more recently, Kamenetz, *Stalking Elijah*. The celebrity-driven kabbalistic renaissance in America of the late 1990s has been extensively documented in the popular press. Hundreds of centers all over the world have been opened for its non-traditional study, and literally thousands of Internet websites offer courses, pamphlets, cassette tapes, and books. Among the countless journalistic accounts of this media phenomenon are Van Biema, "Pop Goes the Kabbalah," and Musleah, "Accessing the Mysteries of the Kabbalah."

CHAPTER 1: VISIONS OF THE CHARIOT

The most thorough and authoritative commentary on the Book of Ezekiel in English is Greenberg, *Ezekiel*, containing extensive essays on the book's historical background, literary development, and a bibliography current to 1983. For a detailed analysis of the image of the divine Chariot as it first appears in Chapter 1 of the Book of Ezekiel and for a reconstruction of its subsequent development in Jewish tradition, see Halperin, *Faces of the Chariot*. I have used the Revised Standard Version for the biblical quotations in this chapter.

The political background of the immediate pre-exilic period in the kingdom of Judah is sketched in Malamat, "The Last Years." For the well-known archaeological evidence for the Babylonian Exile, see W. F. Albright's classic article "King Joiachin." Among the recent studies of the social status of exiled groups in Babylonia is Eph'al, "The Western Minorities."

The circumstances for the emergence of a mystical apocalypticism in the post-exilic period are described in Hanson, *The Dawn of Apocalyptic*. For the social background of this religious ideology in the Persian period in particular, see Berquist, *Judaism in Persia's Shadow*, and for the Hellenistic period, Hengel, *Judaism and Hellenism*, a two-volume compendium of social, political, and religious history. On the roots of some specific mystical motifs, see Gruenwald, "Reflections on the Nature and Origins of Jewish Mysticism." Perhaps the most thorough treatment of this subject, with an analysis of the relevant literature, is Collins, *The Apocalyptic Imagination*. Moshe Idel deals with the transformation of the identity of a central mystical character in "Enoch is Metatron." In *Faces of the Chariot*,

Halperin notes how the Book of Daniel transforms Ezekiel's original Chariot motif in a new political environment—and literary genre.

Though condemned to the wilderness of Dead Sea Scroll scholarship for his own strong views on the radicalism of the Qumran community, Robert Eisenman is the only scholar, I believe, to have fully expressed the practical, earthly implications of the apocalyptic orientation of the Qumran community. See especially his *Maccabees, Zadokites, and Qumran* and *James the Brother of Jesus*. In a similar vein, Richard Horsley stresses the political dimensions of apocalyptic rhetoric in *Jesus and the Spiral of Violence* and *The Message and the Kingdom*. The political and religious ideology of the First Revolt against Rome has been sketched by Martin Hengel in *The Zealots*, especially as it represents a continuation of earlier religious expressions and trends.

The continuation of messianic hopes even after the bloody defeat of the First Revolt is detailed, with references, in Silver, *A History*. For a comprehensive general survey of the post-70 C.E. period in the Land of Israel, see Alon, *The Jews in Their Land*, and Avi Yonah, *The Jews of Palestine*, for the period after the Bar-Kokhba Revolt. Among the most important recent works on the Second Revolt is Mor, *The Bar Kokhba Revolt*. Two concise and readable introductions to the developments of this period are Schiffman, *From Text to Tradition*, and Shanks, *Christianity and Rabbinic Judaism*.

I am again indebted to Halperin, *Faces of the Chariot*, for his vivid and provocative reconstruction of the central role played by the Chariot vision in the Shavuot synagogue services in Roman Palestine. For the architecture of the ancient synagogue in this period, see the surveys in Levine, "The Revolutionary Effects," and Fine, *Sacred Realm*. The prominent place held by a representation of the zodiac circles in a number of ancient synagogues is assessed by Hachlili, "The Zodiac," and by Ness, "Astrology." For a suggestion about their function and significance, see Dothan, *Hammath Tiberias*: 68–70.

On the general background of the Hekhalot literature and the interpretive problems it has aroused, see, among many, Scholem, *Jewish Gnosticism*; Gruenwald, *Apocalyptic and Merkavah Mysticism*; and Dan, *The Ancient Jewish Mysticism*. Definitive editions of the various texts of the Hekhalot literature have been published in German translation by Schäfer, in his *Hekhalot-Studien*. For his more general survey of the importance of magical practices in this tradition, see his articles "Merkavah, Mysticism, and Magic" and "Jewish Magic Literature." Additional insights into the social context of this magico-mystical activity is provided in Halperin, *Visions of the Chariot*. For a similar sociological approach to the history and function of the Hekhalot literature, see Chernus, "Individual and Community." Another important recent study is Dan, "On the Problem of the Historical Status." The famous talmudic story of the Four Sages who entered Paradise comes from B. Hag. 14b. The English version is quoted in Schwartz, *Gabriel's Palace:* 51–2.

A useful English translation and commentary of the *Sefer Yetzirah* is by Kaplan. For a more skeptical view of the supposed antiquity of mystical reflections on Genesis, see Goshen Gottstein, "Ma'aseh Bereshit."

On the issue of "Godfearers" and relations between Jews and Gentiles throughout the Roman period, see, most recently, Feldman, *Jew and Gentile in the Ancient World.* The messianic texts of the late Roman period are briefly surveyed in Silver, *A History,* and an intriguing reconstruction of Jewish apocalypticism in the decades before the Muslim conquests is provided in the highly controversial book by Crone and Cook, *Hagarism,* which sees Jewish religious influence initially dominant in the anti-Byzantine resistance movement. For one of the original texts, see Lewis, "An Apocalyptic Vision."

The conquest of Jerusalem by Umar ibn al-Khattab and the subsequent social and political changes in Palestine are detailed in Gil, *History of Palestine.* The archaeological evidence is presented in Whitcomb, "Islam and the Socio-Cultural Transition." Halperin, in *The Faces of the Chariot,* has underlined the Jewish mystical motifs adopted by Early Islam.

For the changing economic and political circumstances of the Jewish communities of Babylonia, see Gafni, *The Jews of Babylonia;* and Neusner, *History of the Jews of Babylonia* and *School, Court, Public Administration.* The rise of the Abbasids and the larger economic implications of the establishment of Baghdad is examined in Hodges and Whitehouse, *Mohammed, Charlemagne, and the Origins of Europe.* The gradual crystallization of dissenting sects and protest movements within Babylonian Jewry is surveyed in volume five of Salo Baron's classic *Social and Religious History of the Jews.*

Among the many surviving works of Jewish magic of Late Antiquity, perhaps the most famous are *Sefer ha-Razim* (English translation by Morgan) and the *Harba de-Moshe,* "The Sword of Moses" (translation included in Gaster and Daiches). Another important text published by Scholem is "Havdalah of Rabbi Akiva." The scholarly literature on popular religion in the talmudic period is considerable. Collections of Aramaic amulets from Nippur were published by Montgomery early in the century in *Aramaic Incantation Texts.* More recently, Naveh and Shaked have analyzed a wide range of materials from Babylonia as well as Egypt and Israel in *Magic Spells and Formulae.* Although later in date, some examples from the Cairo Genizah offer evidence of the coherence of this long tradition of popular Jewish religion; see Schiffman and Swartz, *Hebrew Incantation Texts.* The basic components and formulae of traditional Jewish amulets are analyzed in Frenkel, *The Hebrew Amulet.*

On the character of the international traders originating in Iraq, see

Gil, "Radhanite Merchants." The establishment and expansion of the Jewish community in al-Qayrawan has recently been examined by Ben-Sasson in *Flowering of the Jewish Community.* On the influence and power of the gaonim in Babylonian Jewish society, see Brody, *The Geonim.* For the particular reactions to and participation in mystical pursuits by Sherira Gaon and his son Hai Gaon, see Hildesheimer, *Mystik und Agada.* The text of the report about the North African Baalei Shem and Hai Gaon's response to them is quoted in Scholem, *Major Trends:* 49.

CHAPTER 2: GOD'S MANY FACES

The best single source on Jewish life and communal institutions in Europe up to the Crusades is Roth, *The Dark Ages.* As a volume in the World History of the Jewish People Series, it includes overall thematic surveys of religious, economic, and political history, as well as regional studies. See also Baron, *Social and Religious History,* for an earlier and somewhat less detailed view. Recent studies of aspects of Jewish life in the Middle Ages include Mark Cohen, *Under Crescent and Cross,* and, particularly for the uneasy integration of Jews into the increasingly monetarized commercial economy of Europe, Little, *Religious Poverty and Profit.*

The traditions and culture of the Jews of southern Italy in the early Middle Ages are explored in the essays on "Italy in the Dark Ages" and "The Beginning of Hebrew Poetry in Italy" in Roth, *Dark Ages.* An English translation and commentary to the Megillat Yuhasin is provided by Salzman, *Chronicle.* The quotation on the spiritual gifts of Amittai's sons comes from Salzman, *Chronicle:* 62. For more background on the magical practices associated with Abu Aharon and the family of Amittai, see Dan's article, "The Beginnings of Jewish Mysticism in Europe" in Roth, *Dark Ages.*

On the life and writings of Shabbetai Donnolo, see Scharf, *The Universe.* The story of the Four Captives is contained in the Sefer ha-Kabbalah of Abraham ibn Daud, and was translated into English and accompanied by commentary by Gerson Cohen, *A Critical Edition:* 46–49, 63–67.

The most exhaustive study of the historical background of the Kalonymus family is Grossman, "Immigration." For more general background on the history of the Jews in the Carolingian empire, see Schwarzfuch's essay, "The Jews Under the Carolingians," in Roth, *Dark Ages,* and Baron, *Social and Religious History.* For an intriguing archaeological analysis of the growth of trade in Dark Age Europe, see Hodges and Whitehouse, *Mohammed, Charlemagne.* Archbishop Agobard's contemptuous description of Jewish worship based on the Shi'ur Komah comes from his tract *De judaicis superstitionibus,* "On the Superstitions of the Jews." For background of Agobard's life and descriptions of his other writings, see Cabaniss, *Agobard.*

The literature on the Crusades is extensive, but for the specific theme of the destruction of Jewish communities within Europe, see Chazan, *In the Year 1096* and *European Jewry*. For first-hand accounts of the massacres, see Eidelberg, *Jews and the Crusaders*. The account by Baron in *Social and Religious History*, Vol. IV, stresses the leadership role taken in the Rhineland by Kalonymus ben Meshullam.

A basic if somewhat uncritical examination of the spiritual and supernatural beliefs of the Hasidei Ashkenaz is Trachtenberg, *Jewish Magic*. See also Nigal, *Magic, Mysticism*, for the wider impact of magical beliefs on Jewish tradition. For Ivan Marcus's interpretation of the social significance of the medieval Ashkenazi Hasidic movement, see his "The Historical Meaning of the Hasidei Ashkenaz" and "The Politics and Ethics of Pietism." His more comprehensive work on the Hasidei Ashkenaz is *Piety and Society*. An English translation and commentary on Sefer Hasidim has been published by Finkel. Scholem's chapter on the Hasidei Ashkenaz in *Major Trends* was the first major historical study; the account of the penitential ritual appears on p. 106. For Judah the Hasid's objection to profiteering, see Marcus, "Politics and Ethics": 234–235.

On the general background of religion and society in Languedoc and the rise of the Cathars, see Wakefield, *Heresy, Crusade*; Costen, *Cathars*; and Sumption, *The Albigensian Crusade*. Some possible theological connections between the Cathars and the early kabbalists are explored in Shachar, "Catharism." For a thoughtful historical reconstruction of the development of Jewish mysticism from the esotericism of the Yordei Merkabah to the redactors of the Sefer Bahir, see Gruenwald, "Jewish Mysticism." A recent English translation of the Sefer Bahir, with commentary, has been published by Kaplan.

In his authoritative analysis of the Sefer Bahir in *Origins of the Kabbalah*, Scholem speculated that at least some of the sources for the present text came from the Near East. An intriguing suggestion that the kabbalistic Tree of Life can be traced back to ancient Mesopotamia was made by Parpola in "The Assyrian Tree of Life." For an entirely different explanation of the origin of the Tree of Life motif, see Wolfson, "The Tree That Is All."

The most detailed examination of the mystical thought of the first kabbalists in Provence is Scholem, *Origins of the Kabbalah*. Twersky, *Rabad of Posquières*, provides a biographical study of one of the early leaders of this movement. On the writings of a particular group of Provençal mystics, see Verman, "The Evolution of the Circle of Contemplation." For an analysis of the tensions within the Jewish community of Provence in the wake of the Albigensian Crusade that led to public attacks on the Kabbalah by Rabbi Meir ben Simon, see Stein, *Jewish-Christian Disputations*. Rabbi Meir's scornful comments on the Sefer Bahir are quoted in Neubauer, "The Bahir."

CHAPTER 3: LIGHT AGAINST DARKNESS

The basic work on Jewish society in late medieval Spain remains Baer, *A History of the Jews*. For readable introductions, see Gerber, *The Jews of Spain*, and Sachar, *Farewell España*.

Scholem devoted a series of lectures at the Hebrew University to the unique mystical developments in Gerona; they were published as *The Kabbalah in Gerona*. The last chapter of his *Origins of the Kabbalah* is also devoted to the Gerona school, the influence of their ideas, and the controversies they aroused. The quotation on the first use of the term "Kabbalah" in its later sense was quoted in *Origins*: 38. The importance of outreach to the general public by the kabbalists of Gerona is stressed by Dan, *Jewish Mysticism and Jewish Ethics*. The letter of Rabbi Isaac to his former students in Gerona is quoted in Scholem, *Origins*: 394–395. For background on the politics and culture of the kingdom of Catalonia-Aragon in this period, see Hillgarth, *The Problem*, and Burns, *The Worlds of Alfonso the Learned*.

On the unique, yet influential brand of meditative kabbalah founded in Barcelona by Abraham Abulafia, see Idel, *The Mystical Experience* and *Studies in Ecstatic Kabbalah*.

Among Scholem's early interests in his historical study of the Kabbalah was the origin of the intensely dualistic brand of mystical speculation that arose in Castile in the early thirteenth century. His pioneering article—actually a monograph—on the works of the ha-Cohen brothers of Soria is "The Kabbalah of Rabbi Jacob." This kabbalistic school has also been the subject of numerous studies by Joseph Dan; see his "Emergence of Messianic Mythology" and "Samael, Lillith, and the Concept of Evil." For an assessment of the originality of the concept of evil in early Castilian Kabbalah, see Oron, "Castilian Kabbalah."

One of the great mysteries in the study of the history of the Kabbalah is the extent to which widely scattered groups of Jewish mystics were in contact. Kanarfogel, "Rabbinic Figures," attempts to trace some connections in the period leading up to the fourteenth century.

A partial English translation of the Zohar is Sperling and Simon, *The Zohar*. A topical arrangement of translated passages, with comprehensive introductions and extensive bibliography, can be found in Tishby, *The Wisdom of the Zohar*. For selections of excerpts, with introductions, see Matt, *Zohar*; and Scholem, *Zohar*. The process of assembling the traditions incorporated in the Zohar is reconstructed by Liebes in "How Was the Zohar Composed?" This essay and several others on the history and ideology of the Zohar were collected in his book *Studies in the Zohar*.

For a readable survey of the broader background of Castilian society during the period of the Reconquista and before, see MacKay, *Spain in the Middle Ages*, as well as his collected essays in *Society, Economy, and Religion*. For the court ideology and political career of Alfonso X, see Burns, *The*

Worlds of Alfonso and *Emperor of Culture;* O'Callaghan, *The Learned King;* and Socarras, *Alfonso X.* For the king's legal innovations with regard to the Jews of his kingdom, see Carpenter, *Alfonso X and the Jews.*

The pioneering study of the politics of the later Zoharic works is Baer, "The Historical Background." For parallel protest movements within the church, see Little, *Religious Poverty.* The leadership of Don Todros and the rise and disappearance of the Prophet of Avila is detailed in Baer, *History.* For the messianic fervor of the time and its associated texts, see Silver, *History.*

CHAPTER 4: CONFRONTING THE DEMONS

The travels of Rabbi Isaac of Acre to Castile in search of the origins of the Zohar were first explored in Scholem, *Major Trends.* The reported admission by Rabbi Moses de Leon that *he* was the author of the Zohar is quoted on pp. 190–191. The complex process of authorship, as noted above, is analyzed in Liebes, "How Was the Zohar Written?"

For the physical persecution and ideological process of demonization experienced by the Jews of Europe — as well as for the Jewish experience under Islam — see Cohen, *Under Crescent and Cross.* See also the still classic work by Trachtenberg, *The Devil and the Jews.* For a recent exhaustive study of the roots of anti-Semitism and anti-Jewish laws and policies in Spain, see Netanyahu, *The Origins of the Inquisition.*

Theological developments among the Jews of medieval Spain are traced in Oron, "Doctrine of Evil." Earlier attempts by modern scholars to analyze the background of the messianic enthusiasm of the period are analyzed by Schatz in "Toward the Character." A recent and enlightening study of the religious ritual and expression of the *conversos* is Gitlitz, *Secrecy and Deceit.*

For the practical implications of heavenly advisors and divine revelation in Sefer ha-Meshiv, see Idel, "Inquiries in the Doctrine" and "The Attitude to Christianity." The various versions of the story of Joseph della Reina are analyzed in Dan, "The Story of Rabbi Joseph."

The course of the final liquidation of the Jewish community in Spain is detailed in Baer, *History.* Baer also identified a particular brand of messianic anticipation that arose among the Jews of Spain at this time. See his "Messianic Movement." Other important studies of kabbalistic messianism in the fifteenth and early sixteenth centuries are Aescoly, *Jewish Messianic Movements,* and Silver, *History.* An important article recently translated into English is Tishby, "Acute Apocalyptic Messianism." For an enlightening discussion of the wider cultural and political background of Jewish messianic movements in this period, see Ruderman, "Hope Against Hope."

The recent scholarly estimates of the numbers of Jews involved in the exile from Spain are compared and assessed in Gitlitz, *Secrecy and Deceit.* On the economic implications of the expansion of the Ottoman Empire around the time of the expulsion from Spain, see Brummett, *Ottoman Seapower.* A good introduction to the history of Ottoman Jewry is Shaw, *The Jews.*

An English translation of the journal of David Reubeni was published in *Jewish Travellers.* For varying opinions about Reubeni's origins and identity, see Aescoly's commentary on Reubeni's journal, *The Story of David Reubeni,* and Cassuto, "Who Was David Reubeni?," who argues forcefully for Reubeni's Ethiopian origin.

On Solomon Molcho's apocalyptic ideology and its possible sources, see Schatz, "The Influence of Gnostic Literature." Moshe Idel has examined the importance of magic in the Renaissance and its influence on the legend of Rabbi Joseph della Reina, the career of Solomon Molcho, and the important kabbalistic work Sefer ha-Meshiv in "Jewish Magic" and "Solomon Molcho as a Magician." The first scholar to stress the importance of the Sefer ha-Meshiv for the Balkan kabbalists was, of course, Scholem, in his pioneering article "The 'Maggid' of R. Yosef Taitazak."

Two basic works on the establishment of a Jewish textile industry in the Ottoman provinces of the Balkans following the expulsion from Spain are Avitzur, "Toward a History of the Woolen Textile Industry," and Schochet, " 'Royal Garments' in Salonika." For a more general evaluation of the importance of the industry and its changing fortunes, see Braude, "Salonika Textile Industry." An important reference for the social and political — as well as economic — history of the Iberian immigrants to the Ottoman Empire, including details of the textile industry, is Ankori, *From Lisbon to Salonika.* For a rich collection of artifacts and analysis of material culture, see Juhasz, *Sephardi Jews.*

For the details of the early kabbalistic brotherhoods in the Balkans, see Werblowsky, *Joseph Karo.* The fact that the Golden Age of Safed has its roots in these earlier mystical associations has not always been stressed enough. Rachel Elior has attempted to reconstruct one facet of the theology of these groups in her article "The Doctrine of Transmigration." For an analysis of Alkabetz's farewell sermon in Salonika, see Pachter, "R. Shelomo Alkabetz's Departure Sermon." The excerpt from Alkabetz's letter describing Caro's encounter with the heavenly intermediary is quoted in Jacobs, *Jewish Mystical Testimonies:* 122–151.

CHAPTER 5: A MYSTICAL CITY

Among the earliest and most basic works on the Golden Age of Safed is Schechter, "Safed in the Sixteenth Century." For the general history of the city from ancient times to the twentieth century, see Schur, *History of Safed.* An excellent introduction to the kabbalistic innovations of the sages of

Safed is Fine, *Safed Spirituality*. On the circumstances and effects of the Ottoman Conquest and subsequent violence in Safed, see the conflicting views of David, "Additional Evidence," and Tamar, "On the Jews of Safed." For the wider imperial background, see Har-el, *Struggle for Domination*.

The basic works on the economic history of Safed in the sixteenth century are still Avitsur, "Safed," and Caanani, "Economic Life." Avitsur, in particular, provides detailed information on the scope and production stages of the Safed textile industry. The report of Rabbi Moses Basola on the prosperous commercial life in the city was quoted in Schur, *History of Safed:* 51. I have translated it from Hebrew.

In the last few decades, new information on sixteenth-century Safed has been drawn from the Ottoman archives and tax registers, see Cohen and Lewis, *Population and Revenue* and, more recently and more specifically, Rhode, "The Geography." The best source on the commercial involvements and procedures of Mediterranean Jewry is still Goitein, *A Mediterranean Society*. See also Toaff and Swarzfuchs, *The Mediterranean and the Jews*.

Abraham David has written extensively on the dramatic population changes in Safed in the first half of the sixteenth century and their relation to the immigration of Marranos to Ottoman Palestine. See especially his articles "Demographic Changes" and "Safed as a Center" and his book *Immigration and Settlement*.

The unique character of Rabbi Jacob Berav's academy in Safed is explored in Demitrovsky, "The Academy of Rabbi Jacob Berav." The course of the semikhah controversy and its deeper political implications for the relative authority of the leadership in Safed and in Jerusalem are discussed by Benayahu, "The Revival of Ordination"; Katz, "The Ordination Controversy"; and Cover, "Bringing the Messiah." Caro's career in Safed (as well as his earlier career in the Balkans) is described in Werblowsky, *Joseph Karo*.

The most recent biography and assessment of the thought of Moses Cordovero is Sack, *The Kabbalah of Rabbi Moshe Cordovero*. The earlier standard work is Ben-Shlomo, *The Theological Doctrine*.

On the cult of the saints in Galilee that would later become a central feature of kabbalistic devotions, see Reiner, *Pilgrims and Pilgrimage*. The transformation of older practices is described in Benayahu, "Devotion Practices." For some of the surviving compositions of Cordovero's mentor Alkabetz, see Werblowsky, "A Collection of Prayers." The quotations from Cordovero's dairies on the gerushin were published in Werblowsky, *Joseph Karo:* 51–53. His admonition to humility is quoted from the English translation of *Tomer Devorah* in Miller, *Palm Tree:* 122.

The methods of diffusion of Cordoverian Kabbalah is examined in

Robinson, "Moses Cordovero and Kabbalistic Education." For an English translation of Cordovero's Palm Tree of Deborah, see Miller, *The Palm Tree*. Another kabbalistic handbook, Cordovero's *Or Ne'erav*, "Pleasant Light," has recently been translated into English by Robinson. For the social setting of the popularity of Cordoverian—and, eventually, Lurianic Kabbalah in Italy—see Bonfil, *Jewish Life*. For a specific case of influence, see Tishby, "Rabbi Moses Cordovero."

Information on ethnic relations and community administration within the Jewish population of Safed is provided in David, "Demographic Changes," and Rozen, "Status of the *Mustarabim*." Lamdan has recently reassessed the question in "Inter-communal Relations."

The background of Judah Abelin's attack on the scholar-entrepreneurs in Safed is described in detail in Benayahu, "The Tax Concession." This entire episode can perhaps best be seen in the context of the larger conflicts within sixteenth-century Jewish society throughout the Mediterranean; see Elior, "Struggle," and Hacker, "Intellectual Activity."

CHAPTER 6: LIFTING THE SPARKS

For the wider political and socio-economic background of Safed's Golden Age, see the essays in Kunt and Woodhead, *Süleyman the Magnificent*.

Benayahu, *Sefer Toldot Ha-Ari*, attempts to disentangle the thicket of legends that arose around the memory of Isaac Luria. For a critical examination of the biographical legends of the Ari and the archival sources for his early life, see David, "Halakhah and Commerce." Additional documentary evidence for the commercial activity of the Ari can be found in Schochetman, "New Sources." The economic activities of Egyptian Jewry in general are explored by Goitein, *Mediterranean Society*; and for the sixteenth century in particular, see David, "Jews in Egypt."

The main outlines of Lurianic Kabbalah are discussed by Scholem in *Major Trends*: 244–286, and in *Sabbatai Sevi*: 27–44, with particular emphasis on its eventual impact on popular piety. Jacobson, "Aspect of the Feminine," analyzes Luria's sexual imagery. For an attempt at a comprehensive description, see Tishby, *Doctrine of Evil*. Jacobs has attempted an assessment of the theological impact of Lurianic Kabbalah in "The Uplifting of Sparks." A recent reassessment of the relationship of Lurianic Kabbalah to Scripture is Magid, "From Theosophy to Midrash."

The story of Vital's first meeting with Luria is recounted in Patai, *The Jewish Alchemists*: 340. Much of the surviving information on Luria's teachings is based on the writings of his students, particularly Vital. For an attempt to identify some of his authentic teachings, see Scholem, "Luria's Authentic Kabbalistic Writings."

Praise for Luria's legendary psychic and spiritual abilities is quoted in Benayahu, *Sefer Toldot Ha-Ari*: 156–8. For some of the unique spiritualist techniques and supernatural phenomena ascribed to Luria and the other kabbalists of sixteenth-century Safed, see Fine, "The Art of Metoposcopy," and Patai, "Exorcism and Xenoglossia."

On Luria's theories of reincarnation—as interpreted by Vital—see *Sha'ar ha-Gilgulim.* Scholem provides the wider background in his classic article on the theme of reincarnation in Jewish mysticism in the chapter "Transmigration of Souls" in his collection of lectures *On the Mystical Shape.* On the association of the spirits of ancient sages with particular localities in the vicinity of Safed, see Moskowitz, *Discovery of the Tombs of the Saints.* Another important source is Ish-Shalom, "Holy Tombs." A modern handbook, sold to the faithful at Meron by the Committee for the Rescue of Ancient Tombs, is entitled *Sefer Kadmonenu.* Luria's practice of *yihudim* is discussed extensively in Fine, "The Contemplative Practice."

The tale of the Ari's appeal to his disciples to depart at once for Jerusalem is quoted in Schwartz, *Gabriel's Palace* quoted 86.

Clear evidence in the rabbinic responsa of the deteriorating economic and political conditions at the end of the sixteenth century has been assembled by Bashan in "The Economic and Political Crisis." The most important source for understanding the wider economic context of the collapse of the Safed textile industry is Braude, "International Competition."

The text of the secret agreement between Haim Vital and some of the Ari's disciples was first published by Rabinowitz in "From the Genizah of Stolyna." Scholem added an extensive historical commentary in "Document of Association." For the influence of the Ari on his disciples, see Meroz, "Faithful Transmission." The definitive historical analysis of the diffusion of the Ari's reputation is Benayahu, *Sefer Toldot Ha-Ari.* The messianic expectations connected with the circle of the Ari are discussed in Tamar in "Luria and Vital." For the ambitions of Haim Vital after the death of the Ari, see Tamar's article "Messianic Dreams and Visions." Although Scholem doubted that the greatest popularizer of Lurianic Kabbalah, Israel Sarug, was ever a disciple of the Ari ("Israel Sarug"), Idel has recently suggested that Sarug was deeply influenced by the mystical theology of sixteenth-century Jerusalem circles in "Between the Kabbalah of Jerusalem."

For the subsequent theological transformations of the original doctrines, see Jacobson, *From Lurianic Kabbalah,* and Jacobs, "Lifting the Sparks."

CHAPTER 7: THE FORGOTTEN LEGACY

The single most important source on the history and implications of the Sabbatean movement is Scholem's authoritative and magisterial *Sabbatai Sevi.* Among his earlier studies on aspects of the subject are "Redemption

Through Sin" and "The Crypto-Jewish Sect of the Dönmeh," both published in *The Messianic Idea.* For a provocative assessment of the Sabbatean movement by a New Testament scholar, see Davies, "From Schweitzer to Scholem." One conspicuous aspect of the aftermath of the apostasy of Sabbetai Zvi — the ideological purge of any Jews suspected of being "soft" on Sabbateanism — is explored in Carlebach, *Pursuit of Heresy.*

For a recent assessment of the changing economic conditions in Izmir — the boyhood home of Sabbetai Zvi and the center of intense support for his movement — see Goffman, *Izmir and the Levantine World.* The physical description of Sabbetai Zvi was written by Abraham Cuenque, a follower and eyewitness. It is quoted in Scholem, *Sabbatai Sevi:* 189.

On the continuing impact of "practical" Kabbalah in Eastern Europe after the demise of the Sabbatean movement, see Etkes, "The Role of Magic."

The historical circumstances of the rise of Eastern European Hasidism and the historical figure of Rabbi Israel ben Eliezer have recently been explored by Rosman in *Founder of Hasidism,* with extensive bibliography. See also Dinur, "The Messianic-Prophetic Role," and Elior, "Hasidism," for a reassessment of Scholem's view of the place of Hasidism in the history of Jewish mysticism.

For classic works on the spiritual contributions of modern Hasidism, see Buber, *Origin and Meaning of Hasidism* and *Tales of the Hasidim,* and Heschel, *Circle of the Baal Shem Tov.* Scholem explored the role of the Zaddik in early Jewish mysticism in the chapter "The Righteous One" in *On the Mystical Shape.* See also Green, "Typologies of Leadership."

The ideological and political struggles between Hasidic leaders and the rabbinical authorities are detailed in Schochet, *The Chasidic Movement,* and Mahler, *Hasidism.*

EPILOGUE: THE KABBALAH REBORN

Among the important studies of Christian Kabbalah and its influence on European Renaissance culture and literature are Blau, *Christian Interpretation;* Wirszubski, *Pico della Mirandola;* and Idel, "Magical and Neoplatonic Interpretations of Kabbalah." Another basic source is Scholem's *Encyclopedia Judaica* essay on "Christian Kabbalah" reprinted in *Kabbalah,* pp. 196–201.

On the tradition of the Golem, see Scholem's classic article "The Golem" in *On the Kabbalah and Its Symbolism* and his later, wry note "The Golem of Prague and the Golem of Rehovot" in *The Messianic Idea.* Another essential source is Idel, *Golem.*

For an example of the kabbalistic practices of Rabbi Shalom Sharabi and his followers at the Bet El Yeshiva in Jerusalem, see Jacobs, *Jewish Mystical Testimonies:* 192–207.

Scholem dealt with the implications of the career of Jacob Frank in his essay "Redemption Through Sin" in *The Messianic Idea*. An enlightening interpretation of the political context of Frankism can be found in Levine, "Frankism as Worldly Messianism."

One of the main debates in the intellectual history of Jewish studies is the extent to which the Kabbalah was viewed as destructive superstition by scholars in the nineteenth century. Some provocative themes in the modern study of the history of Jewish mysticism are explored in Strousma, "Gnosis and Judaism." Scholem made no secret of his feeling that his work was a long-needed corrective to the earlier negative views. See his essay "Scholarship and the Kabbalah" in *Kabbalah* and "The Science of Judaism" in *The Messianic Idea*. This view is shared, but nuanced, by Tishby, *Wisdom of the Zohar* 1:43–50. For a different perspective, see Idel, *Kabbalah:* 7–10.

For a memorable vignette of Scholem, see Weiner, *9 1/2 Mystics.* The circumstances of his early life and turn to the study of the Kabbalah are described in Scholem's autobiography, *From Berlin to Jerusalem.* See also Biale, *Gershom Scholem* and "Gershom Scholem on Jewish Messianism" for the place of Scholem in modern Jewish intellectual history.

Among the most prominent modern Jewish mystics and religious thinkers in the Land of Israel was Rabbi Abraham Isaac Kook; for recent scholarly assessments, see Kaplan and Shatz, *Rabbi Abraham Isaac Kook.* On the political and territorial dimensions of the teachings of his son Rabbi Zvi Yehudah Kook, see Tal, "Foundations of a Political Messianic Trend," and Sprinzak, *The Ascendance:* 43–51.

For a journalistic account of the study of Kabbalah among the rich, famous, and spiritually famished, see Chun, "Ab Kab," and Eisen, "Jewish Mysticism."

BIBLIOGRAPHY

Adler, Elkan Nathan. *Jewish Travellers in the Middle Ages.* New York: Dover Publications, 1987.

Aescoly, Aaron. *Jewish Messianic Movements.* Jerusalem: Mosad Bialik, 1956. [Hebrew]

————. *The Story of David Reubeni, from the Oxford Manuscript.* Jerusalem: Mosad Bialik, 1993. [Hebrew]

Albright, W. F. "King Joiachin in Exile." *Biblical Archaeologist* 5 (1942): 49–55.

Alon, Gedaliah. *The Jews in Their Land in the Talmudic Age.* Cambridge, MA: Harvard University Press, 1980.

Alter, Robert. *Necessary Angels: Tradition and Modernity in Kafka, Benjamin, and Scholem.* Cambridge, MA: Harvard University Press, 1991.

Avi-Yonah, Michael. *The Jews of Palestine: A Political History from the Bar Kokhba War to the Arab Conquest.* Oxford: Blackwell, 1976.

Avitsur, Shmuel. "Safed—Center of the Manufacture of Woven Woolens in the Sixteenth Century." *Sefunot* 6 (1962): 41–70. [Hebrew]

———. "Toward a History of the Woolen Textile Industry in Salonika." *Sefunot* 12 (1971–1978): 147–169. [Hebrew]

Baer, Yitzhak. "The Historical Background of the 'Raya Mehemna.'" *Tarbiz* 5 (1939–40): 1–44. [Hebrew]

———. *A History of the Jews in Christian Spain.* 2 vols. Philadelphia: Jewish Publication Society of America, 1961–66.

———. "The Messianic Movement in Spain in the Period of the Exile." *Me'assef Zion* 5 (1933): 73–77. [Hebrew]

Baron, Salo Wittmayer. *A Social and Religious History of the Jews.* Philadelphia: Jewish Publication Society, 1937–60.

Bashan, Eliezer. "The Economic and Political Crisis in the Ottoman Empire Beginning in the Last Third of the Sixteenth Century, in Light of the Responsa Literature." *Proceedings of the Sixth World Congress of Jewish Studies*, Vol. 2: 107–115. Jerusalem: World Association for Jewish Studies, 1985. [Hebrew]

Ben-Sasson, Menachem. *The Flowering of the Jewish Community in the Lands of Islam: Qayrawan, 800–1057.* Jerusalem: Magnes Press, 1996. [Hebrew]

Ben-Shlomo, Yosef. *The Theological Doctrine of Moses Cordovero.* Jerusalem: Mosad Bialik, 1965. [Hebrew]

Benayahu, Meir. "Devotion Practices of the Kabbalists of Safed in Meron." *Sefunot* 6 (1962): 9–40. [Hebrew]

———. "The Revival of Ordination in Safed." Pp. 248–269 in *Sefer Yovel le-Yitzhak Baer* (Shmuel Etinger, ed.). Jerusalem: Israeli Historical Society, 1960. [Hebrew]

———. *Sefer Toldot Ha-Ari.* Jerusalem: Yad Itzak Ben-Zvi, 1967. [Hebrew]

———. "The Tax Concession Enjoyed by the Scholars of Safed." *Sefunot* 7 (1963): 103–117. [Hebrew]

Berquist, Jon L. *Judaism in Persia's Shadow: A Social and Historical Approach.* Philadelphia: Fortress Press, 1995.

Biale, David. "Gershom Scholem on Jewish Messianism." Pp. 521–550 in *Essential Papers on Messianic Movements and Personalities in Jewish History* (Mark Saperstein, ed.). New York: New York University Press, 1992.

———. *Gershom Scholem: Kabbalah and Counter-history.* Cambridge, MA: Harvard University Press, 1979.

Blau, Joseph L. *The Christian Interpretation of the Cabala in the Renaissance.* New York: Columbia University Press, 1944.

Bloom, Harold (ed.). *Gershom Scholem.* New York: Chelsea House Publishers, 1987.

Bokser, Ben Zion. *The Jewish Mystical Tradition.* New York: The Pilgrim Press, 1981.

Bonfil, Robert. *Jewish Life in Renaissance Italy.* Berkeley, CA: University of California Press, 1994.

Braude, Benjamin. "International Competition and Domestic Cloth in the Ottoman Empire, 1500–1650: A Study in Undevelopment." *Review* II:3 (Winter 1979): 437–451.

———. "The Salonika Textile Industry in the Economy of the Eastern Mediterranean." *Pe'amim* 15 (1983): 82–95. [Hebrew]

Brody, Robert. *The Geonim of Babylonia and the Shaping of Medieval Jewish Culture.* New Haven, CT: Yale University Press, 1998.

Brummett, Palmira. *Ottoman Seapower and Levantine Diplomacy in the Age of Discovery.* Albany, NY: State University of New York Press, 1994.

Buber, Martin. *The Origin and Meaning of Hasidism.* New York: Horizon Press, 1960.

———. *Tales of the Hasidim.* 2 vols. New York: Schocken Books, 1947–48.

Burns, Robert I. (ed.). *Emperor of Culture: Alfonso X the Learned of Castile and His Thirteenth-Century Renaissance.* Philadelphia: University of Pennsylvania Press, 1990.

———. *The Worlds of Alfonso the Learned and James the Conqueror: Intellect and Force in the Middle Ages.* Princeton, NJ: Princeton University Press, 1985.

Cabaniss, Allen. *Agobard of Lyons, Churchman and Critic.* Syracuse, NY: Syracuse University Press, 1953.

Canaani, Yaacov. "Economic Life in Safed and its Environs in the Sixteenth Century and the First Half of the Seventeenth Century." *Meassef Zion* 6 (1933): 172–217. [Hebrew]

Carlebach, Elisheva. *The Pursuit of Heresy: Rabbi Moses Hagiz and the Sabbatian Heresies.* New York: Columbia University Press, 1990.

Carpenter, Dwayne E. *Alfonso X and the Jews: An Edition of and Commentary on Siete Partidas 7.24 "De los Judios."* Berkeley, CA: University of California Press, 1986.

Cassuto, M. D. "Who was David Reubeni?" *Tarbiz* 32 (1963): 339–358. [Hebrew]

Chazan, Robert. *European Jewry and the First Crusade.* Berkeley, CA: University of California Press, 1987.

———. *In the Year 1096: The First Crusade and the Jews.* Philadelphia: Jewish Publication Society of America, 1996.

Chernus, Ira. "Individual and Community in the Redaction of the Hekhalot Literature." *Hebrew Union College Annual* 52 (1981): 253–274.

Chun, Rene. "Ab Kab. Celebrities and the Fashion Elite Study the Jewish Scripture Kabbalah." *New York Magazine.* April 22, 1996: 16–17.

Cohen, Amnon, and Lewis, Bernard. *Population and Revenue in the Towns of Palestine in the Sixteenth Century.* Princeton, NJ: Princeton University Press, 1978.

Cohen, Gerson D. *A Critical Edition With a Translation and Notes of the Book of Tradition (Sefer ha-Kabbalah) by Abraham Ibn Daud.* Philadelphia: Jewish Publication Society of America, 1967.

Cohen, Mark R. *Under Crescent and Cross: The Jews in the Middle Ages.* Princeton, NJ: Princeton University Press, 1994.

Collins, John J. *The Apocalyptic Imagination: An Introduction to the Jewish Matrix of Christianity.* New York: Crossroad, 1992.

Committee for the Rescue of Tombs of the Ancients in Eretz Israel. *Sefer Kadmonenu.* Jerusalem: Committee for the Rescue of the Tombs of the Ancients, 1987.

Cooper, David A. *God Is a Verb: Kabbalah and the Practice of Mystical Judaism.* New York: Riverhead Books, 1997.

Costen, Michael. *The Cathars and the Albigensian Crusade.* Manchester, UK: Manchester University Press, 1997.

Cover, Robert. "Bringing the Messiah Through the Law: A Case Study." Pp. 201–217 in *Religion, Morality, and the Law* (J. Roland Pennock and John W. Chapman, eds.). New York: New York University Press, 1988.

Crone, Patricia, and Cook, Michael. *Hagarism: The Making of the Islamic World.* Cambridge: Cambridge University Press, 1977.

Dan, Joseph. *The Ancient Jewish Mysticism.* Tel Aviv: MOD Books, 1993.

———. "The Emergence of Messianic Mythology in the Thirteenth-Century Kabbalah in Spain." Pp. 57–68 in *Occident and Orient: A Tribute to the Memory of A. Scheiber.* Leiden: E.J. Brill, 1988.

————. *Gershom Scholem and the Mystical Dimension of Jewish History.* New York: New York University Press, 1987.

————. *Jewish Mysticism and Jewish Ethics.* Seattle: University of Washington Press, 1986.

————. "On the Problem of the Historical Status of the *Yordei ha-Merkabah.*" *Zion* 60 (1995): 179–199.

————. "Samael, Lilith, and the Concept of Evil in the Early Kabbalah." *Association for Jewish Studies Review* 5 (1980): 17–40.

————. "The Story of Rabbi Joseph de la Reyna." *Sefunot* 6 (1962): 311–326. [Hebrew]

David, Abraham. "Additional Evidence on the Attacks against the Jews of Safed in 1517." *Cathedra* 8 (1979): 190–194. [Hebrew]

————. "Demographic Changes in the Safed Jewish Community of the Sixteenth Century." Pp. 83–93 in *Occident and Orient* (Robert Dan, ed.). Leiden: E.J. Brill, 1988.

————. "Halakhah and Commerce in the History of the Ari." *Jerusalem Studies in Jewish Thought* 10 (1992): 287–297. [Hebrew]

————. *Immigration and Settlement in Eretz Israel in the Sixteenth Century.* Jerusalem: Rubin Mass, 1993. [Hebrew]

————. " 'The Jews in Egypt Are Bankers and Merchants.' " *Pe'amim* 51 (1992): 107–123. [Hebrew]

————. "Safed as a Center for the Return of Marranos in the Sixteenth Century." Pp. 183–204 in *Society and Community* (Abraham Haim, ed.). Jerusalem: Misgav Yerushalaim, 1991. [Hebrew]

Davies, W. D. "From Schweitzer to Scholem: Reflections on Sabbatai Svi." Pp. 335–374 in *Essential Papers on Messianic Movements and Pe'rsonalities in Jewish History* (Mark Saperstein, ed.). New York: New York University Press, 1992.

Dimitrovsky, Haim. "The Academy of Rabbi Jacob Berav." *Sefunot* 7 (1983): 41–102. [Hebrew]

Dinur, Ben-Zion. "The Messianic-Prophetic Role of the Baal Shem Tov." Pp. 377–88 in *Essential Papers on Messianic Movements and Personalities in Jewish History* (Mark Saperstein, ed.). New York: New York University Press, 1992.

Dothan, Moshe. *Hammath Tiberias.* Jerusalem: Israel Exploration Society, 1983.

Eidelberg, Shlomo. *The Jews and the Crusaders: The Hebrew Chronicles of the First and Second Crusades*. Hoboken, NJ: Ktav Publishing House, 1996.

Eisen, Robert. "Jewish Mysticism: Seeking the Inner Light." *Moment* 22:1 (February 1997): 38–42; 82.

Eisenman, Robert. *James the Brother of Jesus*. New York: Viking, 1996.

———. *Maccabees, Zadokites, Christians, and Qumran: A New Hypothesis of Qumran Origins*. Leiden: E.J. Brill, 1983.

Elior, Rachel. "The Doctrine of Transmigration in *Galya Raza*." Pp. 243–269 in *Essential Papers on Kabbalah* (Lawrence Fine, ed.). New York: New York University Press, 1995.

———. "Hasidism—Historical Continuity and Spiritual Change." Pp. 303–323 in *Gershom Scholem's Major Trends in Jewish Mysticism 50 Years After* (Peter Schäfer and Joseph Dan, eds.). Tübingen: J.C.B. Mohr, 1993.

———. "The Struggle Over the Status of the Kabbalah in the Sixteenth Century." *Jerusalem Studies in Jewish Thought* 1 (1981): 177–190. [Hebrew]

Eph'al, Israel. "The Western Minorities in Babylonia in the Sixth-Fifth Centuries B.C.: Maintenance and Cohesion." *Orientalia* 48 (1978): 74–90.

Epstein, Perle. *Kabbalah: The Way of the Jewish Mystic*. Boston: Shambala, 1988.

Etkes, Immanuel. "The Role of Magic and Baalei Shem in Ashkenazic Society in the Late Seventeenth and Early Eighteenth Centuries." *Zion* 60 (1995): 69–104. [Hebrew]

Feldman, Louis H. *Jew and Gentile in the Ancient World: Attitudes and Interactions from Alexander to Justinian*. Princeton, NJ: Princeton University Press, 1993.

Fine, Lawrence. "The Art of Metoposcopy: A Study in Isaac Luria's Charismatic Knowledge." *AJS Review* 11 (1986): 79–101.

———. "The Contemplative Practice of Yihudim in Lurianic Kabbalah." Pp. 64–98 in *Jewish Spirituality: From the Sixteenth-Century Revival to the Present* (Arthur Green, ed.). New York: Crossroad, 1987.

———. *Safed Spirituality*. New York: Paulist Press, 1984.

Fine, Steven (ed.). *Sacred Realm: The Emergence of the Synagogue in the Ancient World*. New York: Oxford University Press, 1996.

Finkel, Avraham Yaakov. *Sefer Chasidim, The Book of the Pious.* Northvale, NJ: Jason Aronson, 1997.

Frenkel, David A. *The Hebrew Amulet.* Jerusalem: Institute for Jewish Studies, 1995. [Hebrew]

Friedman, Richard Elliott. *The Disappearance of God: A Divine Mystery.* Boston: Little, Brown, and Co., 1995.

Gafni, Yeshayahu. *The Jews of Babylonia in the Talmudic Period: Social and Spiritual Life.* Jerusalem: Merkaz Zalman Shazar, 1990. [Hebrew]

Gaster, Moses, and Daiches, Samuel. *Three Works of Ancient Jewish Magic.* Sussex, UK: Chuthonios Books, 1986.

Gerber, Jane S. *The Jews of Spain: A History of the Sephardic Experience.* New York: The Free Press, 1992.

Gil, Moshe. *A History of Palestine, 634–1099.* Cambridge: Cambridge University Press, 1992.

———. "The Radhanite Merchants and the Land of Radhan." *Journal of the Economic and Social History of the Orient* 17 (1974): 299–328.

Gitlitz, David M. *Secrecy and Deceit: The Religion of the Crypto-Jews.* Philadelphia: Jewish Publication Society of America, 1996.

Goffman, Daniel. *Izmir and the Levantine World, 1550–1650.* Seattle: University of Washington Press, 1990.

Goitein, S. D. *A Mediterranean Society: The Jewish Communities of the Arab World as Portrayed in the Documents of the Cairo Geniza.* Berkeley, CA: University of California Press, 1967.

Goshen Gottstein, Alon. "Is *Ma'aseh Bereshit* Part of Ancient Jewish Mysticism?" *The Journal of Jewish Thought and Philosophy* 4 (1995): 185–201.

Greeberg, Moshe. *Ezekiel, 1–20. The Anchor Bible,* Vol. 22. Garden City, NY: Doubleday, 1983.

Green, Arthur. "Typologies of Leadership and the Hasidic Zaddiq." Pp. 127–156 in *Jewish Spirituality: From the Sixteenth-Century Revival to the Present* (Arthur Green, ed.). New York: Crossroad, 1987.

Grossman, Avraham. "The Immigration of the Kalonymus Family from Italy to Germany." *Zion* 40 (1975): 154–185. [Hebrew]

Gruenwald, Ithamar. *Apocalyptic and Merkavah Mysticism.* Leiden: E. J. Brill, 1980.

―――. "Jewish Mysticism in the Transition from the Sefer Yetzirah to the Sefer ha-Bahir." *Jerusalem Studies in Jewish Thought* 6 (1986): 15–72. [Hebrew]

―――. "Reflections on the Nature and Origins of Jewish Mysticism." Pp. 25–48 in *Gershom Scholem's Major Trends in Jewish Mysticism 50 Years After* (Peter Schäfer and Joseph Dan, eds.). Tübingen: J.C.B. Mohr, 1993.

Gurary, Noson. *Chasidism: Its Development and Practice.* Northvale, NJ: Jason Aronson, 1997.

Hachlili, Rachel. "The Zodiac in Ancient Jewish Art: Representation and Significance." *Bulletin of the American Schools of Oriental Research* 228 (1977): 61–77.

Hacker, Joseph. "The Intellectual Activity of the Jews in the Ottoman Empire during the Sixteenth and Seventeenth Centuries." Pp. 95–135 in *Jewish Thought in the Seventeenth Century* (Isadore Twersky and Bernard Septimus, eds.). Cambridge, MA: Harvard University Press, 1987.

Halperin, David J. *The Faces of the Chariot: Early Jewish Responses to Ezekiel's Vision.* Tübingen: J.C.B. Mohr, 1988.

Hanson, Paul D. *The Dawn of Apocalyptic.* Philadelphia: Fortress Press, 1975.

Har-el, Shai. *Struggle for Domination in the Middle East: The Ottoman-Mamluk War, 1485–91.* Leiden: E.J. Brill, 1995.

Hengel, Martin. *Judaism and Hellenism.* Philadelphia: Fortress Press, 1974.

―――. *The Zealots: Investigations into the Jewish Freedom Movement in the Period from Herod I until 70 A.D.* Edinburgh: T.&T. Clark, 1989.

Heschel, Abraham Joshua. *The Circle of the Baal Shem Tov: Studies in Hasidism.* Chicago: University of Chicago Press, 1985.

Hildesheimer, Esriel Erich. *Mystik und Agada im Urteile der Gaonen R. Schreira und R. Hai.* Frankfurt: J. Kaufmann, 1931.

Hillgarth, J. N. *The Problem of a Catalan Mediterranean Empire 1229–1327.* London: Longman, 1975.

Hodges, Richard, and Whitehouse, David. *Mohammed, Charlemagne, and the Origins of Europe.* Ithaca, NY: Cornell University Press, 1983.

Horsley, Richard A. *Jesus and the Spiral of Violence.* San Francisco: Harper & Row, 1987.

Horsley, Richard A., and Silberman, Neil Asher. *The Message and the Kingdom*. New York: Putnam, 1997.

Idel, Moshe. "The Attitude to Christianity in Sefer ha-Meshiv." *Immanuel* 12 (1981): 77–95.

———. "Between the Kabbalah of Jerusalem and the Kabbalah of R. Israel Sarug." *Shalem* 6 (1992): 165–173. [Hebrew]

———. "Enoch Is Metatron." *Immanuel* 24/25 (1990): 220–240.

———. *Golem: Jewish Magical and Mystical Traditions on the Artificial Anthropoid*. Albany, NY: State University of New York Press, 1990.

———. "Inquiries into the Doctrine of the Sefer ha-Meshiv." *Sefunot* 17 (1983): 185–266. [Hebrew]

———. "Jewish Magic from the Renaissance Period to Early Hasidism." Pp. 82–117 in *Religion, Science, and Magic* (Jacob Neusner, Ernest S. Frerichs, and Paul Flesher, eds.). New York: Oxford University Press.

———. *Kabbalah: New Perspectives*. New Haven, CT: Yale University Press, 1988.

———. "The Magical and Neoplatonic Interpretations of the Kabbalah in the Renaissance." Pp. 186–242 in *Jewish Thought in the Sixteenth Century* (Bernard D. Cooperman, ed.). Cambridge, MA: Harvard University Press, 1983.

———. *The Mystical Experience in Abraham Abulafia*. Albany, NY: State University of New York Press, 1988.

———. "Solomon Molcho as a Magician." *Sefunot* 18 (1985): 193–219. [Hebrew]

———. *Studies in Ecstatic Kabbalah*. Albany, NY: State University of New York Press, 1988.

Ish-Shalom, Michael. *Holy Tombs: A Study of Traditions Concerning Jewish Holy Tombs in Palestine*. Jerusalem: Rabbi Kook Foundation and the Palestine Institute of Folklore and Ethnology, 1948. [Hebrew]

Jacobs, Louis. *Jewish Mystical Testimonies*. New York: Schocken Books, 1977.

———. "The Uplifting of Sparks in Later Jewish Mysticism." Pp. 99–126 in *Jewish Spirituality: From the Sixteenth-Century Revival to the Present* (Arthur Green, ed.). New York: Crossroad, 1987.

Jacobson, Yoram. "The Aspect of the 'Feminine' in the Lurianic Kabbalah." Pp. 239–255 in *Gershom Scholem's Major Trends in Jewish Mysticism 50 Years After* (Peter Schäfer and Joseph Dan, eds.). Tübingen: J.C.B. Mohr, 1993.

———. *From Lurianic Kabbalism to the Psychological Theosophy of Hasidism.* Tel Aviv: Ministry of Defence, 1986. [Hebrew]

Juhasz, Esther. *Sephardi Jews in the Ottoman Empire: Aspects of Material Culture.* Jerusalem: Israel Museum, 1990.

Kamenetz, Roger. *Stalking Elijah: Adventures with Today's Jewish Mystical Masters.* San Francisco: HarperSanFrancisco, 1997.

Kanarfogel, Ephraim. "Rabbinic Figures in Castlian Kabbalistic Pseudepigraphy: R. Yehudah He-Hasid and R. Elhanan of Corbeil." *Jewish Thought and Philosophy* 3 (1993): 77–109. [Hebrew]

Kaplan, Arieh (trans.). *The Bahir.* York Beach, ME: Samuel Weiser, 1979.

———. *Sefer Yetzirah: The Book of Creation.* York Beach, ME: Samuel Weiser, 1997.

Kaplan, Lawrence J., and Shatz, David (eds.). *Rabbi Abraham Isaac Kook and Jewish Spirituality.* New York: New York University Press, 1995.

Katz, Jacob. "The Ordination Controversy Between R. Jacob Berab and R. Levi b. Habib." *Zion* 16 (1951): 28–45. [Hebrew]

Kunt, Metin, and Woodhead, Christine (eds.). *Süleyman the Magnificent and His Age: The Ottoman Empire in the Early Modern World.* London: Longman, 1995.

Lamdan, Ruth. "Inter-communal Relations in Safed after the Expulsion from Spain—A New Look." *Pe'amim* 72 (1997): 75–83. [Hebrew]

Levine, Hillel. "Frankism as Worldly Messianism." Pp. 283–300 in *Gershom Scholem's Major Trends in Jewish Mysticism 50 Years After* (Peter Schäfer and Joseph Dan, eds.). Tübingen: J.C.B. Mohr, 1993.

Levine, Lee I. "The Revolutionary Effects of Archaeology on the Study of Jewish History: The Case of the Ancient Synagogue." Pp. 166–189 in *The Archaeology of Israel* (Neil Asher Silberman and David A. Small, eds.). Sheffield, UK: Sheffield Academic Press, 1997.

Lewis, Bernard. "An Apocalyptic Vision of Islamic History." *Bulletin of the School of Oriental and African Studies* 13 (1950): 321–324.

Lewis, Bernard, and Cohen, Amnon. *Population and Revenue in the Towns of Palestine in the Sixteenth Century.* Princeton, NJ: Princeton University Press, 1978.

Liebes, Judah. "How Was the Zohar Composed?" *Jerusalem Studies in Jewish Thought* 8 (1989): 1–71. [Hebrew]

———. "New Directions in the Study of the Kabbalah." *Pe'amim* 50 (1992): 150–170. [Hebrew]

———. *Studies in the Zohar.* Albany, NY: State University of New York Press, 1993.

Little, Lester K. *Religious Poverty and the Profit Economy in Medieval Europe.* Ithaca, NY: Cornell University Press, 1978.

MacKay, Angus. *Society, Economy, and Religion in Late Medieval Castile.* London: Variorum Reprints, 1987.

———. *Spain in the Middle Ages: From Frontier to Empire, 1000–1500.* London: Macmillan Press, 1993.

Magid, Shaul. "From Theosophy to Midrash: Lurianic Exegesis and the Garden of Eden." *AJS Review* 22 (1997): 37–75.

Mahler, Raphael. *Hasidism and the Jewish Enlightenment: Their Confrontation in Galicia and Poland in the First Half of the Nineteenth Century.* Philadelphia: Jewish Publication Society of America, 1985.

Malamat, Abraham. "The Last Years of the Kingdom of Judah." Pp. 205–221 in *The World History of the Jewish People. The Age of the Monarchies: Political History.* Vol. IV/1 (A. Malamat, ed.). Jerusalem: Massada, 1981.

Marcus, Ivan G. "The Historical Meaning of the Hasidei Ashkenaz: Fact, Fiction, or Cultural Self-Image." Pp. 103–114 in *Gershom Scholem's Major Trends in Jewish Mysticism 50 Years After* (Peter Schäfer and Joseph Dan, eds.). Tübingen: J.C.B. Mohr, 1993.

———. *Piety and Society: The Jewish Pietists of Medieval Germany.* Leiden: E.J. Brill, 1981.

———. "The Politics and Ethics of Pietism in Judaism: The Hasidim of Medieval Judaism." *Journal of Religious Ethics* 8 (1980): 227–258.

Matt, Daniel C. *The Essential Kabbalah.* San Francisco: HarperSanFrancisco, 1996.

———. *God and the Big Bang: Discovering Harmony Between Science and Spirituality.* Woodstock, VT: Jewish Lights Publishing, 1996.

———. *Zohar, The Book of Enlightenment.* New York: The Paulist Press, 1983.

Meroz, Ronit. "Faithful Transmission versus Innovation: Luria and His Disciples." Pp. 257–274 in *Gershom Scholem's Major Trends in Jewish Mysticism 50 Years After* (Peter Schäfer and Joseph Dan, eds.). Tübingen: J.C.B. Mohr, 1993.

Miller, Moshe (trans.). Rabbi Moshe Cordovero, *The Palm Tree of Devorah.* Spring Valley, NY: Targum/Feldheim, 1993.

Montgomery, James. A. *Aramaic Incantation Texts from Nippur.* Philadelphia: University Museum, 1913.

Mor, Menachem. *The Bar-Kokhba Revolt, Its Extent and Effect.* Jerusalem: Yad Izhak Ben-Zvi, 1991. [Hebrew]

Morgan, Michael A. *Sefer ha-Razim: The Book of Mysteries.* Chico, CA: The Scholars Press, 1983.

Moskowitz, Zvi. *Discovery of the Tombs of the Saints.* Jerusalem: Privately published, 1966. [Hebrew]

Musleah, Rahel. "Accessing the Mysteries of the Kabbalah." *Publishers Weekly.* October 13, 1997: 48–50.

Navek, Joseph, and Shaked, Saul. *Magic Spells and Formulae: Aramaic Incantations of Late Antiquity.* Jerusalem: The Magnes Press, 1993.

Ness, Lester. "Astrology in Judaism in Late Antiquity." *Archaeology in the Biblical World* 2 (1992): 44–54.

Netanyahu, Benzion. *The Origins of the Inquisition in Fifteenth Century Spain.* New York: Random House, 1995.

Neubauer, Adolf. "The Bahir and the Zohar." *Jewish Quarterly Review* 4 (1892): 357–368.

Neusner, Jacob. *A History of the Jews of Babylonia.* Chico, CA: Scholars Press, 1984.

———. *School, Court, Public Administration: Judaism and Its Institutions in Talmudic Babylonia.* Atlanta, GA: Scholars Press, 1987.

Nigal, Gedalyah. *Magic, Mysticism, and Hasidism: The Supernatural in Jewish Thought.* Northvale, NJ: Jason Aronson, 1994.

O'Callaghan, Joseph F. *The Learned King: The Reign of Alfonso X of Castile.* Philadelphia: University of Pennsylvania Press, 1993.

Oron, Michael. "Castilian Kabbalah—Continuation or Revolution? A Study of the Concept of Evil Among the Castilian Kabbalists." *Jerusalem Studies in Jewish Thought* 6 (1987): 383–392. [Hebrew]

———. "The Doctrine of Evil and Redemption in the *Sefer ha-Pli'ah* and the *Sefer ha-Kanah.*" *Da'at* 8 (1982): 87–93. [Hebrew]

Pachter, Mordecai. "R. Shelomo Alkabetz's Departure Sermon from Salonika to Eretz Israel." *Shalem* 5 (1987): 252–263. [Hebrew]

Parpola, Simo. "The Assyrian Tree of Life: Tracing the Origins of Jewish Monotheism and Greek Philosophy." *Journal of Near Eastern Studies* 52 (1993): 161–208.

Patai, Raphael. "Exorcism and Xenoglossia among the Safed Kabbalists." *Journal of American Folklore* 91 (1978): 823–833.

———. *The Jewish Alchemists.* Princeton, NJ: Princeton University Press, 1994.

Rabinowitz, Zeev. "From the Genizah of Stolyna." *Zion* 2 (1940): 125–132. [Hebrew]

Reiner, Elhanan. *Pilgrims and Pilgrimate to Eretz Yisrael, 1099–1517.* Ph.D. diss., Hebrew University of Jerusalem, 1988. [Hebrew]

Rhode, H. "The Geography of the Sixteenth-Century Sancak of Safed." *Archivum Ottomanicum* 10 (1985): 179–218.

Robinson, Ira. "Moses Cordovero and Kabbalistic Education in the Sixteenth Century." *Judaism* 39 (1990): 155–162.

———. *Moses Cordovero's Introduction to Kabbalah: An Annotated Translation of his Or Ne'erav.* Hoboken, NJ: KTAV, 1994.

Rosman, Moshe. *Founder of Hasidism: A Quest for the Historical Ba'al Shem Tov.* Berkeley, CA: University of California Press, 1996.

Roth, Cecil (ed.). *The Dark Ages: Jews in Christian Europe, 711–1096.* New Brunswick, NJ: Rutgers University Press, 1966.

Rozen, Minna. "Status of the Mustaravim and Relations Between Communities in the Jewish Population of Eretz Israel from the End of the Fifteenth Century to the End of the Sixteenth Century." *Cathedra* 17 (1980): 73–89. [Hebrew]

Ruderman, David. "Hope Against Hope: Jewish and Christian Messianic Expectations in the Late Middle Ages." Pp. 185–202 in *Exile and Diaspora.* Jerusalem: Ben-Zvi Institute, 1991.

————. *Kabbalah, Magic, and Science: The Cultural Universe of a Sixteenth Century Jewish Physician.* Cambridge, MA: Harvard University Press, 1988.

————. *A Valley of Vision: The Heavenly Journey of Abraham ben Hananiah Yagel.* Philadelphia: University of Pennsylvania Press, 1990.

Sachar, Howard M. *Farewell España: The World of the Sephardim Remembered.* New York: Random House, 1994.

Sack, Bracha. *The Kabbalah of Rabbi Moshe Cordovero.* Beersheva: Ben-Gurion University Press, 1995.

Salzman, Marcus. *The Chronicle of Ahima'az.* New York: AMS Press, 1966.

Schäfer, Peter. *Hekhalot-Studien.* Tübingen: J. C. B. Mohr, 1988.

————. "Jewish Magic Literature in Late Antiquity and Early Middle Ages." *Journal of Jewish Studies* 41 (1990): 75–91.

————. "Merkavah, Mysticism, and Magic." Pp. 59–78 in *Gershom Scholem's Major Trends in Jewish Mysticism 50 Years After* (Peter Schäfer and Joseph Dan, eds.). Tübingen: J.C.B. Mohr, 1993.

Schäfer, Peter, and Joseph Dan (eds.). *Gershom Scholem's Major Trends in Jewish Mysticism 50 Years After.* Tübingen: J.C.B. Mohr, 1993.

Scharf, Andrew. *The Universe of Shabbetai Donnolo.* New York: Ktav Publishing House, 1976.

Schatz, Rivkah. "Influence of Gnostic Literature on the Sefer ha-Mefoar of Shlomo Molcho." *Jerusalem Studies in Jewish Thought* 6 (1987): 235–267. [Hebrew]

————. "Toward the Character of the Politico-Messianic Outbreak after the Expulsion from Spain." *Da'at* 11 (1983): 53–66. [Hebrew]

Schechter, Solomon. "Safed in the Sixteenth Century." (Originally published in 1908). Pp. 202–306 in *Studies in Judaism.* New York: Athenaeum, 1970.

Schiffman, Lawrence H. *From Text to Tradition: A History of Second Temple and Rabbinic Judaism.* Hoboken, NJ: Ktav Publishing House, 1991.

Schiffman, Lawrence H., and Swartz, Michael D. *Hebrew and Aramaic Incantation Texts from the Cairo Geniza.* Sheffield, UK: JSOT Press, 1992.

Schochet, Azriel. "'Royal Garments' in Salonika." *Sefunot* 12 (1971–78): 171–189. [Hebrew]

Schochet, Elijah Judah. *The Chasidic Movement and the Gaon of Vilna.* Northvale, NJ: Jason Aronson, 1994.

Schochetman, Eliav. "New Sources from the Geniza for the Commercial Activity of the Ari in Egypt." *Pe'amim* 16 (1983): 56–64. [Hebrew]

Scholem, Gershom. "Document of Association of the Students of the Ari." *Zion* 2 (1940): 133–160. [Hebrew]

———. *From Berlin to Jerusalem: Memories of My Youth.* New York: Schocken Books, 1980.

———. "Havdalah of Rabbi Akiva. A Source for Jewish Magic of the Geonic Period." *Tarbiz* 50 (1980–81): 243–281. [Hebrew]

———. "Israel Sarug—A Student of the Ari?" *Zion* 3–4 (1940): 214–243. [Hebrew]

———. *Jewish Gnosticism, Merkabah Mysticism, and Talmudic Tradition.* New York: Jewish Theological Seminary of America, 1960.

———. *Kabbalah.* New York: Meridian, 1978.

———. *The Kabbalah in Gerona.* Jerusalem: Akademon, 1964. [Hebrew]

———. "The Kabbalah of Rabbi Jacob and Rabbi Issac, Sons of Rabbi Jacob ha-Cohen." *Mada'ei Yahadut* 2 (1927): 165–293. [Hebrew]

———. "The 'Maggid' of R. Yosef Taitazak and the Revelations Attributed to Him." *Sefunot* 11 (1971–1978): 69–112.

———. *Major Trends in Jewish Mysticism.* New York: Schocken Books, 1971.

———. *The Messianic Idea in Judaism.* New York: Schocken Books, 1971.

———. *On the Kabbalah and Its Symbolism.* New York: Schocken Books, 1969.

———. "On Luria's Authentic Kabbalistic Writings." *Kiryat Sefer* 19 (1953): 184–199.

———. *On the Mystical Shape of the Godhead.* New York: Schocken Books, 1991.

———. *The Origins of the Kabbalah.* Princeton, NJ: Jewish Publication Society and Princeton University Press, 1987.

———. *Sabbatai Sevi, The Mystical Messiah.* Princeton, NJ: Princeton University Press, 1973.

———. *Zohar, The Book of Splendor.* New York: Schocken Books, 1949.

Schur, Nathan. *History of Safed.* Tel Aviv: Dvir, 1983. [Hebrew]

Schwartz, Howard. *Gabriel's Palace: Jewish Mystical Tales.* New York: Oxford University Press, 1993.

Shachar, Shulamit. "Catharism and the Origin of the Kabbalah in Languedoc." *Tarbiz* 40 (1970–71): 483–507. [Hebrew]

Shanks, Hershel (ed.). *Christianity and Rabbinic Judaism: A Parallel History of Their Origins and Early Development.* Washington, DC: Biblical Archaeology Society, 1992.

Shaw, Stanford J. *The Jews of the Ottoman Empire and the Turkish Republic.* New York: New York University Press, 1991.

Silver, Abba Hillel. *A History of Messianic Speculation in Israel.* Boston: Beacon Press, 1959.

Socarras, Cayetano J. *Alfonso X of Castile: A Study in Imperialistic Frustration.* Barcelona: Hispam, 1975.

Sperling, Harry, and Simon, Maurice (trans.). *The Zohar.* 5 vols. London: The Soncino Press, 1984.

Sprinzak, Ehud. *The Ascendance of Israel's Radical Right.* New York: Oxford University Press, 1991.

Stein, Siegfried. *Jewish-Christian Disputations in Thirteenth-Century Narbonne.* London: H.K. Lewis, 1969.

Strousma, Gedaliahu G. "Gnosis and Judaism in Nineteenth Century Christian Thought." *Jewish Thought and Philosophy* 2 (1992): 45–62.

Sumption, Jonathan. *The Albigensian Crusade.* London: Faber & Faber, 1978.

Tal, Uriel. "Foundations of a Political Messianic Trend in Israel." Pp. 492–503 in *Essential Papers on Messianic Movements and Personalities in Jewish History* (Mark Saperstein, ed.). New York: New York University Press, 1992.

Tamar, David. "Luria and Vital as the Messiah Ben Joseph." *Sefunot* 7 (1963): 167–177. [Hebrew]

———. "The Messianic Dreams and Visions of Rabbi Haim Vital." *Shalem* 4 (1984): 211–229. [Hebrew]

———. "On the Jews of Safed in the Days of the Ottoman Conquest." *Cathedra* 11 (1981): 181–182. [Hebrew]

Tishby, Isaiah. "Acute Apocalyptic Messianism." Pp. 259–286 in *Essential Papers on Messianic Movements and Personalities in Jewish History* (Mark Saperstein, ed.). New York: New York University Press, 1992.

————. *The Doctrine of Evil and Klippah in the Kabbalah of the Ari.* Jerusalem: Magnes Press, 1984. [Hebrew]

————. "Rabbi Moses Cordovero as He Appears in the Treatise of Rabbi Mordecai Dato." *Sefunot 7* (1963): 119–165. [Hebrew]

————. *The Wisdom of the Zohar.* 3 vols. Oxford: Oxford University Press, 1989.

Toaff, Ariel, and Schwarzfuchs, Simon (eds.). *The Mediterranean and the Jews: Banking, Finance, and International Trade (XVI–XVIII Centuries).* Ramat Gan, Israel: Bar-Ilan University Press, 1989.

Trachtenberg, Joshua. *The Devil and the Jews.* New York: World Publishing Company, 1961.

————. *Jewish Magic and Superstition: A Study in Folk Religion.* New York: Behrman's Jewish Book House, 1939.

Twersky, Isadore. *Rabad of Posquières: A Twelfth-Century Talmudist.* Cambridge, MA: Harvard University Press, 1962.

Van Biema, David. "Pop Goes the Kabbalah." *Time.* November 24, 1997: 92.

Verman, Mark. "The Evolution of the Circle of Contemplation." Pp. 163–177 in *Gershom Scholem's Major Trends in Jewish Mysticism 50 Years After* (Peter Schäfer and Joseph Dan, eds.). Tübingen: J.C.B. Mohr, 1993.

Vital, Haim. *Sha'ar ha-Gilgulim.* Jerusalem: Hemed Press, 1971. [Hebrew]

Wakefield, Walter L. *Heresy, Crusade, and Inquisition in Southern France, 1100–1250.* Berkeley, CA: University of California Press, 1974.

Weiner, Herbert. *9 1/2 Mystics: The Kabbalah Today.* New York: Holt, Rhinehart, and Winston, 1969.

Werblowsky, R. J. Zwi. "A Collection of Prayers and Devotional Compositions by Solomon Alkabetz." *Sefunot 6* (1962): 135–183. [Hebrew]

————. *Joseph Karo, Lawyer and Mystic.* Oxford: Oxford University Press, 1962.

Whitcomb, Donald. "Islam and the Socio-Cultural Transition of Palestine — Early Islamic Period (638–1099 CE)." Pp. 488–501 in *The Archaeology of Society in the Holy Land* (Thomas E. Levy, ed.). London: Leicester University Press, 1995.

Wirszubski, Chaim. *Pico della Mirandola's Encounter with Jewish Mysticism.* Cambridge, MA: Harvard University Press, 1989.

Wolfson, Elliot R. *Along the Path: Studies in Kabbalistic Myth, Symbolism, and Hermeneutics*. Albany, NY: State University of New York Press, 1995.

———. *Circle in the Square: Studies in the Use of Gender in Kabbalistic Symbolism*. Albany, NY: State University of New York Press, 1995.

———. *Through a Speculum That Shines: Vision and Imagination in Medieval Jewish Mysticism*. Princeton, NJ: Princeton University Press, 1994.

———. "The Tree That Is All: Jewish-Christian Roots of a Kabbalistic Symbol in *Sefer ha-Bahir*." *Jewish Thought and Philosophy* 3 (1993): 31–76.

INDEX

ABOUT THE AUTHOR

Neil Asher Silberman is an author and historian with a special interest in the history, archaeology, and politics of the Near East. His books include *The Message and the Kingdom* (with Richard A. Horsley) and *The Hidden Scrolls.* A contributing editor for *Archaeology* magazine, he lives in Connecticut.